THE SINS OF THE FATHERS

THE
SINS
OF THE
FATHERS

TURKISH DENIALISM AND
THE ARMENIAN GENOCIDE

SIOBHAN NASH-MARSHALL

A Herder & Herder Book
The Crossroad Publishing Company
New York

A Herder & Herder Book
The Crossroad Publishing Company
www.crossroadpublishing.com

© 2017 by Siobhan Nash-Marshall.

The text of this book is set in 12/15 Adobe Garamond Pro.

Composition by Rachel Reiss
Cover design by Sophie Appel

Library of Congress Cataloging-in-Publication Data
available upon request from the Library of Congress.

ISBN 978-0-8245-2378-7

Books published by The Crossroad Publishing Company may be purchased at special quantity discount rates for classes and institutional use. For information, please e-mail sales@CrossroadPublishing.com.

CONTENTS

Noi fummo i Gattopardi, i Leoni
Quelli che ci sostituiranno saranno gli sciacalletti, le iene.
—Giuseppe Tomasi di Lampedusa, *Il Gattopardo*

We were the Leopards, the Lions
Those who replace us will be the little jackals, the hyenas

For Mary T. Clark R.S.C.J.
with love

In the absence of justice, what is
sovereignty but organized robbery?
—St. Augustine

FOREWORD

Three growing convictions drove me to write this book. The first is that philosophers played a crucial role in both the Armenian Genocide and Turkish denial. I am increasingly confident that philosophy's hands are, as it were, bloody. The second is that the philosophical approach to reality that led to the genocidal policies of the Ottoman Turks and to Turkish denial, the approach that views human life and historical truth as insignificant, that does not consider its own pronouncements disproven by concrete facts, that considers the use of the principle of non-contradiction in the *real world* optional, is still informing our world. The third is that philosophy cannot correct those mistakes that led it to play an instrumental role in the genocidal policies of the twentieth century if it does not intellectually address concrete historical reality: historical truth.

For millennia, Western thinkers have struggled with concrete facts. The temptation to claim that only the "ideal"—the immutable, the universal, the intellectually known—is real has been with philosophy since Parmenides declared the concrete world to be an illusion those many thousands of years ago. It was not until the modern world that this temptation led to the sustained attempt not just to ignore concrete facts and realities, but to consider concrete reality raw material that needed to be molded into a rationally appropriate reality.

Although Descartes claimed that it would be "unreasonable" for a single person to "reform a state by changing it from the foundations up, overturning it in order to rebuild it," he not only thought that it was necessary to do so. He set the stage for the "overturnings" and "rebuildings"—or *revolutions*, as they have come to be known—that characterized modern history. In his search for certainty, he defined a universal method for the human mind. If followed, he claimed, human beings would avoid all mistakes. His application of his own method led him to split the concrete material world (the *res extensa*) from the world of reason (the *res cogitans*), the world of experience from the world of thought. It led him to conclude both that concrete facts—that experiences—could not disprove the validity of thoughts and that concrete facts were themselves inherently valueless. The experience of vivisecting animals did not convince him to revisit his claim that animals could not feel pain. Squeals and howls were, he confidently reported, mechanical responses. Nor did the squeals and howls convince him that there was something about concrete reality that should be respected.

The allure of Descartes's approach was fatal to the unfolding of Western thought. It was devastating to the world. It led Western thought to hold that only its rational pronouncements had value, and that those pronouncements—especially when they concerned the value inherent in actually existent material realities—could only be refuted by other rational pronouncements, and not by concrete evidence concerning those material realities. It led the *Encyclopédistes*, their heirs, and their admirers, the German idealists, to try to "overturn" the world "in order to rebuild it" according to rational standards: to remake the world in the image and likeness of their ideas. That that *overturning* and shaping required the destruction of human lives and ancient cultures was insignificant to them. Their rational pronouncements told them that *le Roi Capet* and the *Vendeans* had no inherent value. They also demonstrated that *les aristocrates* and *les catholiques* were both evil. They were both impediments to the establishment in France of what truly had value: the *Philosophes'* rational order.

There is no logical or formal distinction between *overturning* an *Ancien Régime* through slaughter and *destroying a people and culture*: a *genos*. If one believes that an ideal can justify slaughtering a king, his court, and those who would defend him, that a class of people's death is a necessary condition of making the world conform to a rational idea, one cannot not justify *genocide*.

The Armenians were not the first victims of modern philosophy's *demiurgical designs*. They were, however, the victims through whom these *demiurgical designs* were radicalized: became the raw expression of wills unmoored from any sort of truly rational ideal. The Armenian Genocide that has played out for over a century marks the moment in which the entire world consented (and still consents) to the sacrifice of an entire people and culture to an anti-ideal: to a radical group's will to power. It marks the moment in which the entire world consented (and still consents) to the sacrifice of a *genos* to a *falsehood*. It marks the moment when the world consented (and still consents) to the sacrifice of history itself and the truth. It is not by chance that the Armenian Genocide was so quickly and carefully reproduced by the Nazis. Hitler bargained that once the world consented to allowing one radical group's will to power to ravage a people, appropriate its wealth and native lands, destroy its culture, deny its history, and lie about its own past, it would have to allow a second radical group the same privilege. If the Turks could do it, why not the Germans?

One look at our world today shows that we are still living under the shadow not just of modern philosophy's *demiurgical designs*, but of the world's consent to the sacrifice of the Armenians. The Allies did put an end to Hitler's attempt directly to emulate the Young Turks and Mustafa Kemal and construct his lasting *Reich* for the German *Volk*. They did not put an end to the principles that led Hitler to believe that he could and should construct that Reich. The belief that concrete things and realities have no inherent value and should be molded into appropriate entities is alive and active in our world, as is the rejection of concrete facts. What is more terrifying is that the contemporary rejection of value and fact is not being advocated in the name of some universally accepted (or acceptable) value or purpose. Those who today ignore the facts and actively try to mold things and realities seem to believe that there is no such thing as a universal value or purpose at all. The "how" they are accomplishing what they want, as Orwell claimed years ago, is clear. The "why" is an inarticulable mystery.

Returning to these whys is the task of philosophy, as is the pressing matter of addressing the principles that led us to this moment. For philosophy to do so, for its questions to lead to the wisdom that discovering those whys requires, it must begin by addressing what actually is: the world, with all of its wounds and warts, and all of its wondrous causes. If it begins with anything else—the possible, the imaginary—it ends up in a rabbit hole. One cannot determine the principles and purpose of the non-real. It is nonsensical. One cannot really explain why you cannot chop off nobody's head at the door. It should be obvious. If it is not, then one cannot make it so through a theory.

This book is part of my attempt to address and repair philosophy's betrayal. Its specific aim is twofold. It is philosophically to reflect on the causes of what cannot but be considered an ongoing *horrendous evil*—the Armenian Genocide and Turkish denialism—in order for the truth to be known and for the love of wisdom to remember that it works with humility in service of historical truth. It is also to gather the data for a more systematic study of the betrayal of philosophy.

Chapter 1

HOMELANDS, GENOCIDE, AND DENIAL

A few years ago, I wrote a long article in which I argued that there are cases of genocide denial that are acts of genocide.[1] The article examined a single, but extraordinarily significant, instance of such denial: an official letter sent in 1990 by His Excellency the Ambassador of the Republic of Turkey, Nüzhet Kandemir, to Professor Robert J. Lifton of the City University of New York.[2]

The letter was only accidentally extraordinary. The envelope in which it was sent—mistakenly, one assumes—contained two documents in *addition* to the official letter, that in every other meaningful way resembles the scores of letters sent by the government and representatives of the Republic of Turkey to scholars who have written about the Armenian Genocide. Those two documents were:

---

1. I wrote the article with Rita Mahdessian, whom I also thank for her valuable contribution to the present book. See Siobhan Nash-Marshall and Rita Mahdessian, "Lies, Damned Lies, and Genocide," *Metaphilosophy*, 44.1–2 (2013), 116–44.

2. The letter is a response to a chapter in Professor Lifton's book *The Nazi Doctors: Medical Killing and the Psychology of Genocide* (New York: Basic Books, 1986) that includes a discussion of the parallels between the Armenian Genocide and the Holocaust. For the text of the letter and the additional documents, see Roger W. Smith, Eric Markusen, and Robert Jay Lifton, "Professional Ethics and the Denial of the Armenian Genocide," *Holocaust and Genocide Studies*, 9 (1995), pp. 1–22. I shall henceforth refer to this article as SML.

1. a private memorandum written by an American academic—
   Professor Heath W. Lowry of Princeton University[3]—and
   addressed to Ambassador Kandemir;

and

2. a draft of the letter that Ambassador Kandemir eventually
   sent to Professor Lifton, which was written by Professor
   Lowry at the behest of the ambassador.

The additional documents, which Professor Lifton received and
published, prove many things. The most important of these, when
one's goal is to try to understand Turkish denial of the Armenian
Genocide, are two:

a. that the government of the Republic of Turkey had engaged
   an American academic in order to help it quash scholarly

---

3. Professor Heath W. Lowry has had an interesting career. In 1983 he was one
of the key figures involved in establishing the Institute of Turkish Studies
at Georgetown University, which was paid for by a grant from the Turkish
government. He worked at the U.S. State Department's National Foreign Affairs Training Center, where he taught U.S. diplomats scheduled for assignment in Turkey. In 1985 he was one of the specialists in Turkish Studies who
signed a petition requesting that the U.S. House of Representative's resolution
condemning genocide not include the Armenian Genocide, which the petition stated was "the result of 'intercommunal warfare' complicated by 'disease,
famine, suffering and massacres.'" From 1993 to 2013, Professor Lowry was
the Atatürk Professor of Ottoman and Modern Turkish Studies at Princeton
University. He was the Director of the Program of Near Eastern Studies at
Princeton from July 1994 to June 1997. After he was hired by Princeton, Professor Lowry publicly admitted that his memorandum to Ambassador Kandemir was a mistake. He added that he did not believe that there was enough
evidence to back the claim that the CUP had committed genocide, but that
he would readily admit that what happened to the Armenians was genocide
if the state archives of Russia, the Ottoman Empire, and the archives of the
Armenian revolutionary organizations "point to genocide." See, e.g., http://
www.nytimes.com/1996/05/22/nyregion/princeton-is-accused-of-fronting-for-
the-turkish-government.html. See also SML, pp. 4–6.

recognition of the Armenian Genocide and comparisons
between the Armenian Genocide and the Holocaust;[4]

and

b. that the ambassador and Professor Lowry both knew that
the Armenian Genocide is a historical reality, although
they both publicly denied that it is.[5]

---

4. See SML, p. 6, the first lines of Prof. Lowry's Memorandum to Ambas-
    sador Kandemir: "Per your request conveyed to me by Ms. Hilal Baskal of
    your staff, I have located and read Lifton's *The Nazi Doctors*, with an eye to
    drafting a letter for your signature to the author." See also SML, p. 8: "Our
    problem is less with Lifton than it is with the works upon which he relies.
    Lifton is simply the end of the chain, that is, from now on we will see all
    works on the genocide of the Jews, including references such as those made
    by Lifton on the basis of the works by Dadrian, Fein, Kuper, Hovannisian,
    et al. Though this point has been repeatedly stressed both in writing and
    verbally to IADA-Ankara, we have not yet seen as much as a single article by
    any scholar responding to Dadrian (or any of the others as well). I strongly
    recommend that it be pointed out to Ankara that Lifton's book is simply
    the end result of the Turkish failure to respond in a prompt fashion to the
    Dadrian articles and the Fein and Kuper books." See SML, pp. 6–9.

5. There are three facts that indicate that both Prof. Lowry and Ambassador
    Kandemir knew that the Armenian Genocide is a historical reality. The
    first concerns the object of their collaboration in the case of the Lifton let-
    ter. The ambassador (and the government of Turkey) hired Professor Lowry
    not to discover and promulgate the truth regarding the fate of the Arme-
    nians of Western Armenia (the *six Armenian vilayets*), but to respond to
    the claims of those scholars who demonstrate that there was an Armenian
    Genocide and compare the Armenian Genocide to the Holocaust. See the
    previous footnote on this point. The second fact concerns the way in which
    (Lowry and) Ambassador Kandemir responded to Professor Lifton. Their
    letter does not respond to Lifton's claim that there was an Armenian Geno-
    cide with rational arguments grounded in readily accessible evidence that
    would disprove Lifton's claim. It simply accuses Lifton of poor scholarship
    and suggests that he read material written by known genocide negationists.
    For a more articulate discussion of these points, see my "Lies, Damned
    Lies, and Genocide." The third fact is in a sense even more astounding.
    In the most significant part of his private memorandum to Ambassador
    Kandemir, Prof. Lowry actually refers to the Armenian Genocide as the

Through a long and very technical argument that dealt primarily with lying, the types and characteristics of non-verbal linguistic actions, the reasons why non-verbal linguistic actions can be criminal, and the UN Genocide Convention, my article demonstrated that the Turkish ambassador's letter was an act of genocide in its own right[6]:

> [It] intentionally stated something that could destroy the mental sanity of an ethnic, religious, social and cultural group *in order* also *to* destroy the mental sanity of that ethnic group: the Armenians.[7]

The UN Genocide Convention defines the intentional infliction of mental harm upon an ethnic group perpetrated with the intent to destroy that ethnic group as genocide.[8]

"genocide," thereby privately acknowledging that what had happened to the Armenians was indeed a genocide. See SML, p. 8: "In summation, what we are faced with here are seven references (comprising about one full page of text) in a book of 561 pages. They are based almost exclusively on the articles by Dadrian (each of which have [sic] been the subject of detailed memos by this writer in past years), together with references to the work of Helen Fein (whose book includes a full chapter on the Armenian Genocide) and Leo Kuper (whose book contains a very long chapter on the Genocide). Stated differently, Lifton, in his book published four years ago in 1986, is simply using the existing literature on the Holocaust and Genocide."

Further evidence that Prof. Lowry knows that there was an Armenian Genocide was given to me by Taner Akçam. He once told me in conversation that the professor had helped him to discover some crucial documents that demonstrated the CUP's intent to commit genocide on the Armenians.

6. The claim that verbal pronouncements can be *acti rei* is not original to me. Defamation, inciting a crime, abetting, yelling "fire" in a crowded building when there is no fire are all verbal acts that are crimes. Nor, as I shall discuss in the next chapter, is the claim that genocide denial can be an act of genocide original to me.

7. "Lies, Damned Lies, and Genocide," p. 143.

8. See Article II of the UN Genocide Convention: "In the present Convention, genocide means any of the following acts committed with intent to destroy,

What I would like to do in this book is to revisit the issue in order better to qualify how and why the Republic of Turkey's policy of genocide denial—which is exhibited among other places in Ambassador Nüzhet Kandemir's letter to Professor Lifton—is genocide.[9] Taking my cue from Professor Lifton, when in response to the ambassador's letter he claims that "genocide does not end with its last human victim: denial continues the process,"[10] I shall argue that the Republic of Turkey's policy of genocide negationism not only "continues the process" of the Armenian Genocide of 1915. It is an *integral part* of the very genocide that it denies occurred.

The primary premises of my argument will be three propositions:

1. Denial of genocide was part of the original genocidal intent and plan formulated and implemented by the *İttihat ve Terakki Cemiyeti* (Committee of Union and Progress; henceforth CUP) that was governing the Ottoman Empire during World War I and whose object was the deportation and extermination (*deghahanoutiun* and *tseghaspanoutiun*) of Western Armenians.

2. The object of the CUP's genocidal plan was (and continues to be) pursued by the governments of the successor state to the Ottoman Empire: the governments of the Republic of Turkey.

---

in whole or in part, a national, ethnical, racial or religious group, as such: (b) Causing serious bodily or mental harm to members of the group."

There are a number of studies on the damage that negationism inflicts upon the survivors of a genocide and their victims. For a poignant study of the effects of genocide denial in the case of the Armenian Genocide, see Aida Alayarian, *Consequences of Denial: The Armenian Genocide* (London: Karnac Books, 2008).

9. For a wonderful historical examination of denial in the case of Turkish-Armenian relations, see Fatma Müge Göçek, *Denial of Violence: Ottoman Past, Turkish Present and the Collective Violence against Armenians, 1789–2009* (New York: Oxford University Press, 2014). I shall henceforth refer to this book as DV.

10. SML, p. 14.

3. The object of the CUP's genocidal plan was (and continues to be) implemented by the governments of the Republic of Turkey for the very same reasons for which the CUP first formulated and implemented its genocidal plan during World War I.

Frameworks, false distinctions, and history

My propositions would challenge not just the dominant historical stance that treats the Armenian Genocide and Republic of Turkey's official policy of genocide denial as fundamentally distinct events. They would challenge at least some aspects of nearly all of the canonical beliefs concerning the Armenian Genocide itself, starting with its dates.

Historians commonly claim that that the Armenian Genocide began in 1915, shortly after the Ottoman Empire entered World War I, and ended with the signing of the Treaty of Lausanne in 1923.[11] This cannot be right if the Republic of Turkey's policy of

---

11. It is a *topos* in literature on the Armenian Genocide that the genocide took place between 1915 and 1923. Raymond Kévorkian's magisterial *The Armenian Genocide* (New York: I.B. Tauris & Co. Ltd., 2011), for instance, incorporates the dates in its very structure. Part IV of the work is called "In the Vortex of the War: The First Phase of the Genocide" and, as the title suggests, deals with 1915. The book ends with the rise of Mustafa Kemal and establishment of the Republic of Turkey in 1923.

  Recent scholarship has challenged the once believed to be hard distinction between pre-Republican and post-Republican Turkey. It has shown that there is a great deal more continuity between the "Ikinci Meşrutiyet" (Second Constitutional Period) (1908–1918), "Milli Miicadele" (National Struggle) (1919–1923), and "Cumhuriyet" (Republic) (after 1923) than was previously acknowledged. See, e.g., Erik J. Zürcher, "The Ottoman Legacy of the Turkish Republic: An Attempt at a New Periodization," *Die Welt des Islams*, N.S. 32.2 (1992), pp. 237–53. This has important consequences for the matter at hand. If there is continuity between the plans and projects of pre- and post-Republican Turkey, then there is no reason to claim that the genocidal plans of pre-Republican Turkey ended in 1923. Indeed, recent

genocide denial is an *integral part* of the Armenian Genocide, and the Republic of Turkey is still actively denying that the Armenian Genocide took place. If these last two claims are true, the Armenian Genocide must still be taking place.

I do not mean by this last statement (or my three propositions) to suggest that Armenians continue to be slaughtered today in the land and highlands east of Anatolia, or deported therefrom, that Aleppo is still surrounded by Ottoman concentration camps filled with starving Western Armenians, or that Deir-es-Zor, Raqqa, and Ras-al-Ayn are still red with fresh Armenian blood. I do not think that it is reasonable to question the historical fact that the deportation and extermination of the vast majority of Western Armenians took place between 1915 and 1923.[12]

---

scholarship is increasingly demonstrating the contrary. It has been shown, for instance, that the demographic engineering inherent in the Armenian Genocide continued well past 1923. See, e.g., Uğur Ümit Üngör, "Turkey for the Turks," in Ronald Grigor Suny, Fatma Müge Göçek, and Norman M. Naimark (eds.), *A Question of Genocide: Armenians and Turks at the End of the Ottoman Empire* (Oxford/New York: Oxford University Press, 2010), pp. 287–305. I shall henceforth refer to this book as AQG.

12. As Talaat Pasha's "black book," or *Report on the Armenian Genocide*, demonstrates, the greater part of the extermination and deportation of those Armenians who lived in those eastern provinces of the Ottoman Empire— the *six Armenian vilayets*—part of which Turkey would now want to call "Eastern Anatolia," had been completed by the end of 1917. See Ara Sarafian, *Talaat Pasha's Report on the Armenian Genocide*, 1917 (London: Gomidas Institute, 2011). The years 1918–1923 were also unquestionably painful, devastating, and bloodstained for the Armenians, who were not just reeling from the unimaginable horrors of a full-blown annihilation campaign in the western part of their ancestral lands, but realized that they were still not safe from those who had organized and run that campaign. They were hunted in the eastern part of their ancestral lands—in the Caucasus—where they were forced to raise an army out of what was left of their people and defend both themselves and the last little portion of their historic homeland, part of which the world today still recognizes as their own. See, e.g., Vahakn Dadrian, *The History of the Armenian Genocide: Ethnic Conflict from the Balkans to Anatolia to the Caucasus* (Providence/Oxford: Berghahn Books, 1995), pp. 347–76. See also Richard Hovannisian, *The*

Nor do I want with my propositions in any way to minimize the horrors or criminality of the physical destruction of the Armenians: the savage murders of the men, the unthinkable bestiality visited upon Armenian women and children during their death marches, in orphanages, in concentration camps, and in extermination zones. Armenians, as Wegner claimed, died "all of the deaths of the world, the deaths of all centuries."

My propositions are meant to challenge the dominant belief that the Armenian Genocide began and ended with the physical eradication of the Armenians from that part of their historical homeland in the lands and highlands east of Anatolia that were called "Armenia" until the 1930s. They are meant also to challenge the implicit presuppositions of that belief: that the Armenian Genocide was nothing but the physical destruction of an enormous number of people who belonged to the Armenian *genos*. I want with my propositions to challenge the framework with which scholars have approached both the Armenian Genocide and Turkish negationism.

Many years ago, those who gazed at the skies believed that Venus morning-star and Venus evening-star were different celestial bodies. The ancient Greeks gave Venus morning-star and Venus evening-star different names. They called Venus morning-star *Phosphorous* (Φωσφόρος), which means "bearer of light." The Latins called it *Lucifer*. The Greeks called the evening-star *Hesperus* (Ἕσπερος). The Latins called it *Vesper*. As was their wont, the Greeks and Latins personified both *Phosphorous* and *Hesperus* and gave all sorts of mythical explanations to account for their existence. Some ancients

---

Republic of Armenia, Vol. I (Los Angeles/Berkeley: University of California Press, 1971); Vol. II (Los Angeles/Berkeley: University of California Press, 1982); Vols. III & IV (Los Angeles/Berkeley: University of California Press, 1996). They were again hunted down in their western highlands and Cilicia. Those who had returned to their homeland after the end of World War I were once more chased out, or simply killed. The armies of the powers that promised to protect them left them to fend for themselves. On this, see, e.g., Karnig Panian, *Goodbye Antoura: A Memoir of the Armenian Genocide.* (Stanford, CA: Stanford University Press, 2015). See footnote 56 on p. 32.

claimed that *Phosphorus* and *Hesperus* were half-brothers. One of the "brothers," it was added, was the son of a mortal, while the other brother was the son of a god. The ancients associated one of the brothers with those who out of envy strive to rise above their stations but are beaten back. They linked that brother with Icarus and his mad flight. The myths were all very poetic and beautiful.

They were also built on a false distinction: a distinction that does not correspond to a real difference *in re*. Once the Greeks learned from the Babylonians that *Phosphorous* and *Hesperus* were actually one and the same celestial body, they renumbered the planets and changed their interpretations of the ancient myths. In so doing, they not only corrected a mistake. They paved the way for Ptolemy, Copernicus, Kepler, Newton, and Einstein. None of these men could have formulated his astronomical theories had his predecessors not realized that *Phosphorous* and *Hesperus* were one and the same planet: Venus.

The same thing happens (or should happen) anytime we learn that we have built those theories with which we attempt to understand a given fact, thing, or event upon a false distinction. Once we realize that we have done so, we must change our definitions, reevaluate our beliefs, and reformulate our theories concerning the facts. It is well worth the effort if our aim is to know the truth.

The distinction between the Armenian Genocide and the Republic of Turkey's official policy of genocide denialism is, I shall argue, a false distinction. That false distinction keeps us from understanding both the genocide and negationism.[13] It hinders our caring for the open wound.

---

13. Taner Akçam mentions another such dichotomy in the case of the Armenian Genocide. The dichotomy concerns the two-truth approach to the Armenian Genocide and its two-evidence backing. See Taner Akçam, *The Young Turks' Crime Against Humanity: The Armenian Genocide and Ethnic Cleansing in the Ottoman Empire* (Princeton/Oxford: Princeton University Press, 2012 [henceforth cited as CAH]), pp. xxii–xxiii: "Until recently there have been two opposing assessments of the Ottoman and Turkish state archives. According to the 'official Turkish position,' what happened to the Armenians

Genocide and its explanation

As my propositions suggest, I shall also address two deeper matters in this book. The first is that horrible question that cannot but haunt Armenians: *Why?* Why the genocide? Why did the Ottoman Turkish triumvirate of CUP men—Talaat Pasha, Enver Pasha, and Cemal Pasha—order that the Armenians be eradicated from their homeland? Why have the successor governments of the Republic of Turkey been so vehement in their denial of their orders? Why have they spent millions upon millions of dollars in an attempt to sabotage genuine scholarly research on the Armenian Genocide and public knowledge thereof?[14] Why their brash threats to governments that officially acknowledge that the Armenian Genocide is a historical fact?[15] Why the ongoing ballet of Turkish ambassadors

---

was a tragic but unintended by-product of the war, and there is no reliable evidence of a deliberate policy of systematic killing. In this view the only source of reliable evidence on the topic is the Prime Ministerial Archive in Istanbul.... Conversely, those who maintain that the policies towards the Armenians constituted genocide dismiss the Ottoman archives as an unreliable source of information.... In this work I hope to have demonstrated, for the first time, the falseness of this apparent contradiction."

14. For a brief overview on this topic, see SML, pp. 2–5. One of Turkey's most bizarre attempts to quash public knowledge of the Armenian Genocide was the *Time*-DVD scandal. The June 5, 2005, Europe edition of the magazine included an anti-Armenian propaganda DVD paid for by the Ankara Chamber of Commerce. The ostensible purpose of the DVD was the promotion of tourism in Turkey. It was included in a tourism leaflet. On October 18, 2005, *Time*, among other things, published a letter of apology for the DVD, stating that "the so-called documentary portion of the DVD presents a one-sided view of history that does not meet our standards for fairness and accuracy, and we would not have distributed it had we been aware of its content. Unfortunately, the DVD was not adequately reviewed by anyone at TIME because it was believed to be a benign promotion piece."

15. The latest such threats took place after the Vatican, Austria, Germany, Luxembourg, Brazil, Belgium, Bulgaria, Paraguay, and Germany acknowledged the Armenian Genocide. Prime Minister Erdogan's threat to the Vatican, for instance, was: "I condemn the pope and would like to warn him not to make similar mistakes again," http://www.newsweek.com/turkeys-

recalled from those nations that officially declare that the slaughter of Armenians that began in 1915 was a genocide?[16] Why Article 301 in the Turkish Penal Code?[17] Why the destruction of Armenian

---

erdogan-i-condemn-pope-over-armenia-genocide-comment-322275. For Erdogan's remarks in response to the statement on the Armenian Genocide by the Prime Minister of Belgium, see http://www.dailystar.com.lb/News/Middle-East/2015/Jun-20/303063-turkey-slams-belgian-pm-over-armenian-genocide-remarks.ashx. Erdogan's response to Putin's statement on the Armenian Genocide was: "Taking into account the mass atrocities and exiles in the Caucasus, Central Asia and Eastern Europe committed by Russia for a century, the collective punishment methods such as Holodomor, as well as inhumane practices, especially against Turkish and Muslim people in Russia's own history, we consider that Russia is best-suited to know exactly what 'genocide' and its legal dimensions are," http://www.al-monitor.com/pulse/originals/2015/04/turkey-russia-armenia-ties-lost-magic.html#. The response to Germany by Mevlüt Çavuşoğlu, the foreign minister of Turkey, was: "The way to close the dark pages of your own history is not by defaming the histories of other countries with irresponsible and baseless decisions." In Ankara, Prime Minister Binali Yildirim stated: "There is no shameful incident in our past that would make us bow our heads," http://www.nytimes.com/2016/06/03/world/europe/armenian-genocide-germany-turkey.html?_r=0.

16. In 2015 Turkey recalled its ambassadors from at least four nations—the Vatican, Austria, Luxembourg, and Brazil—once these officially acknowledged the Armenian Genocide as a historical fact. In 2016, Turkey recalled its ambassador to Germany after the Bundestag passed a motion acknowledging not just that what had happened to Western Armenians was genocide, but also the German Reich's instrumental role in genocide.

17. Article 301 of the Turkish penal code has been used to suppress mention of the Armenian Genocide in Turkey. Numerous people, including Orhan Pamuk, Elif Shafak, Hrant Dink, and Taner Akçam, have been charged with "violating it" for offending "Turkishness" by mentioning or hinting at the Armenian Genocide. In the case of Taner Akçam, the European Court for Human Rights found that Article 301 violates the European Convention on Human Rights. See http://www.raoulwallenberg.net/news/european-court-of-human-rights-rules-in-favor-of-armenian-genocide-scholar-taner-akcam/. For a legal analysis of Article 301, see Bülent Algan, "The Brand New Version of Article 301 of Turkish Penal Code and the Future of Freedom of Expression Cases in Turkey," *German Law Journal*, 9.12 (2008), pp. 2237–51. For an interesting analysis of the way in which Article 301 has altered the way in which contemporary Turks approach the topic of the Armenian Genocide, see Nazan Maksudyan, "Walls of Silence:

monuments?[18] Why the renaming of ancient Armenian—and Greek—towns, cities, and locations?[19] Why the attempt to change the scientific names of animals and plants when these contain a reference to *Armenia*?[20] Why the painful pseudo-history that they have both imposed within their borders and attempted to transmit to the Western world?[21]

The second matter concerns the related questions: *What* and *How*? What acts did and does the Armenian Genocide include? Did it include just the slaughter and deportation of the Armenians? Or does it also include the denial, the threats, and Article 301? Did it include the confiscation and appropriation of Armenian property? Did it include the Turkification of Armenians? Did it include the destruction of Armenian monuments? Does it include the pseudo-history? Just how broad is the Armenian Genocide? Or, put differently, *how* did (and do) the successive governments of Turkey perpetrate the Armenian Genocide?

Translating the Armenian Genocide into Turkish and Self-Censorship," *Critique*, 37.4 (2009), pp. 635–49. I shall touch upon one of the sentences of a case of "violation" of Article 301 later on in the book.

18. Incalculable damage to the Armenians and to the world has been done through this destruction. For a very fine overview, see William Dalrymple, *From the Holy Mountain: A Journey Among the Christians of the Middle East* (New York: Henry Holt & Co., 1997). See also http://armenianweekly.com/2011/08/01/searching-for-lost-armenian-churches-and-schools-in-turkey/. See also http://virtualani.org/tomarza/index.htm. For a more comprehensive study of the importance of Armenian architecture, see, e.g., Adriano Alpago-Novello, *The Armenians* (New York: Rizzoli International, 1986).

19. See, e.g., Kerem Öktem, "The Nation's Imprint: Demographic Engineering and the Change of Toponymes in Republican Turkey," *European Journal of Turkish Studies*, 7 (2008).

20. See, e.g., http://news.bbc.co.uk/2/hi/europe/4328285.stm.

21. Pseudo-history in this context is ambiguous. There is the pseudo-history involved in the Republic of Turkey's active denialist agenda. There is also the pseudo-history involved in the fascinating "ur-Turkish" myth, commonly called the Turkish "History Thesis." I shall discuss both the denialist agenda and the myth later in this book. They are linked. For a quick account of the denialist pseudo-history, see SML, pp. 2–5.

Scholars who respond to these questions normally presuppose things such as:

1. Only those acts that physically destroy a *genos* can be acts of genocide.[22]
2. The Armenian Genocide took place between 1915 and 1923.

Thus they have, by and large, responded to the *what* and *how* questions regarding the Armenian Genocide by describing the barbarity of the slaughter and deportation of Western Armenians. They have generally distinguished the *whys*. They have treated the *why* of the Armenian Genocide as though it were unrelated to the *whys* of subsequent Turkish denial, destruction of Armenian monuments, toponymical and zoonymical alterations, and pseudo-history.

These responses are inherently flawed. Their assumptions are flawed.[23] What is more important is that these responses (and their presuppositions) overlook the unmistakable connection between

---

22. This can, for instance, be seen in the way in which Taner Akçam implicitly defines genocide in his very good book, *A Shameful Act: The Armenian Genocide and the Question of Turkish Responsibility* (New York: Metropolitan Books, 2006), henceforth cited as ASA. Throughout his chapter on "Turkish Nationalism," Akçam documents the various ways in which the CUP began to Turkify Anatolia before the outbreak of World War I. Such measures included the imposition of the Turkish language in schools and the "elimination of Christians." The latter "were implemented in the Aegean region" against the Greeks, he claims, "in the Spring of 1914" (p. 103). According to the UN Genocide Convention, both forced assimilation and "elimination" and "cleansing" are acts of genocide. Yet Akçam does not consider them such. In the chapter called "What Led to the Decision for Genocide" he explicitly asks "why the measures against the Armenians took a genocidal form compared to Greek massacres and expulsions" (p. 111). Akçam returns to this issue in CAH, pp. xxvii–xxxii.

23. There is much more to the crime of genocide than the physical destruction of a people. The second article of the UN Genocide Convention does not give a complete list of acts that are to be considered genocidal. It does claim that such things as the deliberate infliction of "mental harm" and

those Turkish actions that have elicited the *whys*. All of these actions share the same efficient, formal, and final causes. All were (or are being) performed by the successive and successor governments of what cannot but be considered one and the same political entity. All targeted (or target) the same group of people: the Armenians. All had (or have) the same object: they would expunge Armenian-*ness* from what was known until very recently as Armenia: Armenian lives, Armenian cemeteries, Armenian culture, Armenian history, Armenian architectural accomplishments, Armenian names.

To distinguish what is not distinct—which is what treating the *whys* of the genocide as separate questions does—is to make a false distinction. This specific false distinction obfuscates both the genocide and its denial.

One of the essential characteristics of a successful explanation of any phenomenon or event is *exhaustiveness*. A successful explanation must account for all of the relevant data and facts concerning that phenomenon or event that it wants to explain. Lawyers know this. It is the reason why they fight to have facts excluded from the evidence of a case. Excluding facts alters explanatory theories. Facts excluded can make the difference between a theory that overwhelmingly demonstrates a person's guilt and a theory that would make a person's guilt admit of reasonable doubt.

Take Hanioğlu's account of the rise of the "national Muslim/ Turkish bourgeoisie" during World War I. That rise, the Turkish historian claims, resulted from an "official policy" of the CUP that "helped Turkish entrepreneurs establish companies and banks with the word 'national' in their title," "created an array of other economic institutions in support of their policies," and passed the

---

the "forcible transference of children" from one *genos* to another are to be considered genocidal. See http://www.hrweb.org/legal/genocide.html.

The second assumption above does not just seem to presuppose that *genocide* is to be equated with the physical destruction of a people. It also seems to presuppose that materially and temporally distinct acts are necessarily really distinct. I shall deal with this issue in Chapter 3 of this book.

"Temporary Law for the Encouragement of Industry" in 1913. The CUP was initially unsuccessful, Hanioğlu states:

> Until the full switch to "National Economics," the results of this legislation were meager; in 1915, Muslim entrepreneurs owned only 42 companies in the empire, as compared with 172 firms listed under non-Muslim ownership. In March 1915, the government amended the law to reinforce its unwritten agenda, restricting privileges to "Ottomans" which in practice meant Muslims, and to Ottoman joint stock companies. As a consequence, by 1918 the picture had changed dramatically. A host of new companies and factories established by Muslims gave them the upper hand in the economy.[24]

What Hanioğlu fails to mention in this account of the dramatic turnaround in the proprietorship of Ottoman industries and banks—over 80% of which belonged to foreigners or Christians in 1915[25]—is that in 1915 the CUP did not just "switch to 'National

---

24. M. Şükrü Hanioğlu, *A Brief History of the Late Ottoman Empire* (Princeton/Oxford: Princeton University Press, 2008), p. 190. I shall henceforth refer to this book as LOE.

25. See Erik J. Zürcher, *The Young Turk Legacy and Nation Building: From the Ottoman Empire to Atatürk's Turkey* (London/New York: I.B. Tauris & Co., 2010), p. 111: "Three quarters of the Young Turks grew up in the 1880s and 1890s in the Balkans, Aegean or Istanbul. Consequently, they witnessed at close range the rise of the Christian bourgeoisie in the towns and cities of the empire. The area they hailed from had been integrating into the European economy since the late eighteenth century and trade with Europe had increased at a high rate since the 1830s. It was primarily the Christian middle class that profited, sometimes working with European economic interests, sometimes in competition with them. From the mid-1890s the pace of integration picked up, and by the end of the century the overwhelming majority of the industrial establishments of the empire were in the hands of foreigners or local Christians. The two categories overlapped to a certain extent because many among the Christians who had earlier acquired protection of a European power later opted for full foreign

Economics.'" On May 27, 1915, it also *happened* to pass the *Tehcir Law* (*tehcir kanunu*), which "authorized" the deportation of all Armenians in the Ottoman Empire. It also *happened* to confiscate all "abandoned" Armenian properties.[26] The "Directorate of Tribal and Immigrant Settlement" of the Interior Ministry sent around the fifteen articles, which regulated the redistribution of Armenian properties to Muslims, on May 30, 1915.[27]

It is only because he omitted these relevant facts that the Turkish historian could claim that CUP *economic* policies were the cause of the rise of the "national Muslim/Turkish bourgeoisie." The omission of relevant facts skews our understanding of events.[28]

In the same way, to treat the relevant facts concerning the Armenian Genocide as though these included only the physical destruction of Western Armenians—their deportation and extermination—is to exclude relevant facts from the evidence. It is *a priori* to make for an unsuccessful explanation of the Armenian Genocide.

To understand the Armenian Genocide, one must explain *all* of the relevant facts concerning Turkey's treatment of Armenians. These do not just include the deportation and extermination of

---

citizenship." I shall henceforth refer to this book as YTL. One of the causes of the economic power of the Christians of the empire was the Armenian *zartonk*. I will speak of this in Chapter 5.

26. The Greeks were also victims of the CUP's economic bullying. See, e.g., Erik J. Zürcher, *Turkey: A Modern History* (London/New York: I.B. Tauris, 2004) [henceforth HMT], p. 126: "CUP secretary (and later president of the Turkish Republic) Mahmut Celâl (Bayar) drove at least 130,000 Greeks from the Western coastal regions into exile in Greece."

27. See, on this, Taner Akçam and Umit Kurt, *The Spirit of the Laws: The Plunder of Wealth in the Armenian Genocide* (New York/Oxford: Berghahn, 2015). Akçam and Kurt point out that the May 30 decree was not the first one through which Armenian property was confiscated. There were two previous CUP decrees passed on May 17 and 23.

28. As is obvious, the skewing in this case is particularly grave. Hanioğlu's claims would be comical if it were not for the fact that they are backed by the Republic of Turkey. One of the primary uses to which Armenian wealth was put was to constitute a Muslim Turkish bourgeoisie.

Western Armenians. They also include Turkey's confiscation and appropriation of Armenian property, its subsidizing and promoting pseudo-history, its disbursing millions of dollars for its negationist campaign, its political bullying, its toponymical and zoonymical name-changing, and its putting on trial those writers and historians in Turkey who would mention the Armenian Genocide for having violated Article 301 of the Turkish Penal Code. To understand the Armenian Genocide, in other words, one must address all of the *whats* and answer all of the *whys*.

The key here are the *whys*. One understands events by understanding their causes. This is especially true for intentional acts.

Genocide, Evil, and the Limits of Rational Explanations

There are limits to an account of the causes of genocide. Genocide is a horrendous instance of moral evil. One of the distinguishing characteristics of moral evils is irrationality.[29] Moral evils are, in a very real sense, quite literally unthinkable.[30] They are the fruits

---

29. This is best seen if one compares evil with its contrary opposite: the good. The primary causes of morally good acts are always intelligible. This is why there can be such a thing as ethics. The necessary condition of any ethics—eudaemonistic, deontological, utilitarian, or anything else—is that moral acts are informed by principles that can be rationally formulated. If this is so, and if moral evils are the contrary opposite of moral goods, what informs them *cannot* be principles that can be rationally formulated. This fact made Plato claim that evil is simply caused by ignorance. It led Augustine to claim that evil is both a privation and *disordered*.

30. The fact that moral evils are in a sense unthinkable does not stop the human will from choosing to pursue them. Nor does it consequently diminish a person's responsibility for his morally evil actions. Simply put, rationality is not a necessary condition of human action. We can very well know that a given course of action is nonsensical and still choose to pursue it. We can act knowing that we will "pay for it later." The fact that we can do so, and do so knowing that we are, makes us fully responsible for our acts. Aristotle attempts to deal with the mystery here in Book VII of the *Nicomachean Ethics*.

of wills informed by minds that have ceased to function properly, of emotions gone wild. What is unthinkable cannot literally be understood.

Does ISIS's destruction of the walls of Niniveh, Nimrud, Palmyra, Apamea, and the ancient temple complex at Hatra really make sense? Surely, something profoundly irrational lies at the heart of the orgy of violence raging in the Middle East today, and at the root of ISIS's urgent need to show it on YouTube. The foundations of the current goings-on in the Middle East are so far removed from anything remotely related to human rationality that they defy belief. It is no wonder that Western people on the whole choose today to ignore the Middle East. The occurrences there seem less real than H.G. Wells's *War of the Worlds*.

There was something insane lurking beneath Hitler's quest for racial purity in Germany.[31] How can someone have striven to make a country that has notoriously shifted borders and been overrun by invasions in the last millennium racially pure? How—given German history—can anyone have believed that there was such a thing as a "racially pure" German *Herrenvolk* (the master race), that it had descended from the last survivors of Atlantis,[32] and have set up the *Lebensborn* (fount of life) reproduction program that would ensure that race's continuation?[33] How can anyone have taken seriously

---

31. See, on this, Robert J. Lifton, *Nazi Doctors*, part I, esp. pp. 22–45, wherein Lifton shows just how absurd and horrendous the Nazi biological quest was.

32. See, e.g., Heather Pringle, *The Master Plan: Himmler's Scholars and the Holocaust* (New York: Hyperion, 2006), pp. 60–61.

33. The program, which was apparently the brainchild of Heinrich Himmler, not only fostered the birth of "racially pure" children of unwed mothers, who were then raised in Germanizing orphanages in Germany and Norway. It also attempted to Germanize tens of thousands of children whom the Nazis kidnapped from countries they had conquered (e.g., Latvia, Estonia, Poland, Russia, Yugoslavia) because, as Himmler put it, "It is our duty to take [the children] with us to remove them from their environment.... Either we win over any good blood that we can use for ourselves and give it a place in our people, or we destroy this blood." Those kidnapped or bred children who were not deemed "worthy" were killed. The exact number

the mad and macabre teachings of the pseudo-scientific *Forschungs und Lehrgemeinschaft das Ahnenerbe* (Research and Teaching Community of the Ancestral Heritage), the Nazi program that sent research teams throughout the world to study the "inheritance of the Aryan forefathers"?[34]

There is something profoundly irrational underlying both the Armenian Genocide and Turkish denial thereof. The latter has for years been the butt of sarcastic editorials that ridicule

what Turkey does every time a foreign government dares to challenge its discredited claim that the Armenians perished in the cruel fog of World War I, and not in a premeditated attempt to eradicate a people.[35]

The foundation of the decision to insist—loudly and repeatedly—that Armenian Genocide claims are "based on biased, distorted and various subjective political motives," when historians and the facts overwhelmingly prove otherwise, cannot be rational. Nor

---

of children kidnapped is unknown. Nazis destroyed their records of this program. The Norwegian government's postwar response to the children born in the Nazi Lebensborn clinics there was particularly nasty. After the war, it branded them as "children of the enemy" and institutionalized many of them in mental hospitals. On this subject, see, e.g., http://www.nytimes.com/2002/12/16/world/norway-tries-to-resolve-a-lasting-nazi-legacy.html. Anni-Frid Lyngstad, one of the singers in the successful Swedish pop group ABBA, is one of the "Tyskerbarnas"—"children of the Germans." See http://www.theguardian.com/world/2002/jun/30/kateconnolly.theobserver. For a fuller account of the program and its aftermath, see Marc Hillel and Clarissa Henry, *Of Pure Blood*, trans. Eric Mossbacher (New York: Pocket Books, 1978). See also Catrine Clay and Michael Leapman, *Master Race: The Lebensborn Experiment in Nazi Germany* (London/New York/Sydney/Toronto: BCA, 1995).

34. On this topic see Pringle, *The Master Plan: Himmler's Scholars and the Holocaust*.

35. "Yes, It's Genocide," *New York Times* editorial, June 3, 2016, http://www.nytimes.com/2016/06/03/opinion/yes-its-genocide-armenia-germany-turkey-erdogan.html?src=recg.

could the foundation of the monstrous decision to slaughter an entire nation have been.

At the root of ISIS's apocalyptic venture, Hitler's millenarian dreams, and Turkey's perpetration and denial of the Armenian Genocide lie irrational choices to attain absurd ends through any and all howsoever horrendous means.[36] These choices and ends mark the limit of our capacity to comprehend moral evil. They are what any attempt to understand the *whys* of horrendous moral evils must recognize as the *foundation* of that evil, *unintelligible,* and just plain *wrong.*[37]

---

36. In light of this, it came as no surprise to me to hear from Dr. Amal Marogy that the Western philosopher ISIS most often cites is Jean-Paul Sartre, who insisted that in order for a person to be truly free, his choice needed necessarily to precede the understandable or rational, i.e., his essence.

37. The great risk in trying to understand the irrational choices that lie at the heart of great moral evils is obsession. It is especially the victims of these great moral evils who run this risk. Pain and the profound human reluctance to admit that human beings can act irrationally would push them past the limits of rational explanation. This is when obsession is born. Victims grapple for reasons that would explain the evil they suffered. They are invariably frustrated: no irrational choice admits of a rational explanation. Frustration causes further pain and the further need to understand the causes of the evil suffered. It can become a vicious cycle. The cycle keeps the evil present.

The attempt to understand those irrational choices that led to moral evils also engenders conspiracy theories. This is why they proliferate in the aftermath of great or well-known moral evils. The absence of a plausible justification for moral evils makes any harebrained theory that would call upon hidden powers or mysterious alliances to make sense of them attractive. Any explanation is better than no explanation to the mind that seeks explanations. The fact that the explanations are groundless and indemonstrable often seems to those who would seek them only to confirm their worth. An excellent example of the mechanism at play here is the Kennedy assassination. That murder seems so senseless that any number of conspiracy theories have sprouted in its wake. Oliver Stone's impossibly long movie on the subject presents one such theory. There are literally thousands more. There are those who would call on Fidel Castro, the KGB, the Mafia, the CIA, and so forth.

The fact that we cannot rationally grasp the deepest roots of moral evils also ensures that the horror of genocide is passed down from father to son.

Dealing with the irrationality of evil

It is only once we have recognized that what informs the actions of criminals is not a rational mind, but a will fettered by twisted and intractable emotions, that we can properly respond to them.

It is not just hypocrisy that keeps the leaders of the Western world from stopping ISIS, its slaughter of Christians, and destruction of the foundations of Western civilization. It was not just hypocrisy that kept them from stopping Hitler until long after he had begun to devastate Europe and annihilate the Jews. Human beings are, in general, loath to believe that their kind can act for systematically unintelligible reasons. To do so contradicts a basic assumption upon which all humanity must rely in order to be able to live. We cannot at once believe that all of our neighbors and colleagues always lie, that all salesmen are greedy thieves, that all drivers are suicidal maniacs and all mailmen lecherous rapists, and live in society. We would go crazy if we did. We must assume that human beings fundamentally act in accordance with basic rational and ethical principles: that moral failures are exceptions.[38] It takes time for us to allow ourselves to believe that a specific person or organization can choose systematically to act irrationally: to pursue insane goals for insane reasons and with insane means.[39]

---

38. Marilyn Adams makes this point admirably. She points out that questioning that the world in which we live adheres to rational principles is quite literally insane. See Marilyn Adams, *Horrendous Evils and the Goodness of God* (Ithaca/London: Cornell University Press, 1999), p. 143: "Experiencing the world as ordered in a way that is congruent enough with reality is constitutive of human sanity. Experiencing the world as chaotic, or losing one's taste for orderings that match up with the 'objective' world, is part of what it is to be insane."

39. How else are we to explain the facts that: German Jews did not respond to the tightening of the Nazi noose despite their knowledge of the Armenian Genocide, or that those Jews who were prisoners at Theresienstadt did not believe Siegfried (Vítězslav) Lederer, who had escaped from Auschwitz, when he told them that the latter was a horrendous extermination camp? On the first point see Wolf Gruner, "'Peregrinations into the Void?':

It took years for Western leaders to realize that Hitler not only meant to follow through with the delirious rantings of *Mein Kampf* and the 25 *Points* of the *Nazi Party Manifesto*, but would use any and all means to do so. When they finally declared war on Hitler *four years* after he raised an army and *three years* after he used that army to remilitarize the Rhineland, they still had not really understood that Hitler would break his word, even when doing so put his entire enterprise at risk;[40] perpetrate unimaginable horrors, even when it meant sacrificing valuable manpower that he could have used to conquer and maintain the *Lebensraum* (living space) he had repeatedly declared the German people deserved;[41] and that he would continue his obsessive destruction long after he knew that he was doomed.[42]

German Jews and Their Knowledge about the Armenian Genocide during the Third Reich," *Central European History*, 45 (2012), pp. 1–26. On the second point see George E. Berkley, *Hitler's Gift: The Story of Theresienstadt* (Boston: Branden Books, 2001), p. 180.

40. Would Stalin have signed the Molotov-Ribbentrop Pact if he expected Hitler to break it? Did it make sense for Hitler to break the Nonaggression Pact that he and Stalin had signed? Breaking this pact opened a new front for him, led him to repeat Napoleon's mistake, and arguably marked the beginning of his end.

41. The number of soldiers involved in exterminating Jews is astounding. Christopher R. Browning claims that "By the end of 1941, the strength of these units was 33,000; by the end of 1942, 300,000." See "The Nazi Decision to Commit Mass Murder: Three Interpretations: The Euphoria of Victory and the Final Solution: Summer–Fall 1941," *German Studies Review*, 17.3 (1994), p. 475.

42. This is particularly clear in the case of Hungarian Jews. In 1944, when it was clear that the Nazis would lose the war, the Hungarian government—Hungarian Admiral Miklos Horthy and Prime Minister Miklos Kallay—tried to negotiate a separate peace with the Allies. In response to this, the Nazis invaded Hungary in March 1944. They sent Eichmann to Budapest to organize the deportation and extermination of Hungarian Jews. Eichmann continued the deportations after heavy Allied bombings, and after the destruction of the railroads there. See, on this point, Hannah Arendt, *Eichmann in Jerusalem: A Report on the Banality of Evil* (New York/London: Penguin Books, 2006), pp. 200ff.

Hindsight would tell us that by 1939, the Allies had all of the evidence they needed to understand all of these things. Hitler had by then already acted on at least two of the points he outlined in his *Manifesto*, although it was completely unreasonable for him to have done so. In 1935 he promulgated the racial laws to "protect German blood" and announced that he would reintroduce military conscription, although this violated the terms of the Treaty of Versailles, and should have triggered an immediate military response from England and France. In 1936 he sent troops to the Rhineland, which was an even more flagrant violation of the Treaty of Versailles and Pact of Locarno.[43] In 1938 he annexed Austria and grabbed the Sudetenland. In January 1939 he declared that he intended to exterminate the Jews.[44] Hindsight, as they say, is 20/20. Foresight and mid-sight are not.

Dealing with moral evil not only requires understanding what we are not built to understand: the irrational. It requires opposing what seems to be a contradiction: systematized folly, organized insanity, methodical madness. Above all, it requires accepting that there are limits to what our rational arguments can accomplish. We cannot respond to horrendous moral evils by attempting to reason with those who would perpetrate them. To do so would be to presuppose that the foundations of the decisions to perpetrate

---

43. Hitler's remilitarization of the Rhineland on March 7, 1936, was a brazen violation of both the Treaty of Versailles of 1919 and the Locarno Pact of 1925. The Treaty of Versailles explicitly stated that Germany's failure to abide by the terms of the treaty "in any manner whatsoever" would be "regarded as committing a hostile act...and as calculated to disturb the peace of the world." It was a huge risk for Hitler. Had France and England immediately responded, World War II might not have taken place.

44. See, e.g., Christian Gerlach, "The Wannsee Conference, the Fate of German Jews, and Hitler''s Decision in Principle to Exterminate All European Jews," *Journal of Modern History*, 70.4 (1998), p. 784: "It is well known that Hitler, in an infamous speech to the Reichstag on January 30, 1939, had spoken as follows: 'If the world of international financial Jewry, both in and outside of Europe, should succeed in plunging the nations into another world war, the result will not be the Bolshevization of the world and thus a victory for Judaism. The result will be the extermination of the Jewish race in Europe.'"

horrendous evils are reasonable. This presupposition is false, even when pride keeps those political leaders who should realize that it is from admitting as much.

This is why the *appeasement* tactics that three British prime ministers used in their attempts to stop Hitler did not work. Their tactics presupposed that Nazi plans and aspirations were informed by decisions that were fundamentally reasonable. The fact that they failed simply confirms that their presupposition was false.

It is also why attempts to institute international panels of historians that would review evidence concerning the Armenian Genocide are doomed to fail. They presuppose that a reasonable decision lies at the foundation of the Republic of Turkey's decision to deny that the Armenian Genocide took place. The fact that this is not the case is proven by countless facts: the fact that historians have overwhelmingly demonstrated and accepted that the eradication of Armenians in World War I constituted a genocide; the fact that Raphael Lemkin, the Polish-Jewish jurist who coined the term *genocide* and formulated the juridical definition of the crime, explicitly stated that what had happened to the Armenians was a *genocide*; the fact that in the aftermath of World War I Sultan Mehmet VI Vahdeddin, albeit under pressure, condemned those who had perpetrated the extermination of the Armenians; the fact that courageous Turkish lawyers, journalists, and professors have risked condemnation by their own nation in order to demonstrate it; the fact that where there was once a flourishing Armenian *millet* that lived in their ancestral lands, there are only ghosts; the fact that more than twenty percent of the population of Anatolia and the Eastern Provinces was Christian in 1910, and that today less than one percent of the inhabitants of those lands is Christian.

My argument and its assumptions

I shall articulate the main argument of this book in the next five chapters. Working my way backward, I shall start with genocide denial and argue that it can be of two main sorts: *post-genocidal* and *intra-genocidal* denial. As the terms suggest, *post-genocidal denial* claims that a genocide did not take place after the completion of the genocide, while *intra-genocidal denial* takes place during the genocide whose reality it denies. In the following chapter I shall turn to the question that gave rise to this book: Was the act of genocide committed by Ambassador Nüzhet Kandemir of the Republic of Turkey when, in his letter to Professor Lowry, he denied that the Armenian Genocide took place, a new genocide? Was it, in other words, *post-genocidal denial* or *intra-genocidal denial*? I shall discuss the criteria with which to answer that question, and compare materially and temporally distinct acts and really distinct acts. I shall argue with Aristotle that acts are distinguished by their objects and not their means or time of execution. After that, I shall reformulate my primary question and split it into three parts:

1. What was the object of the CUP's (Committee of Union and Progress's) campaign against the Armenians?
2. Why was that their object?
3. What is the object of the successor governments of the Republic of Turkey when they deny that the Armenian Genocide took place, change toponyms and attempt to change zoonyms, and articulate pseudo-history?

I shall answer these questions in Chapters 4, 5, and 6. In Chapter 7 I shall state my conclusions.

Three technical points before I present my case. First, I shall take genocide to be that crime that is defined by the UN Convention on Genocide. I sympathize with the many scholars who have explicitly and implicitly attempted to correct the political or theoretical inadequacies of that convention.[45] I also believe that it is silly to quibble

---

45. See my "Genocide," *The New Catholic Encyclopedia of Philosophy Supplement* 2009 (Detroit: Gale, 2009), pp. 387–91.

with the definition of genocide while one is discussing its application. One of the necessary requisites of a rational dialogue concerning the application of a term is that the term have a set, accepted meaning. Rejecting—or worse, stealthily revising the proper definition of a term while one is discussing its application—is babelic.

Second, I understand why historians might complain that the use of legal terms such as "genocide" has politicized historical accounts of the Holocaust and the Armenian Genocide.[46] I also happen to believe that one cannot politicize what is inherently political; that both the Holocaust and the Armenian Genocide were inherently political events that took place in eras dominated by political philosophy; and, consequently, that the scholar should fear avoiding political or legal terms in his accounts of these genocides, as opposed to fearing using them. Avoiding terms when they designate essential characteristics or causes of a given event or state of affairs—much like not giving an exhaustive account of the data or facts that one's theory is meant to explain—is misleading. It obfuscates rather than clarifies.

This is not the place to discuss this matter with the seriousness that it deserves. But I cannot help asking myself how one can avoid politics (and philosophy) when one's subject matter is twentieth-century European and Middle Eastern history.

One of the quips with which philosophy professors can and should respond to what has become *the* unavoidable question at parties, in the classroom, or on trains—"What does one do with philosophy?"—is "cause mayhem." In all seriousness, anyone who knows twentieth-century history should realize that he cannot

---

46. See, e.g., Donald Bloxham, "The First World War and the Development of the Armenian Genocide," in AQG, especially the final three paragraphs, where Bloxam states among other things that: "the historiography of the Shoah today is more mature and less politicized than that of the Armenian genocide"; that "Part of the interpretative problem is that 'genocide' is more a legal term than an historical one, designed for the ex post facto judgements of the courtroom rather than the historian's attempts to understand events"; that "In the historiography of the Armenian genocide the writing of reconstructive history has too often been subordinated to ahistorical ends."

make sense of the unimaginable amount of blood spilt throughout it and in most corners of the globe without referring to philosophers. British politicians have, on the whole, lived and died by Mill and Bentham. Lenin, Stalin, Mao, Pol-Pot, Ceausescu, Mengistu, Enver Hoxha, and Tito, to mention a few of the twentieth century's powerful dictators, were all followers of that philosopher student of Hegel named Karl Marx. Hitler, though he loved Nietzsche, the Van Gogh of philosophy, was also a socialist and relied heavily upon Marx. So too did Mussolini, who was also a socialist and, apparently, one of the great experts on socialist literature. Halide Edib writes in her memoirs that her first husband, Salih Zeki, was an avid reader of August Comte.[47] So was Ahmed Riza, one of the founders of the CUP. Prince Sabahattin loved Edmond Demolins. Ziya Gökalp, one of the primary ideologues of the CUP, loved Fichte and Bergson and was a devotee of Émile Durkheim. Yusuf Akçura, another of the CUP's leading ideologues, was a disciple of Albert Sorel. The thinker who most influenced the leaders of the CUP was apparently Gustave LeBon.

The twentieth century was the playground of nineteenth-century philosophy. This is not just true because the thought of one century often guides the events of the following century. The specific concerns of nineteenth-century philosophy made its influence on the unfolding of the twentieth century overwhelming. The very point of philosophy for many nineteenth-century thinkers was not the "love of wisdom," but guiding the progress of human beings and society toward their ideal states—hence their discussions of the stages of mankind, the process of history, class rights, capital, nationhood, *volksgeist, volk,* education, and so forth.[48]

---

47. Halide Edib, *Memoirs of Halidé Edib* (New York/London: The Century Company, 1926), p. 204. I shall henceforth refer to this book as HW.

48. Many factors played into the transformation of philosophy into a demiurge-like dream. One was certainly the French Revolution. The German Idealists thought that event was crucial. That revolution, too, had causes. One of them seems to have been Descartes's Nero-like dream of destroying and rebuilding cities in order to make them more intelligible to him. Cer-

Nineteenth-century philosophers could not agree on how to guide the progress of man. Nor could they agree on the *ideal* human state. They often did make plans, though, and these were implemented in the twentieth century by the Lenins and Maos, Hitlers and Francos, Castros and Kim Jong-Uns. Philosophical politics—notions of personhood, nationhood, sovereignty, natural rights, class rights, *volk*, borders, and autonomy—were the warp and weft of early twentieth-century history. Armenian, Turkish, and German history are no exception to the rule.

How one can avoid politics (and philosophy) when one's subject matter is twentieth-century European and Middle Eastern history? M. Şükrü Hanioğlu drives this point home for the history of the Turks:

> Foreign visitors were often stunned by the extent to which works of nineteenth-century [sic] French materialism, such as d'Holbach's *Système de la Nature*, held sway over the Ottoman educated class. One observed that every graduate of the new imperial schools seemed to emerge "a materialist, and generally a libertine and a rogue." The rise of an educated class reared on popular materialist ideas created the conditions for an explosion of Ottoman materialist activity in the last two decades of the nineteenth century, which in turn would exert a profound influence over both the intellectual progenitors of the Young Turk Revolution and the founders of modern Turkey.[49]

---

tainly a good case can be made that nineteenth-century thinkers wanted to do just that: turn human beings and society into images of their own ideas. Descartes's dream also has its necessary conditions: his dualism and its claim that the *res extensa* was inherently valueless; the rise of empirical sciences and their distinction between primary and secondary qualities, and the consequent problem of the knowability of the other, which still haunts many contemporary thinkers. Much can and should be said about this.

49. Hanioğlu, LOE, p. 101. Baron d'Holbach was an eighteenth-century French *Encyclopédiste*.

And again:

> The importance of the acceptance of a hybrid doctrine
> based on eighteenth-century French materialism and
> nineteenth-century German *Vulgärmaterialismus* by a
> large segment of the Ottoman intelligentsia should not
> be underestimated. This was one instance where ideas
> mattered a great deal: for the winds of materialism con-
> tinued to blow long after the Young Turk Revolution
> and into Republican times, exerting a profound influ-
> ence on the Weltanschauung of the founders of the
> Republic and on the ideology they fashioned to build
> modern Turkey.[50]

Nor can one sidestep the term "genocide," or other legal terms
such as "expropriation" and "deportation" when dealing with early
twentieth-century Armenian and Turkish history any more than
one can sidestep the terms "genocide," "deportation," and "expropriation" when one deals with twentieth-century German, Jewish, and Polish history, or twentieth-century Soviet and Ukrainian
history. Twentieth-century Armenian and Turkish, German and
Polish, Russian and Ukrainian history is fundamentally philosophical-political. Laws are the grammar of politics, legal terms its
language. To attempt to approach twentieth-century history without using legal terms is to attempt to approach it without using
its own language and grammar. It is tantamount to attempting
to understand Italian Renaissance painting without mentioning
colors or lighting.

That twentieth-century history informs current politics is also
an unavoidable fact. Twentieth-century implementations and en-
forcements of philosophical-political visions on peoples and on
land were often harsh, reckless, and terribly inconclusive. We have
inherited pressing political, geographical, and juridical problems

---

50. Hanioğlu, LOE, p. 138.

throughout much of the globe. Crimea and the Ukraine, Syria and Iraq, are just the tip of the iceberg.

The fact that the immediate roots of many current political problems lie in the politics enacted at the beginning of the twentieth century entails that our studies of that moment in history have a great deal of present political relevance. This is especially true when one focuses on Armenian and Turkish twentieth-century history. This does not mean that we can or should attempt to pacify current political players by attempting to de-politicize their pasts. It is historically inaccurate, and politically dangerous. It is above all untrue and unjust.

Truth and justice in matters historical, legal, and moral are not just honorable goals for scholars disinterestedly to pursue. The contribution that scholars—and only scholars—can make with respect to them is indispensable not just to the courtroom, but more so to society. Plato and Aristotle, not to mention Seneca and Boethius, Aquinas and Dante, all clearly demonstrate that the moment one relegates what is most noble in the human being— his desire for the true, the beautiful, and the good—to ivory towers, chaos cannot but erupt in the lands surrounding those towers. Lifton and his colleagues Smith and Markusen make the point very eloquently:

> Scholarship is, or should be, a quest for truth. What scholars write and say in that quest matters a great deal. Directly or indirectly, our words contribute to a shared consciousness—to the constellation of beliefs that a society forms in connection with issues of any kind. Scholars' contributions to that shared consciousness become especially important in relation to a society's struggles with large, disturbing, and threatening historical events.[51]

---

51. SML, p. 16.

The third point concerns Halide Edib Adivar's biography, *Memoirs of Halidé Edib*, which I shall be citing extensively.[52] Edib was a complex person. She was a successful writer.[53] She was a teacher. She was a feminist. She was primarily a politician. She was one of the central figures in the Turkish nationalist movement.[54] She played a key role in the definition and imposition of "Turkish identity" in Anatolia.[55] Her memoirs are an important source for those

---

52. I would like to thank Eileen Romano for sending me a copy of this biography. It is in part thanks to her that I began to reflect upon the issues that I am discussing in this book.

53. For an overview of Edib's literary production, see, e.g., Emel Sönmez, "The Novelist Halide Edib Adivar and Turkish Feminism," *Die Welt des Islams*, N.S. 14.1 (1973).

54. See Alexander Safarian, "On the History of Turkish Feminism," *Iran & the Caucasus*, 11.1 (2007), p. 145, n. 10: "During many years Halide Edib closely cooperated with Ziya Gökalp and was one of the activists of the Pan Turkist movement. She was among the founders of the strongly nationalistic and influential society *Yeni lisan* ('New Language') (together with Ziya Gökalp, Ata Gunduz, Abdullah Cevdet, and Husein Cahid). The society was established by the initiative of Ziya Gökalp and pursued the following aims: (1) The purging from Turkic life of foreign and pernicious influences, revival of the old Turkic (Asiatic) culture, and purification of the Turkish language by eliminating Persian and Arabic loan-words; (2) Scientific determination of the ethnic and cultural community of all 'Turanians', i.e. Turks, Mongols, Tunguz, Finno-Ugric and other Uralo-Altaic peoples; etc." (see S.A. Zenkovsky, *Pan-Turkism and Islam in Russia* [Cambridge, MA: Harvard University Press, 1960], pp. 107, 299). Safarian reports that "The name of Halide Edib was mentioned in *Tiirkciiliigiin Esaslan* ('The Principles of Turkism') by Ziya Gökalp as one of the writers that had rendered an exclusive service to Turkism." He cites Ziya Gökalp, *Tiirkciiliigiin Esaslan* (Istanbul, 1961), p. 11.

55. Edib had what one might think of as a revolutionary *salon* in Constantinople, which she also discusses in her *Memoirs*. With Yusuf Akçura and Ziya Gökalp, she founded the *Halka Doğru* (Towards the People) movement, whose object was to nationalize the Anatolian masses. It is because of her role in the establishment of "Turkish identity" (Edib was called "Mother of the Turk" for her novel *Yeni Turan*) that Cemal Pasha asked her to direct the forcible Turkification of Armenian children at the orphanage of Antoura. Robert Fisk considers her direction of that orphanage genocidal.

who want to understand the Armenian Genocide. They also reflect her complexity as a person. They are more political than they are historical. This makes them at once difficult to interpret and an excellent source of information for the scholar who wishes to understand the Armenian Genocide as long as he remembers that they are the work of light and shadows: the work of a politician.[56]

See "Living Proof of the Armenian Genocide," *The Independent*, March 9, 2010.

56. One obvious sign of the politics inherent in Edib's biography is her account of her direction of the orphanage at Antoura. A comparison of her and Karnig Panian's account (*Goodbye, Antoura*) speaks volumes about the light and shadows of Edib's biography.

Chapter 2

"DENIAL CONTINUES
THE PROCESS"

In their public response to Ambassador Kandemir's letter, Professor Lifton and his colleagues Professors Smith and Markusen claim that "genocide does not end with its last human victim: denial continues the process."[1] Their claim is embedded in a thoughtful reflection on the "ways in which the denial of genocide causes 'violence to others'" and can be considered a "form of contribution to genocidal violence" in its own right.[2]

The authors identify two primary ways in which genocide denial "continues the process" of genocide:

    1. it instigates future genocides;

and

    2. it assails the victims of genocide with new genocidal violence.

The first of these ways is well known to those who have reflected on genocide:

> By absolving the perpetrators of past genocides from responsibility for their actions and by obscuring the reality of genocide as a widely practiced form of state policy in

---

1. SML, p. 14.

2. SML, pp. 13–14.

the modern world, denial may increase the risk of future
outbreaks of genocidal killing.[3]

The authors need not even have formulated this conclusion in
the conditional tense. History demonstrates that both "absolving
the perpetrators of past genocides from responsibility for their actions" and "obscuring the reality of genocide" *actually do* and *have*
set the precedent that encouraged the repetition of genocidal violence.[4] One need look no further than Hitler's Obersalzberg speech
to see this.[5]

---

3. SML, p. 14.

4. Vahakn Dadrian makes this point in his comparison of the Armenian
    Genocide and the Holocaust. He argues that the Allies' failure to prose-
    cute those responsible for the Armenian Genocide, despite their "solemn
    and public pledge" (Dadrian, p. 395), could not but have emboldened
    Hitler. Citing David Matas, he states that "Nothing emboldens a crimi-
    nal so much as the knowledge that he can get away with the crime. This
    was the message the failure to prosecute for the Armenian Massacre
    gave to the Nazis. We ignore the lesson of the Holocaust at our peril"
    (Dadrian, p. 409).

5. For our purpose here, the significant part of the copy of that speech,
    which is commonly referred to as L-3 from its classification at the Nurem-
    berg Trials, is this: "Unsere Stärke ist unsere Schnelligkeit und unsere
    Brutalität. Dschingis Khan hat Millionen Frauen und Kinder in den Tod
    gejagt, bewußt und fröhlichen Herzens. Die Geschichte sieht in ihm nur
    den großen Staatengründer. Was die schwache westeuropäische Zivilisa-
    tion über mich behauptet, ist gleichgültig. Ich habe den Befehl gege-
    ben—und ich lasse jeden füsilieren, der auch nur ein Wort der Kritik
    äußert—daß das Kriegsziel nicht im Erreichen von bestimmten Linien,
    sondern in der physischen Vernichtung des Gegners besteht. So habe
    ich, einstweilen nur im Osten, meine Totenkopfverbände bereitgestellt
    mit dem Befehl, unbarmherzig und mitleidslos Mann, Weib und Kind
    polnischer Abstammung und Sprache in den Tod zu schicken. Nur so
    gewinnen wir den Lebensraum, den wir brauchen. Wer redet heute noch
    von der Vernichtung der Armenier?" (Our strength lies in our speed and
    in our brutality. Genghis Khan sent millions of women and children into
    death knowingly and with a light heart. History sees in him only the
    great founder of states. What weak Western European civilization alleges
    about me does not matter. I have given the command—and I shall have

That genocide denial also assails the victims of genocide with new *genocidal violence* is, perhaps, less evident. It is not thereby less true.

Genocide denial and the violence of lying

That genocide denial is *per se* violent should be obvious to anyone who has reflected on the damage caused by lying.[6] None of us likes to think about it, especially while he is actively engaged in it, but deliberately denying a known truth—or asserting a known falsehood—is inherently violent. Kant makes the point in his characteristically pithy definition of lying: *"Mendacium est falsiloquium in praeiudicium alterius"* [A lie is a falsehood that harms another].[7]

---

anyone who utters one word of criticism shot—for the goal of a war is not reaching certain [geographical] lines, but the physical elimination of the enemy. And so for the present only in the East, I have put my Death-Head units [*Totenkopfverbände*] in place with the command relentlessly and without compassion to kill all men, women, and children of Polish origin and language. Only thus can we win the living space [*Lebensraum*] that we need. Who today speaks about the destruction of the Armenians?"). Much ink has been spilled on this passage. See, e.g., Margaret Lavinia Andersen, "Who Still Talked About the Extermination of the Armenians: German Talk and German Silences," in AQG, pp. 199–220; Hannibal Travis, "Turkey Past and Future: Did the Armenian Genocide Inspire Hitler," *Middle East Quarterly* (Winter 2013), pp. 27–35; Dadrian, pp. 394–412. While its authenticity has been challenged, scholarship has demonstrated the quote is authentic. I shall return to Hitler's quote later in this book.

6. I discussed this more in depth in "Lies, Damned Lies, and Genocide." The backbone of my argument there is that lying can be criminal insofar as it can be an illocutionary act of genocide that has the perlocutionary effect of creating mental harm to its intended victims.

7. Immanuel Kant, "On the Supposed Right to Lie Because of Philanthropic Concerns," *Grounding for the Metaphysics of Morals* (2nd ed.), ed. and trans. James W. Ellington (Indianapolis: Hackett, 1981), p. 64. He adds that "a lie always harms another; if not some other human being, then it

The reason why lies "harm another" is that truth is a necessary condition of the development and proper performance of our characteristically human functions. Aristotle gives two basic definitions of human beings. He claims that we are by nature both "rational animals" and "political"—or what might more precisely be called "civic animals." What he does not add, but could have, is that both as rational and as civic animals, we have a natural inclination toward the truth.

This is self-evident in the case of our rationality. When Aristotle begins the *Metaphysics* with that stunning line, "all men by nature desire to know," he is implicitly claiming that all men by nature desire the truth. Knowledge is by definition the truth. As we cannot develop or properly function as human beings without knowing, neither can we develop or properly function as rational beings without truth. We forget this at our own peril.[8]

---

nevertheless does harm to humanity in general, inasmuch as it vitiates the very source of right."

8. Last year I taught a seminar on boredom. Its purpose was to reflect on the phenomenon of widespread apathy—which is often misclassified as egoism—that is plaguing the Western world, and particularly young adults. The first reading I assigned my class was Harry Frankfurt's "On Bullshit." It began a semester-long discussion on the causes of the apathy that young Western adults manifest. I discovered that young adults today are primarily frightened, lonely, and purposely disengaged. They have (they emphatically and repeatedly stated throughout the semester) heard so much "bullshit" throughout their lives that they do not know what or whom to believe. Nor, they insisted, have they been given the means by which to sort through the "bullshit." Their schooling (they claimed) did not teach them how to think, or even require them to think. Their teachers presented them with data that they had to repeat in order to score well on tests. In the midst of their classes, the teachers would tell the students, "You should write this down. It is going to be on the test." Teachers thereby taught them to master repeating what you are told to say. Given Frankfurt's definition of "bullshit," the students insisted that term be applied to their schooling. Nor did the students have strong families that could compensate for the "bullshit." Most of the students came from broken homes. The combination of weak families, the massive presence of "bullshit" in our world, and test-oriented

Truth is also essential to us as "civic animals." "It would be impossible for men to live together," Aquinas claims, "unless they believed one another, as declaring the truth one to another."[9] How could we buy anything unless we believed that the seller and producer were truthful about the product? How could we eat anything unless we believed the same thing? How could we take public transportation, attend a concert, go to school, or do any one of the thousands of things that we do every day without trusting that those who provide us with services, use our services, and share the services with us are truthful when they suggest that they are driving and taking a bus in order to get to some specific place, performing and attending concerts because they want to play and hear music, teaching and attending class because they love knowledge?

Lies run contrary to our natural inclination toward the truth. They contradict the liar's own natural inclination toward the truth. This is why liars can be lied to. Their natural inclinations lead them to expect others to tell the truth, even though they themselves do not do so.

Above all, lies run contrary to the natural inclinations of those people to whom the lies are told: the passive subjects of the lies. This is why lies harm persons. They subvert our minds and fray our

---

schooling has made young Western adults incapable of trusting themselves as persons who are capable of knowing, and of truly caring for anything. Caring is a risk that requires knowing that you know that what you care about is worth caring about. The "bullshit" has made young adults terrified of reality. So young adults prefer not to engage with reality. They are fully aware of the facts both that they are escaping reality and that they are doing so because they do not think that they are capable of discerning what is true from what is false. They prefer not to care. They prefer "numbness to the appeal of all things," as Abbi Parenteau, one of my students, defined boredom.

9. Aquinas, *Summa Theologica*, II-II, 109: 3, ad 1. Aquinas deduces this from his premise that truth is, in a sense, a social obligation.

relations to reality.[10] It is because they do so that lies are used to enslave people, as Orwell chillingly reminds us.[11]

Acts "done against the inclination of the passive subject" are, as Aquinas claims, by definition violent.[12] They are analogous to pounding square pegs into round holes, giving a cell phone a drink, or using a computer to hit a baseball. They do not just contradict the intended purpose of the objects acted upon. They can deform or break those objects.

Lying is an act of this sort. It contradicts the inclinations of those persons who hear and believe them. It can deform or break those persons who hear and believe them. Lying is inherently violent.

Genocide denial is a subspecies of lying:

---

10. See Harry Frankfurt, *On Truth* (New York: Alfred Knopf, 2009), pp. 78–79: "Lies are designed to damage our grasp of reality. So they are intended, in a very real way, to make us crazy. To the extent that we believe them, our minds are occupied and governed by fictions, fantasies, and illusions that have been concocted for us by the liar. What we accept as real is a world that others cannot see, touch, or experience in any direct way. A person who believes a lie is constrained by it, accordingly, to live "in his own world"—a world that others cannot enter and in which the liar himself does not truly reside. Thus the victim of the lie is, in the degree of his deprivation of truth, shut off from the world of common experience and isolated in an illusory realm to which there is no path that others might find or follow."

11. George Orwell, *1984* (Fairfield, IA: www.1stworldlibrary.org, 2004), p. 46: "The Party said that Oceania had never been in alliance with Eurasia. He, Winston Smith, knew that Oceania had been in alliance with Eurasia as short a time as four years ago. But where did that knowledge exist? Only in his own consciousness, which in any case must soon be annihilated. And if all others accepted the lie which the Party imposed—if all records told the same tale—then the lie passed into history and became truth. 'Who controls the past,' ran the Party slogan, 'controls the future: who controls the present controls the past.' And yet the past, though of its nature alterable, never had been altered. Whatever was true now was true from everlasting to everlasting. It was quite simple. All that was needed was an unending series of victories over your own memory. 'Reality control,' they called it: in Newspeak, 'doublethink.'"

12. Aquinas, *Summa Theologica*, I-II, q. 6, a. 4, ad 2.

The attempt to deny the Holocaust enlists a basic strategy of distortion. Truth is mixed with absolute lies, confusing readers who are unfamiliar with the tactics of the deniers. Half-truths and story segments, which conveniently avoid crucial information, leave the listener with a distorted impression of what really happened. The abundance of documents and testimonies that confirm the Holocaust are dismissed as contrived, coerced, or forgeries and falsehoods.[13]

Lipstadt's point holds not just for Holocaust denial. It holds for all genocide denial. Genocide denial is inherently violent.

Genocidal violence of the denial of genocide

Smith, Markusen, and Lifton discuss different ways in which scholars have justified the claim that the denial of a known genocide is specifically *genocidal* violence. In Erich Kulka's view, they report, it is genocidal because genocide denial is "a repetition in thought of what was enacted earlier as physical deed."[14] Kulka's view seems to be that the genocide denialist uses words in the same way and for the same reason as the genocidal killer uses weapons: he attacks a specific *genos* with them in order to destroy it. The denial of a known genocide "must be viewed," Kulka claims, as an act of "intellectual aggression."[15] Its intent is made manifest by the fact that denial itself defends those who perpetrated the genocide.

Israel Charny defends the claim that genocide denial is *genocidal* by arguing that it attacks the foundations of an ethnic group.

13. Deborah Lipstadt, *Denying the Holocaust: The Growing Assault on Truth and Memory* (New York/London/Victoria/Toronto/Auckland: Plume, 1994), p. 2.

14. SML, p. 14.

15. SML, p. 14.

[Denial] "attacks the historical spirit and morale" of the survivors and the descendants of those killed and places "further burdens on their recovery." In short, denial prevents healing of the wounds inflicted by genocide. Furthermore, it constitutes an "attack on the collective identity and national cultural continuity of the victim people."[16]

The reasoning here points to a basic characteristic of historical facts that concern a *genos*: they are part of that *genos*'s collective memory and, consequently, its identity. Much as one can destroy a person by systematically denying the truthfulness of his memories, so too can one destroy the identity of a *genos* or ethnic group by systematically denying the truthfulness of those historical facts that constitute its history. Just as a person's memories are the foundations of both his knowledge of himself and his identity, the foundations of both a people's knowledge of itself and its identity are its history. This is what the negationist attacks when he denies that a genocide took place: the very foundations of the identity of the *genos* targeted by the genocide. It is because he does this that his violence is *genocidal*.

Deborah Lipstadt views negationism as a sort of character assassination, where the character in question is the character of the people targeted by genocide. Much as rapists often do when, in order to exonerate themselves, they claim that their victims really wanted to be raped, genocide denialists attempt to place the blame of genocidal violence on the victims of the genocide in order to exonerate the genocidal murderers. "Denial aims to reshape history in order to rehabilitate the perpetrators and demonize the victims."[17] Just as the character assassination of an individual is an assault on the identity of a person, so too is the character assassination inherent in genocide negationism an assault on the identity of the *genos* targeted by the genocide. Genocide is precisely the attempt to destroy a *genos*, an ethnic group.

---

16. SML, p. 13.
17. SML, p. 13.

All of these arguments concerning genocide denialism are important. They all point to ways in which denialism "continues the process" of genocide. Yet the account that these scholars propose is, I believe, incomplete. More acts fall under the category "denial of genocide" than the *ex post facto* contemporary attempts to "reshape history in order to rehabilitate the perpetrators and demonize the victims."

Denial of genocide and Theresienstadt

One of the presuppositions of these explanations of the reasons why genocide denial is *genocidal*—"continues the process" of genocide—is *temporal*. They treat genocide denial as something that only take place *after* a genocide has been completed. This can clearly be seen in the passage above, where Smith, Markusen, and Lifton state that negationism would absolve "perpetrators of *past* genocides from responsibility for their actions." It is implicit in Kulka's, Charny's, and Lipstadt's defenses of the claim that genocide denial is genocidal.[18] It can also be seen in Markusen's, Smith's, and Lifton's claim that

> Denial may be thought of as the last stage of genocide, one that continues into the present. A kind of *double killing* takes place: first the physical deed, *followed* by the destruction of *remembrance of the deed*.[19]

---

18. It is not just a presupposition of these defenses. Many accounts of Holocaust denialism trace its origin to the end of World War II. See, for instance, Lipstadt, pp. 49ff. See also Michael Shermer and Alex Grobman, *Denying History: Who Says the Holocaust Never Happened and Why Do They Say It?* (Berkeley/Los Angeles/London: University of California Press. 2009), pp. 39ff; Ted Gottfried, *Deniers of the Holocaust: Who They Are; What They Do; Why They Do It* (Brookfield, CT: Twenty-First Century Books, 2001).

19. SML, p. 13. The italics are mine.

This presupposition is certainly warranted in the case of current Holocaust denialism.[20] It is not always warranted. Genocide denial can take place *while* the genocide is being perpetrated. This is the lesson of *Theresienstadt.*

Theresienstadt "Ghetto" was an elaborate instance of genocide denial. One of its purposes was to provide the Nazis with plausible deniability for their genocidal plans and actions.[21] The Nazis advertised it in Germany as the Jewish "Spa town." They called it the "Paradise Ghetto."[22] Heydrich apparently wanted it to house elderly Jews, decorated Jewish war veterans, and famous Jews—who

---

20. David Irving began his career as a negationist well after the fall of the Third Reich. So too did Robert Faurisson, Richard Verrall, Ernst Zundel, Willis Carto, the Institute of Historical Review, A.R. Butz, Mark Weber, and so forth.

21. The other and primary purpose of the Theresienstadt Ghetto was that it was a transit camp. See Norbert Troller, *Theresienstadt: Hitler's Gift to the Jews*, trans. Susan E. Cernyak-Spatz, ed. Joel Shatzky (Chapel Hill, NC/London: University of North Carolina Press, 1991), p. xxii: "Of the 140,000 people who entered this walled town between November 1941 and April 1945, one month before the Russian army arrived and liberated it, almost 90,000 were sent to their deaths in Auschwitz-Birkenau, Treblinka, and other lesser-known camps; another 35,000 died in the ghetto itself, most from hunger and disease, many of these elderly people and children, and only 16,832 survived, many of whom entered near the end of the war when living conditions had improved and the deportations had practically stopped."

22. See, on this, Berkley, *Hitler's Gift: The Story of Theresienstadt.* In the very first paragraphs Berkley describes the newspaper articles in the German press reporting that "the Fuerher was presenting an entire city to the Jews." He summarizes the condition of the gift: those who accepted had to be elderly German and Austrian Jews, war veterans, prominent Jews, and they had to "sign contracts turning over all their remaining assets to the SS." In return they would move to Theresienstadt and be taken "care of for the rest of their lives." They could even choose their accommodations: SS officials asked them to specify in advance where they wanted their rooms, such as on the lake, by the square, etc. They were encouraged to take their most elegant clothes. Troller gives a brief but painful description of the arrival of those wealthy Jews who believed the Nazi propaganda on Theresienstadt. See Troller, p. 56: "the most elegant ladies—and there were many of them—the most self-assured gentlemen."

would "encourage domestic and foreign inquiry"—from Germany, Austria, and Czechoslovakia.[23] His idea, it seems, was to have a model camp to show those people who might have thwarted the "Final Solution" that there was no foul play in the Nazi regime's treatment of the Jews.[24]

Theresienstadt "Ghetto" had its own Jewish "government," the *Judenältestenrat des Ghetto Theresienstadt*—the Council of Elders of Theresienstadt Ghetto.[25] It had a post office. It had a bank, the

---

23. See, on this, Tara Zahra, *The Lost Children: Reconstructing Europe's Families after World War II* (Cambridge, MA/London: Harvard University Press, 2011), p. 79: "Terezín [Theresienstadt] was, in Ruth Kluger's words, 'a stable that supplied the slaughterhouse,' but it developed a second function as an alibi for the Final Solution. As elderly German and Austrian Jews and decorated World War I veterans ... were forced from their homes in 1941 and 1942, some prominent Nazis intervened on their behalf. Heydrich realized that he could use Terezin to deflect internal criticism about Nazi racial policies. At the Wannsee Conference on January 20, 1942, he specified that German and Austrian Jews over the age of 65, along with decorated and disabled war veterans, would not be deported to the death camps (at least not immediately), but rather 'relocated' to Terezín, where they would (supposedly) live out their retirement in peace. This 'practical solution,' he explained, would 'eliminate the many interventions [on behalf of the Jews] with one stroke.' Prominent Jews whose disappearance might generate unwanted publicity were also deported to the camp." See also Gerlach, p. 771: "Heydrich planned to use the new camp at Theresienstadt in the Protectorate of Bohemia and Moravia to intern Jews who were more than sixty years old or who might be regarded as 'doubtful cases.'"

24. One of the issues that could have thwarted the "Final Solution" were the cases of the so-called *mischlinge*: persons who were part German. They had German relatives, who could and did intervene with the Nazis. See, e.g., Gerlach, p. 779: "Part-Jews and Jewish spouses in mixed marriages had too many non-Jewish relatives and friends. Treating them more harshly could cause too much unrest." Cf. Berkley, p. 57.

25. The Council of Elders, having no real decisional power, had to execute Nazi orders. On this subject see Troller, p. 25: "The so-called Jewish 'self-government' received their curt orders every morning when a small delegation of the Council of Elders had to appear at the SS headquarters and these orders had to be executed without any objection or contradiction. They were immediately handed on, in transcript or so-called file entries, to

Bank der Jüdischen Selbstverwaltung (Bank of Jewish Self-Administration), whose director was the famous Zionist Dr. Desider Friedmann.[26] It even had its own printed currency, the krone, which had a portrait of Moses holding the tablets of the 10 Commandments. It had schools for the children. It had streets with normal-sounding names displayed on wooden signs on the corners. The Ghetto "housed" musicians, artists, actors, scholars. It was "home" to the *Prominenten*—prominent Jews.[27] It had shops.[28] It had a café.

---

the lower echelons of the administration." The power they did have was determining how to execute Nazi orders. Specifically, they had to decide whom to send to the "transports to the East": who would fill the Nazi extermination quotas. Troller describes this very well. See, e.g., p. 35: "Someone saw Eichmann or Möhs go into the Magdeburger central office. Immediate, all-pervading paralysis. Whose turn would it be? Who of my family is on the list? One saw gripping fear in everyone's eyes—with the exception of the 'protected,' of course. The Council of Elders had to bear the burden of having to make the selection for the transport assignment during their nightlong conference." The horror is that the members of the Council of Elders knew what "transportation to the East" entailed. See p. 51: "After a few months (of transports) the Council of Elders knew of the activities in the East, but they said nothing. They even know of how little value was the so-called 'protection' of the AK1 and AK2 [those who were promised that they would never be sent East] was."

26. See Berkley, p. 35: "The bank would employ 50 to 60 people and issue 53 million crowns in notes of 1–100-crown denominations." Upon their arrival, all new "residents" of the concentration camp were compelled to exchange their money and assets into Theresienstadt's Kronen and open an account in the bank. The bank had more than 50,000 accounts. The currency, which was originally called the "Ghetto Krone" and subsequently called the "Theresienstadt Krone," was a farce. Theresienstadt's real currency was food and cigarettes. See Troller, p. 80: "Furnishing a room was paid for with two loaves of bread or twenty cigarettes. These customers were well-to-do. Cigarettes and bread, margarine and sugar, were the common coin of the ghetto. Sixteen cigarettes was the equivalent of a loaf of bread."

27. Berkley gives a good summary of the *prominenten*. They included generals, barons, and baronesses. See Berkley, pp. 10, 92.

28. The "goods sold" in the shops were nothing but that part of the personal belongings of Theresienstadt Ghetto prisoners that the Nazis did not find

Heydrich was long dead—and Eichmann had long been given direct supervision of the Theresienstadt—when King Christian X of Denmark famously forced the Nazis to use the camp for its intended denialist purpose. The king was so upset by the arrest and deportation of those Danish Jews who had not been able to escape to Sweden before the Nazis rounded them up that he insisted that his government and the International Red Cross inspect Nazi concentration camps.

It took the Nazis a month to agree to the visit. The Nazi roundup of Danish Jews took place in early October 1943. Eichmann informed King Christian on November 4 that his representatives would be allowed to see Theresienstadt. The Nazis then took seven months to carry out the *Verschönerungsaktion* (Operation Beautification), whose purpose was to embellish the concentration camp for the Danish and International Red Cross inspection.

They planted trees, set up flowerbeds, and covered the "Town Square" with new grass. They spruced up the bank, stores, and café. They had new façades built for them. They installed new lighting in them. They gave them fresh coats of paint. They ordered new uniforms for the waiters and waitresses. They built a music pavilion and playground for the children. They built dressing rooms and shower stalls at the playing field. They gave Jews access to the town's parks. They called medical doctors from Germany to inspect the hospital. They sent new medical supplies, new crisp linen sheets and pillows. They set up a dentist's office. They ordered new

---

useful. When prisoners, many of whom had been duped into believing that they were moving to a new home, arrived at the Ghetto, they were "processed" through the "Schleuse." Their luggage was taken. Everything valuable or useful was confiscated. See Troller, pp. 58–59: "The rest, the odds and ends, the half-squeezed tubes of toothpaste, lanolin, other kinds of ointments, the candle stubs, the flashlights minus the batteries, matchboxes, mouthwash, pencil stubs, erasers, notebooks, writing paper and thousands of other useless items, rubbish, were sent as merchandise to the 'stores' of the ghetto, where we were allowed to purchase them for bogus money, the ghetto currency."

furniture for the "homes" that were to be inspected. They built new beds. They "gave" new "residents" little plots of land where they could plant "their own" gardens. In the months preceding the visit, the Nazis allowed the inhabitants of the Ghetto to receive the food that was sent to them from abroad, so that the "citizens" of the "self-governed" and "autonomous" Jewish "Paradise town" would look healthier. [29] The Nazis even "beautified" the population of Theresienstadt. Some 7,500 of the "worst looking" Jews were transported to Auschwitz right before the arrival of the Danish and Red Cross delegation, so that the population would be more attractive and the camp not look too crowded. [30]

Maurice Rossel, the Swiss representative of the International Red Cross who accompanied the Danish inspectors of Theresienstadt, was completely deceived by the Nazis' *Verschönerung*. [31] "One found in the ghetto goods that were almost impossible to find in Prague," he claimed, and "the smarter women were all wearing silk stockings, hats, scarves, and carried modern handbags." Their healthcare system was of a quality, he remarked, that had "seldom been seen." The summation of his glowing 15-page report of the treatment of Jews in Theresienstadt Ghetto was that "our amazement was extraordinary to find in the ghetto a city that was leading an almost normal existence." [32] He insisted that there was nothing amiss there. [33] Apparently, the thought that that which looks too good to be true might just be so never crossed his mind.

---

29. The Red Cross visit of June 1944 was not the first visit. The previous year the German Red Cross inspected the camp. Walter Hartmann and Dieter Neuhaus were horrified. See Berkley, pp. 164–65.

30. See Berkley, pp. 168–69.

31. Troller's sarcastic comment on this matter comes after his description of the "merchandise" for sale in the "stores"—see note 26 above—"The Red Cross Commission was impressed" (Troller, p. 59)

32. See Berkley, pp. 177–78.

33. See http://data.ushmm.org/intermedia/film_video/spielberg_archive/transcript/RG60_5019/A67D46B8-2B61-41F6-877D-6FF0E04279F4.pdf. See also Sébastien Farré and Yan Schubert, "L'illusion de l'objectif. Le

The *Verschönerungsaktion* was so successful that the Nazis decided to make a movie so that their deception could reach a wider audience.[34] They wanted the Red Cross, the German people, and neutral countries to "see" that the Jews were happy and well treated. The movie was called *Der Führer schenkt den Juden eine Stadt* ("The Führer Gives the Jews a City").[35] The immaculate working conditions, the healthy men at the forge, the soccer game with its exultant spectators with clearly visible Stars of David, the showers in which one can see healthy naked men, the lectures filled with interested well-dressed and well-nourished people wearing Stars of David, the concerts, the children eating bread and butter, the vegetable gardens that one can see in the movie—not to mention the smiling children in the Red Cross's pictures of the concentration camp—all show how alluring genocide denialism can be. Nowhere does one see a hint of soldiers and machine guns, stripes and

---

délégué du CICR Maurice Rossel et les Photographies de Theresienstadt," *Le Mouvement Social*, 227 (2009), pp. 65–83; Aimé Bonifas, "A 'Paradisacal' Ghetto of Theresienstadt: The Impossible Mission of the International Committee of the Red Cross," *Journal of Church and State*, 34 (1992), pp. 805–18.

34. This was not the first movie the Nazis commissioned to document the "Paradise Ghetto." In 1942 they had asked Irina Dodaleva to make a movie.

35. The actual title of the movie was *Theresienstadt: Ein Dokumentarfilm aus dem jüdischen Siedlungsgebiet* (Terezin: A Documentary Film of the Jewish Resettlement). The name *Der Führer schenkt den Juden eine Stadt* ("The Führer Gives the Jews a City") was apparently given to the movie by survivors of Theresienstadt. The movie was directed by Kurt Gerron, the famous actor and director who played Kiepert, the magician in *The Blue Angel* opposite Marlene Dietrich, was in the original cast of Brecht's *Dreigroschenoper* (*The Threepenny Opera*), and was one of the Jews who was denigrated in that horrendous Nazi propaganda movie *Der Ewige Jude* (1940).

There were several private showings of *Der Führer schenkt den Juden eine Stadt* in April 1945. In the 1960s, part of the movie was discovered in Czechoslovakia. It can be seen at https://www.youtube.com/watch?v=oWGEyxoM_Go.

Gerron (and those whom he filmed) was deported to Auschwitz as soon as he completed the movie. He and his wife were gassed upon their arrival. Gerron's life is the subject of the documentary *Prisoner of Paradise* (2002/3).

starvation, gas chambers and crematoria that we have all come to associate with the Holocaust.[36]

The *Verschönerungsaktion* began in December 1943. The Red Cross visit took place on June 23, 1944. Auschwitz was liberated on January 27, 1945.

Denial and the perpetration of a genocide

There is a second important presupposition in the explanations of the way in which genocide "denial continues the process" of genocide in the literature that I am discussing. They presume that the genocide, whose historical factuality is being denied by the negationist, is an event *distinct* from the act of denying it. These scholars' accounts of denialism, in other words, assume that genocide denial is *not part* of the genocide being denied.

Like the first presupposition, this belief is warranted in the case of post-Holocaust negationism. Robert Faurisson might act like a "paper Eichmann," as Vidal-Naquet claims, for his negationist publications and lectures.[37] But his works are not part of the actual planning and carrying out of the Nazi genocide of Europe's Jews. They do not directly contribute to the Holocaust itself. An *ex post facto* "paper Eichmann" is not Eichmann, or his colleague.

This presupposition is also not always warranted. Just as genocide denial need not take place after a genocide has ended, so too does denial not have to be distinct from—not share the causes of—the genocide whose factuality it denies.

---

36. Bedřich Fritta drew a poignant comment to Kurt Gerron's movie called "Film and Reality," which was recently exhibited in the Jüdisches Museum Berlin. See http://www.jmberlin.de/fritta/en/phantasmagorien.php. For an interesting analysis of the movie, see Brad Prager, "Interpreting the Visible Traces of Theresienstadt," *Journal of Modern Jewish Studies*, 7.2 (2008), pp. 175–94.

37. SML, p. 14.

Theresienstadt "Ghetto" was part of the Holocaust in every significant way in which something can be a proper part of something else. Its efficient cause was the Nazi regime. It was materially and formally part of the Holocaust. It was a place where Jews were imprisoned for being Jews. It was a place where Jews were killed for being Jews. It was a place where Jews died by the tens of thousands. It was a transit camp for Jews who were being sent to the extermination camps. Its purpose was the perpetration of the Holocaust.[38]

Most importantly for the purpose of the present argument, Theresienstadt was masterfully deceptive. As the model camp, it served an important purpose for the Nazis: it lent plausibility to their denial that they were murdering Jews, and thus enabled them to continue to do so. The only reason for the *Verschönerungsaktion* was the continuation of the Holocaust. The Nazis wanted to convince the King of Denmark, the Red Cross, and the German people that their concentration camps were not extermination camps so that they could continue undisturbed to exterminate Europe's Jews. The success of their denial had immediate results. The Danes—Frans Hvass of the Danish Foreign Office, and Dr. E. Juel-Henningsen, an administrator from the Danish Ministry of Health who with Rossel had inspected Theresienstadt "Ghetto"— were so taken in by the *Verschönerung* that they handed in a report entitled "Jewish Paradise on Earth." It convinced the Danish Red Cross to stop insisting that it be allowed to inspect Birkenau Family Camp (BIIb). Himmler responded to Danish silence on Birkenau by ordering the gassing of the family camp there. That took place July 10–12, 1944, just two and a half weeks after the famous Red Cross inspection of Theresienstadt.

---

38. The artists who were imprisoned in Theresienstadt Ghetto left us with testimony of the appalling (and quasi-grotesque) conditions in which the Jews lived. See, for instance, Leo Hass's "Jewish Children Marching in Terezin," painted in 1942, or Bedřich Fritta's "Facades for the International Commission," painted between 1943 and 1944.

Nearly all of the people who were filmed in the movie *Der Führer schenkt den Juden eine Stadt* ("The Führer Gives the Jews a City") were sent to Auschwitz as soon as the movie was finished.

Post-genocide denial and intra-genocide denial

What Theresienstadt makes clear is that there are at least two distinct types of genocide denial, which we might call *post-genocide denial* and *intra-genocide denial*, respectively. The first type of genocide denial is typified by David Irving. He began his public denial of the Holocaust in the 1970s, years after the fall of the Third Reich. The second type of genocide denial is typified by Reinhard Heydrich and Adolf Eichmann. They began to deny that the Holocaust was being perpetrated while they were in the midst of perpetrating it.

The primary difference between *post-genocide denial* and *intra-genocide denial* lies in the relation between that denial and the perpetration of the genocide whose factuality it denies. Heydrich's and Eichmann's genocide denial was a constituent part of the genocide that they helped to perpetrate. Theirs was an instance of *intra-genocidal* negationism. David Irving's denial, on the other hand, while certainly an assault on human dignity, rationality, the foundations of culture, and the Jews, is not a constituent part of the genocide that he denies happened. His is an instance of *post-genocidal* negationism.

On demonstrative and suppressive criminal intents

There are some crimes that call for those who perpetrate them not just to broadcast their actions, but also publicly to acknowledge their responsibility for them. Crimes of civil disobedience, crimes of passion, and acts of terrorism immediately come to mind. Terrorism, according to the official American criminal definition, is the instrumental use of violent crime

1. to intimidate or coerce a civilian population;
2. to influence the policy of a government by intimidation or coercion.[39]

In order to maximize his success, the terrorist must plan and carry out a very public act of destruction—like the destruction of the Twin Towers in New York—and announce that he is responsible for it, as al-Qaeda did. One can neither intimidate nor coerce a population—let alone a government—through invisible crimes, or crimes whose culprits are unknown. Terrorists require publicity. Broadcasting both crime and culprit is part of the criminal intent of acts of terrorism.

Let us call crimes like terrorism *remonstrative crimes* and their intents *remonstrative criminal intents*. We might define them thus: *remonstrative crimes* are those whose success requires public perpetration and acknowledgment; *remonstrative criminal intents* are those that comprise the active divulgation of both crime and culprit.

The vast majority of crimes is not *remonstrative*. In most cases, both publicly perpetrating a crime and proclaiming one's guilt defeat the purpose of the crime. If one murders in order to inherit, both openly doing so and loudly announcing that one has would conflict with the very purpose of the murder. An heir who is convicted of murdering in order to hasten inheriting forfeits his inheritance. Clearly, he cannot want this to happen. It would be contradictory for him to do so, and no one can will a contradiction. Rather, the murdering heir must want to do everything required for his crime to achieve its intended result. He must, as such, want to do everything he can so that he is not caught and convicted. The intent to conceal crime and culpability must, in other words, be inherent in his will to commit the crime. Concealing crime and culpability involves suppressing all evidence of the crime itself (when possible), all evidence that would connect him to his crime, and denying any and all responsibility for the crime. These actions,

---

39. 18 U.S.C. § 2331.

too, must be implicit in the murdering heir's intent to hasten his coming into funds. His inheritance would be assured if both the untimeliness of the bequeather's death and his active involvement in it went undetected.

The same thing holds for theft. A person steals in order to profit from his theft: to keep his loot or sell it. He cannot do this if he is caught stealing. The law acts on the principle that no criminal shall profit from his crime. It forces thieves to return their loot, so the thief must want not to get caught. He must also want to do anything and everything that it takes in order not to get caught. Clearly, he can best get away with his crime if no one knows that he has committed it. He can still get away with it if no one knows that *he* is responsible for it. Thus, the thief's will to commit theft must include denying the theft and his culpability.

If the defining characteristic of *remonstrative crimes* is that their success requires public perpetration and acknowledgment, crimes such as murder and theft are *anti-remonstrative*. They are *stealth crimes*. They are *clandestine crimes*. They are crimes, in other words, for which the culprit (and, ideally, the crime) must remain hidden in order to be completely successful. Let us call them *suppressive crimes*. We might define their intents as *suppressive criminal intents*. They include the suppression and denial of all evidence of both crime and culprit.

Genocide and criminal intent

Genocide is a *suppressive crime*. It is not by chance that the Nazis classified their documents concerning the Holocaust as *Geheime Reichssache* (Secret Reich Business) and used euphemisms like *Sonderbehandlung* (Special Treatment) or *Umsiedlung nach dem Osten* (Resettlement to the East), *Aktion Erntefest* (Operation Harvest Festival), *Aktion Reinhard* (Operation Reinhard), *Die Endlösung der europäischen Judenfrage* (The Final Solution to the European Jewish Question) to describe their genocidal actions. It is not by chance that they ordered *Sonderaktion* 1005 (Special Action 1005) with its *Leichenkommandos* (Corpse Units) to exhume and burn the corpses of the hundreds of thousands of people killed during *Aktion Reinhard.* Hiding their crimes was part of their genocidal intent.

Nazi secrecy was a necessary requisite of their perpetrating the genocide. Had the Holocaust been public knowledge, none of its victims would have boarded the trains, walked under the gates that displayed that horrendous motto *Arbeit macht frei* (Labor Makes One Free), or followed the orders to undress for the disinfecting "showers."[40] The Nazis knew this. This is why they hid each step of their elaborate crime from their victims all the way to the gas chambers.[41] They had musicians play on the platforms for the trains that arrived in Auschwitz. They camouflaged Treblinka as a transit camp.

It was also expedient for the Nazis to hide their crimes from the German population and the rest of the world. They could have stopped the Holocaust.[42] This is why the Nazis officially claimed

---

40. There is direct evidence for this. When the 1,260 children from Bialystok arrived at Theresienstadt, they refused to shower. Their caretakers, who included Franz Kafka's sister Ottilie, finally convinced them to do so. Afterward they learned that the children feared gas. See Berkley, pp. 150–51.

41. One of the horrendous means of deception the Nazis used was postcards. Nazis ordered those Jews who had been deported to "the East" from Theresienstadt, for instance, to write postcards to their family and friends in order to tell them that all was well. The prisoners were allowed to write 30 words. Those postcards often arrived at their destinations after the people who had written them were dead. They convinced the recipients that "transport to the East" did not mean death, though of course it most often did. See, for instance, Hannelore Brenner, *The Girls of Room 28: Friendship, Hope and Survival in Theresienstadt* (New York: Schocken Books, 2009), p. 205. See also Troller, p. 49, and Berkley, p. 153. This was not the only example of the Nazis' use of the postcard technique.

42. Hitler learned that it was important for him to keep the public uninformed of his mass murders in the early days of his euthanasia program. He signed the order for *Aktion* T-4, the German Eugenics killing program, in October 1939, backdating it to September. He officially ordered its cancellation in August 1941. "What eventually persuaded Nazi leaders to cancel the project [*Aktion* T-4] officially was not psychiatric resistance but rather general

that their plan for the Jews was *Umsiedlung nach dem Osten* (Resettlement to the East) and that resettlement was necessary for work-related reasons. They set up Theresienstadt and advertised it as the "spa town" for elderly Jews to complete the cover story. Older Jews could not plausibly be resettled in the east for work-related reasons.

Just as Nazi secrecy was a prerequisite of the short-term success of their genocidal plans, it was a prerequisite of their long-term plans. The Nazis did not want people to know about the genocide. They wanted to avoid getting caught.[43] This is why they used their often ghastly euphemisms in their written communications about the genocide and why they did not keep a clear record of their detailed genocidal plans. It is why they dug up and burned the bodies of the hundreds of thousands of victims of *Aktion Reinhard*. It is why they set up Theresienstadt. It is why they arrested and tortured those artists living in Theresienstadt who documented the horrors going on there.[44] It is why they built their extermination camps in Poland. It is why they began to dismantle their extermination camps while the Russians advanced. It is why they burned documents before the Russians arrived. It is why, up to the very end, with fronts collapsing on every side, they frantically tried to hide those prisoners whom they had not exterminated. They sent the prisoners in Poland on a series of death marches toward Germany. They drowned some of them in the Baltic Sea. The marches lasted until the very end. Four days before the Americans arrived in Buchenwald, the Nazis marched the prisoners away from the front. They marched Dachau's prisoners to Tegernsee on April 26, 1945,

---

resistance among the German people, articulated and heightened by a few courageous Protestant and Catholic religious leaders" (*Nazi Doctors*, p. 89). Hitler did not end his eugenics program after publicly announcing its termination. Eugenics centers such as Hadamar, Hartheim, Sonnenstein, and Bernburg secretly continued to kill persons for years.

43. On this point, one wonders if the 1992 alternative history novel by Robert Harris, *Vaterland*, might not just give the most plausible account of Nazi post-genocidal designs.

44. See Troller, pp. 130–60.

three days before the American liberation of that camp, and four days before Hitler's suicide.

Hiding genocide is part of the intention of those who commit genocide. Genocide is a *suppressive crime*. Not considering genocide a *suppressive crime*—not realizing that denial is an integral part of the intent to commit genocide—can lead to a serious misunderstanding not just of a given genocide, but also of some of the actions through which the genocide was perpetrated. Holocaust denialism demonstrates this. Just as the Red Cross's Maurice Rossel was completely fooled by Theresienstadt, so too are many people misled by hatemongers who claim that things like the Nazi euphemisms and Theresienstadt demonstrate that the Holocaust never took place.

Intra-genocidal negationism feeds *post-genocidal* negationism.

Chapter 3

KANDEMIR'S GENOCIDE: MOTIVES AND ACTS

I had meant for this book to be an article, and in my original plan, the article was to begin with a follow-up question to my first article on negationism. The question I had in mind is this: Granted that Ambassador Kandemir—and the Republic of Turkey in whose name he wrote—committed an act of genocide against the Armenians by denying in his letter to Professor Lifton that the 1915 genocide had taken place, did this letter constitute a *new* genocide against the Armenians?

At first glance, my question looks ridiculous. Ambassador Kandemir sent his letter to Professor Lifton 76 years after the Ottoman Empire entered World War I and 67 years after the signing of the Treaty of Lausanne, between which events the vast majority of the atrocities whose factuality he denies and distorts in his letter took place. Ambassador Kandemir was not yet born when the 1915 Armenian Genocide officially began. Nor was he alive in 1923 when historians claim that that genocide ended. How, then, could his genocide not be distinct from *the* Armenian Genocide? Surely the ambassador could not have participated in the perpetration of a horrendous crime that was arguably completed before he was born.

What is more, the ambassador's acts of commissioning, editing, and signing a letter, which he then had sent to Professor Lifton, do not seem to have anything in common with those crimes committed by Ottoman Turks during World War I and in the years shortly thereafter and whose victims were the Western Armenians. What do commissioning, editing, and signing a letter have to do with hanging innocent men, throwing them down ravines, locking them in buildings that were then set on fire, forcing countless women and children to march through deserts without food or water, raping them, disemboweling them, or any one of the other innumerable atrocities perpetrated against the Western Armenians during World War I? And if these sets of acts have nothing to do with one another, how can the ambassador (and the Republic of Turkey) have committed anything but a new genocide of the Armenians?

The objections here can be simply stated. It seems to be a self-evident truth that:

- Temporally and materially distinct acts cannot be one and the same act.

It would seem to be self-evident that closing a window in New York on January 17, 1995, and assassinating Abraham Lincoln in Ford's Theater in Washington, D.C., on April 14, 1865, cannot be the same act. They are different kinds of acts and acts that took place at different times. But

- The Armenian Genocide and Ambassador Kandemir's genocide are temporally and materially distinct acts.

Therefore, it seems to be self-evident that

- The ambassador's genocide cannot but be a new Armenian Genocide.

End of story, it would seem.

And yet the objections are false. It is not just possible for temporally and materially distinct acts to be parts of one and the same act. Significant human acts all seem to be composed of temporally and materially distinct acts. When I sat on a flight from New York to Los Angeles many months ago, I began to write this book on Turkish negationism and the Armenian Genocide, parts of which

I knew I would read at the genocide conferences at the University of Padova and in Philadelphia, and at the Premio Ostana in Piedmont. I did not then perform acts that are temporally identical to the ones that I am performing now. Many months have elapsed since that flight. Nor did I then perform acts that are materially identical to the ones that I am performing now. On that flight, I read (and annotated) Taner Akçam's *A Shameful Act*. I am not doing the same thing now. This does not mean that I was not writing this book while I was flying to LA those many months ago. Reading, thinking, and taking notes are all *inherent* in the act of writing a book, as little as it may be.

Acts, their objects, and definitions

The point here can be made formally. Acts, as Aristotle and Aquinas often repeated, are distinguished not by their material means, but by their objects. In the case of intentional acts, they are distinguished by their motives or ends.

Teaching is not conversing, though both acts make use of the voice and the spoken word. It is the reason *why* one produces vocal sounds, the goal that one pursues through his speaking, that determines what act one is performing when he speaks. That reason, when one is teaching, is to elicit specific acts of understanding regarding a determinate topic in each of one's audience members. This is not the goal of the acts performed by masters of the art of conversation when they speak. The first thing that those masters would point out concerning the goals of their art is that professors cannot grasp them—let alone pursue them—so long as they view every gathering as an audience and every verbal exchange as a set of discrete propositions that are to be corrected and directed toward imparting a precise lesson. Some professors' ingrown pulpits make them insufferable company outside of the classroom.

Making fine motions with a pen on a piece of paper can be the material component of many distinct acts: writing, drawing, and composing, not to mention doodling. Materially, these acts are indistinguishable. It is their goals that both distinguish them and determine what specific act one is performing when he picks up a pen and puts it to use.

Not understanding this point leads to the sort of pseudo-logical problem for which early medieval thinkers and successful lawyers have justly gotten bad reputations. When I take a pig to the market using a rope, it is really I (and not the rope) who am taking the pig, although I am materially only pulling a rope, and it is the rope that is pulling the pig, as much as those successful defense lawyers, who get paid to obfuscate the obvious point that intentions (and not means) determine human acts, would like to convince us of the contrary.

Objects and intermediate objects

Attaining an end, Aristotle points out in the *Nicomachean Ethics*, can require attaining many subordinate ends that are related to the primary end as bridle making is to riding a horse, as riding a horse can be to giving orders to troops, and as giving orders to troops can be to defending one's country. Indeed, Aristotle argues, no important human end—the object of no important human act—can be directly and immediately attained, or, what is the same thing, the realization of every important human end requires the realization of many materially and temporally distinct ends.

This is why Aristotle wrote the *Nicomachean Ethics* in the first place. His object was not just to define the primary end that every human being "by nature" seeks: happiness. Aristotle wanted also to map out the subordinate ends that each person needs to realize in order to be able to reach that primary end.

Everyone wants to be happy. Happiness is not an end that we can immediately reach by willing it. We can sit in a room and will all we want, but our happiness will not appear like a magic flower sprouted from our wills. Nor is happiness something that we can attain through a single intentional act. We cannot push a button, stretch a leg, or take a pill and produce our own happiness. Happiness must be understood, and its necessary conditions too, in order for it to be attained. "If, like archers, we have a target to aim at," the capacity to shoot an arrow, and the concentration and arm strength to make the shot, "we are more likely to hit the right mark."

Most important human ends are like happiness: they are accomplished through the performance of a series of acts that have distinct subordinate ends. The attainment of most human ends is, in other words, *complex*. One does not write a book, teach a course, prepare a lawsuit, buy an airplane ticket, go shopping, cook dinner, commit murder, or perpetrate a genocide by waving a magic wand, shaking a leg, or performing any other single act.

Objects and the definition of acts

For ends whose attainment is *complex*, it is not the particular subordinate end that one is pursuing that determines the specific act that he is performing. That particular end is pursued *for the sake of* the more important end. It is subordinate to that more important end. In this case, it is the more important end that determines the specific act that one is performing.[1]

---

1. There is an apparent paradox inherent in this account of human acts. If (a) all acts are primarily determined by their more important ends (the ends *for the sake of which* the subordinate ends are sought); and (b) there is a single final end *for the sake of which* all human acts are performed (happiness); then it would follow that (c) all human acts are one and the same act. This conclusion would contradict the obvious fact that there are distinct kinds of human acts. Writing is not eating. Traveling is not sleeping. The paradox is important because it could lead one to reject either or both of Aristotle's claims that (1) acts are distinguished through their objects; and (2) there are hierarchies of ends, and the most important of those pursued determines the nature of one's acts. This is only an apparent paradox. The way to see this is to compare the two different senses in which the clause "*for the sake of which*" is used in the two premises. In the second premise, the *end for the sake of which* acts are performed is natural: it is one that the

What made my acts on the airplane those months ago the act of writing this book is the reason why I read and annotated Akçam's *A Shameful Act.* That reason was understanding the relation between genocide denial and genocide in the case of the Armenian Genocide and sharing that understanding in a publication. I read, took notes, and so forth, *for the sake* of giving a written response to my question regarding Ambassador Kandemir's genocide.

Really distinct and materially and temporally distinct acts

If it is the primary object of one's acts that determines the specific act that one is performing, and the attainment of most human ends is *complex,* it is more than just possible for materially and temporally distinct human acts *not* to be really distinct acts. It is likely that many materially and temporally distinct human acts are the same acts.

I really did write this book that I am now writing when I read and annotated Akçam's *A Shameful Act* those many months ago on the airplane, as odd as it might sound to claim that the act of

---

human nature "by nature" pursued. This means that its pursuit is *per se* unavoidable: it is contingent upon human agency only insofar as conscious human functions determine the mode in which one pursues that end, and not the fact that he does. In the first premise, on the other hand, the *end for the sake of which* subordinate ends are pursued is contingent upon human rational agency; its pursuit is not unavoidable, but is contingent upon both an act of will and, optimally, a preceding act of the mind through which a person understands why that specific end is desirable. Once one distinguishes the two different senses in which the clause *for the sake of which* is meant in the two premises, it is clear that the claim that the first premise—(a) all acts are primarily determined by their more important ends (the ends *for the sake of which* the subordinate ends are sought) is meant to hold only for those acts that human agents do not pursue "by nature." This does not mean that intentional acts are not also performed because one *by nature* seeks happiness. It means that one's natural search for happiness does not determine the nature of those acts through which one does so.

reading is to be considered the act of writing, and that an act performed months ago is the same act that I am performing now. I
really was food shopping when I turned the key in the ignition on
my way to Gristedes, long before I came anywhere near food. I really was food shopping when I swiped my credit card an hour later,
when I signed my name a few minutes after that, when I smelled
the apricots twenty minutes before that, and added numbers in my
head to make sure that I was not being cheated. Turning keys and
signing my name are materially distinct acts. I performed them at
distinct times. They both qualify as the same act of food shopping.
I really was cooking both when I was chopping garlic at 7:10 P.M.
and when I was turning on the oven at 7:30, although the acts,
both temporally and materially speaking, have literally nothing in
common with each other.

Thinking that materially and temporally distinct acts are really
distinct would make grasping most human acts impossible. Am I
really performing distinct acts when I exercise my memory, when
I pick up a plastic and metal thing, when I use my fingers to press
square buttons on it, when I press the thing to my ear with the
palm of my left hand, when my left ear drum vibrates and I hear a
voice coming out of the thing, when I exercise my own vocal cords
and facial muscles and smilingly emit sounds into the thing? Or
am I just performing the complex act of making a phone call?

Objects, subordinate objects, acts, and genocide

Like most human objects, genocide is achieved through the realization of a series of subordinate ends. The perpetration of genocide is
complex. Genocides require decisions, planning, organizing, com-
municating, delegating, coordinating, carrying out orders, round-
ing up human beings, slaughtering them, and more. Each of these
acts constitutes a subordinate end which those who would commit
genocide must pursue in order to realize their goal. Each subordinate goal calls for a set of temporally and materially distinct acts.

The decision to commit genocide can take place long before the actual killing takes place. It does not involve swords, guns, telegraphs, trains, or any one of the other means that have been used materially to carry out genocides. The same thing can be said of the constitution and designation of genocidal corps, of the communication of genocidal orders, of the assessment of the progress of one's actuating his genocidal plan. This does not entail that the acts of deciding to exterminate a *genos*, determining who will do the exterminating, delegating the extermination, and assessing the success of the genocide are not acts of genocide.

It is not just those at the end of the chain, those to whom the physical act of elimination is delegated, who are guilty of genocide. The butchers, it would seem, might be less guilty of genocide than are those persons who performed the first acts involved in the genocide: the deciding, the planning, the organizing, and the delegating. The butchers might not even be individually guilty of genocide at all, though they are certainly individually guilty of murder. Acts are distinguished by objects, and the objects of each of the individual butcher's acts might not be to exterminate an entire race. The butchers taken singly might not even have been let in on the state secret that their acts are being coordinated with a series of other acts which, summed up with theirs, would constitute genocide. The butchers might just be murderers.

This cannot be said of those who decide to commit genocide, plan it, and order its perpetration. Theirs is the genocidal act *par excellence*. It constitutes the end to which all other acts involved in perpetrating a genocide are subordinate.

Ambassador Kandemir's genocide

Aristotle's points on intentional acts have direct bearing on the matter of Ambassador Kandemir's genocide. They indicate that the real question to be asked about that genocide should concern the object of Ambassador Kandemir's denial. What was that object?

And what is that object's relation to the object of those responsible for the Armenian Genocide? Was Kandemir's object subordinate to the same object that was pursued by the Committee of Union and Progress (*İttihat ve Terakki Cemiyeti*, CUP) triumvirate that was ruling the Ottoman Empire in 1915 and that resulted in the genocide of the Western Armenians? Or was Ambassador Kandemir's object completely unrelated to the CUP's genocidal object?

These are the questions that I intend to address in the next three chapters of this book. I shall divide them into three primary questions:

1. What was the object of the CUP triumvirate's actions directed against the Armenians?
2. Why was that their object?
3. What is the object of the successor governments of the Republic of Turkey when they deny the factuality of the genocide?

Chapter 4

THE CUP'S PRIMARY OBJECT

It is no secret that the primary object of the CUP's activities from 1908 onward was to create a "homeland" (*vatan*) for the Turks: to secure a geographical location and to construct therein a lasting nation-state that would save "Turkey for the Turks."[1]

---

1. See, on this point, e.g., Uğur Ümit Üngör, "'Turkey for the Turks': Demographic Engineering in Eastern Anatolia, 1914–1945," in AQG, p. 293: "They [CUP leaders] were convinced that only their vision of saving the country by forcefully transforming it into an ethnically homogenous core state with an ethnically homogenous core population was the only acceptable model for the Ottoman Empire." See also Göçek, DV, p. 161: "The CUP firmly believed in the greatness of its mission, defined as 'saving the country in every which way possible.'" Göçek argues that in 1908 "saving the country" was the only clear point in the CUP agenda. The members of the CUP interpreted that mission in a multitude of ways, and in accordance with "abstract political principles of an earlier form of nationalism, a proto-nationalism predicated on a particular type of brotherhood the parameters of which were still naturalized or unclear" (DV, p. 162). She adds that their mission was quasi-religious. "What connected [CUP members] was ... commitment to high ideals. And this ideal consisted of the love of the fatherland. They were all like believers prostrating themselves in front of the stand of the fatherland. All their hearts beat for martyrdom in defense of their faith. There was nothing they would not have sacrificed for this ideal" (DV, p. 164). Hanioğlu clarifies that the CUP was "an umbrella organization composed of loosely affiliated factions" until 1902, "when a more radical faction, the activist nationalist, gained control of the movement," M. Şükrü Hanioğlu, *The Young Turks in Opposition* (Oxford: Oxford University Press, 1995), p. 213. I shall henceforth refer to this book as YTO. The nationalists, Hanioğlu clarifies, were fiercely nationalistic advocates of aggressive social materialism. Their

The political system that the leaders of the CUP envisioned for their "homeland" was, at least officially, to be modeled on modern European nation-states. Its principles were to be variants of the French Republic's *liberté, égalité,* and *fraternité.* The "homeland" itself was to have three primary characteristics, which the CUP's primary ideologists considered the necessary conditions of a lasting political entity. It was:

1. to be inhabited by an ethnically and culturally homogenous people;
2. to have a nationalized culture; and
3. its culture was to be Turkish.

The "homeland" had a fourth important characteristic:

4. it needed to be *created.*

In 1908, none of the necessary elements of the *vatan* that the leaders of the CUP wanted and planned to create—a specifically Turkish culture, a people whose ethnic identity was primarily determined by that culture, and a determinate geographical location to which that ethnic group was both specifically and exclusively bound—actually existed.[2]

---

nationalism, he claims, was "gradually accomplished between 1902 and 1906, and in 1906 CUP propaganda realized a nationalist focus" (p. 211).

2. This is proven by the fundamental shift in the meaning of the two crucial terms of the CUP objective: "vatan" and "Turk." Clear up to the mid-nineteenth century, the term "vatan"—like the associated term "millet" (nation)— did not have specific political meanings for Ottoman Turks. The former did not define a geographical location in such a way as to claim any sort of connection between a location and a determinate culture, people, or ethnic group—"millet." The latter did not define a people in such a way as to ascribe to it the natural right of sovereignty. The term "vatan"—like the term "millet"—began to take on political connotations shortly after the French Revolution, when Ebukir Ratib Efendi tried to impart what he understood about Revolution to his superiors. See, on this, Fatih Yeşil, "Looking at the French Revolution through Ottoman Eyes: Ebukir Ratib Efendi's Observations," in

As Akçam reconstructs the point: "After 1908, the main goal of the Union and Progress movement was the creation of a modern,

---

Bulletin of the School of Oriental and African Studies (University of London), 70.2 (2007), p. 301: "[Ratib Efendi was] the first Ottoman to use *millet* to describe 'the nation.' In Ottoman political lexicon *vatan* was not the motherland but a place where people lived or were born. *Millet* referred not to a nation in the modern sense of the word but one of the communities, bound together by a common religion, which constituted the population of the Empire. The idea that a particular *vatan* should be populated exclusively by a particular *millet* was totally alien to the Ottoman view of the world.... [H]e has recognized the emergence of a new type of state in Europe, a powerful national state united in one language with a common set of beliefs and values. It is for this reason that he coined the term *millet* to refer to a single European people and *vatan* to refer to their homeland." Ratib Efendi's introduction of the term *vatan* was diffused in the nineteenth century by the "Young Ottoman" Namik Kemal, who appropriated the word. On this topic see Bernard Lewis, "Watan," in *Journal of Contemporary History*, 26.3/4, *The Impact of Western Nationalisms: Essays Dedicated to Walter Z. Laqueur on the Occasion of His 70th Birthday* (1991), pp. 523–33. See also Erik J. Zürcher, HMT, p. 68: "To expound his ideas to an Ottoman public, [the "Young Ottoman"] Kemal created a new vocabulary giving old words new meanings corresponding to the terminology of nineteenth-century liberalism. *Vatan*, the Arabic word for one's birthplace, became the equivalent of the French *patrie*, *hürriyet* (being a free man, not a slave) that of *liberty*, *millet* (community) that of *nation*. This new terminology would be the ideological instrumentarium for later generations of Muslims liberals and nationalists." In the twentieth century, the term became part of CUP vocabulary and acquired openly nationalistic overtones. See Taner Akçam, *From Empire to Republic: Turkish Nationalism and the Armenian Genocide* (London/New York: Zed Books, 2004) [henceforth ER], p. 64: "'Until the 19th century, this concept [*vatan*] ... had been used only in a very narrow sense, indicating place of birth or residence, and commanding some sentimental loyalty.' In the middle of the 19th century, Cevdet Paşa claimed that the word *vatan* never had any other meaning for a Turkish soldier than simply the village square. Even as late as the end of the century the term continued to be used in this sense. For example, Sultan Abdulhamid II said that the '*vatan* is the place where people have gathered together.' 'I cannot understand why someone would be willing to die for it. It is not a good thing for so many people to slaughter one another for the sake of the *vatan*.'"

The word "Turk" underwent a similar transformation. As Akçam reports, "the term 'Turk' had long been used within the Ottoman Empire as a pejorative term. Even travelers had remarked that this word was used in Ottoman

centralized state," in which "all of its citizens would be bound by a shared identity and on the basis of universal equality."[3] The "shared identity" was to be the foundation of the CUP's modern "homeland." It was to provide the "emotional tie" that would bind the citizens of the new "modern, centralized state" both to each other and to that state, thereby guaranteeing the survival of the state itself. It was also to ground the new "modern, centralized state's" granting equality of rights to all of its citizens. CUP leaders "opted to unite the principle of universal citizenship according to which everyone was to be treated equally, with a cultural identity."[4] In the new state, cultural equality was to be the prerequisite of equality before the law.

The importance that the leaders of the CUP accorded the link between a shared cultural identity and the stability of a state—not to mention the specific way in which they understood the terms "cultural identity" and "state"—can be clearly seen in the reflections of Yusuf Akçura, one of the party's primary ideologues, on the causes of the

---

lands as a curse word" (Akçam, ER, p. 66; also, e.g., Göçek, DV, p. 119). The pejorative underpinnings of the word "Turk" resulted from the Tanzimat era's push to modernize the Ottoman Empire. At that time, *"alla Franca,"* meaning "in the French (or Western) way," became a household catchphrase symbolizing progress and superiority, while *"alla Turca"*—meaning "in the Turkish way"—with which the phrase *alla Franca* was counterposed, came to symbolize stagnation and inferiority. The CUP reversed the Tanzimat use of the word "Turk." In its vocabulary, "Turk" came to signify a superior mode of being, an ideal, a battle cry, which was meant to unite not just all the Turks in Anatolia, but all Turkish-speaking people in general.

The shift in the meanings of the terms "vatan," "millet," and "Turk"— or, to be precise, the Ottomans' adoption of modern European political terminology—indicate not just what the CUP's political project was, but also its causes. These were not characteristically Ottoman Turkish. They were the CUP's interpretation of the categories of Western political philosophy. This entails not just the obvious point that modern Turkey was deliberately modeled on Western republics. It entails that its very construction is to be interpreted in light of what Palmer calls the *Great Democratic Revolution.* I shall address this point in Chapter 5.

3. Akçam, ASA, pp. 70–71.
4. Akçam, ASA, p. 72.

instability and fragmentation of the late Ottoman Empire.[5] These, he claimed, were the cultural heterogeneity of the many distinct peoples who lived within the borders of the empire and the cultural disparity between the Ottoman state and its many distinct subject peoples:

> The history, customs, religion, relationships, hopes and dreams, manner of thinking, occupational patterns and levels of civilization of the peoples who were Ottoman subjects were so different from one another that it was strange even to imagine them uniting in some compatible way. What sort of point of contact could a Christian Serb, who farmed on the plains of Kosovo, have with a Muslim Arab who lived as a Bedouin in the deserts of Najd?... I ask: Is it possible to find a single Muslim who would make even the smallest concession from his clearly defined religious identity for the sake of a union?... Within the broad expanses of the Ottoman realm, there are two civilizations, two ways of looking at life and the world, two very different philosophies colliding. Is their coexistence at all possible?[6]

---

5. Yusuf Akçura was a Volga Tatar who moved to Constantinople when he was a child. He attended the Military Academy there and was exiled in 1896 for his involvement with the Young Turks. He fled to Paris, where he linked up with Young Turks. He returned to Constantinople after the 1908 revolution. Although he never formally joined the CUP, he worked very closely with it. He founded what was probably the most important Turkish political journal of the time, *Türk yurdu* (Turkish homeland), which advocated Panturanism. In 1912 he, Ziya Gökalp, and Halide Edib founded the *Halka Doğru* (Towards the People) movement, whose object was to nationalize the Anatolian masses. His distance from the CUP helped him become a key figure both after the Armistice of Mudros and in the Turkish Republic. He was a member of the Grand National Assembly and taught Turkish history at Istanbul University. In 1932 he was appointed the first president of the Turkish Historical Society, where he played a key role in the formulation of the official history of the Republic of Turkey.

6. Yusuf Akçura; qtd. by Taner Akçam, ASA, pp. 71–72.

By identifying the causes of the late Ottoman Empire's fragility, Akçura also intentionally pointed to what he thought were the necessary conditions of a stable Turkish state. These are the obverse of what he believed were the causes of the empire's fragmentation: the cultural homogeneity of both those peoples who live within the borders of a state and the state itself. If those people who are culturally "different from one another" cannot "unite in some compatible way," as the passage would claim, then that "compatible unity" upon which a lasting political entity must be founded can only be obtained if people are not culturally "different from one another." And if, as the passage also claims, those citizens whose identity differs from that of the political entity in which they live will not make "the smallest concession" with respect to their identity "for the sake of" that political entity, and if every political entity is as strong as its citizens' investment in it, then it would follow that a lasting political entity and its citizens must also have one and the same cultural identity.[7] A stable state, in other words, requires a national culture.

The national homogenous cultural identity that the CUP wanted for its new "homeland" was "to be formed around the values of the

---

7. Akçura actually articulated this point in a very influential article, "Üç Tarz-ı Siyaset" ["Three Kinds of Policy"], that he published in Cairo in 1904. In that article, Akçura presents and discusses the three possible political systems with which the Ottoman Empire could ensure its survival: Ottomanism, Islamism, and Pan-Turkish Nationalism. Although Akçura does not explicitly argue that one or the other political systems better served "the interests of the Ottoman state, Islam, and all the Turks," the text makes clear that Akçura believed that the only system that had any chance of success with respect to "the interest of the Ottoman state, Islam, and all the Turks" was Pan-Turkish Nationalism predicated on the racial, ethnic, and cultural unity of the Turks. The article has been reprinted as Yusuf Akçura and Ismail Fehmi, in *Oriente Moderno*, 61:1/12 (1981), pp. 1–20, and again in Ahmet Ersoy, Maciej Górny, and Vangelis Kechriotis (eds.), *Discourses of Collective Identity in Central Southeast Europe (1770–1945): Texts and Commentaries*, Vol. III/1, *Modernism: The Creation of Nation-States* (Budapest/ New York: Central University Press, 2010), pp. 218–27. It is also available online at http://vlib.iue.it/carrie/texts/carrie_books/paksoy-2/cam9.html.

dominant national group."[8] It was, in other words, to be Turkish. This should not be surprising. Ottoman Turks thought of themselves as the *Millet-i Hakime,* or the "ruling race."[9] They held fast to the belief that they were the descendants of those who had conquered and built an empire that at its moment of greatest expansion stretched from Algeria to the gates of Vienna.[10] They "accepted Turkish domination of the Ottoman Empire as a situation so natural and obvious as to not merit discussion."[11] The Ottoman Empire's *millet* system sustained this belief. "The Turkish people," as Edib makes the case,

> were used to respecting the lives and the property of a minority, who were almost like religious trusts to them and who went their way without sharing the military burdens of the *ruling race. This tolerance had its roots in the chivalrous attitude of the master to the inferior* as well as in the broad spirit of Islam toward alien religions.[12]

Leaving aside the why of the CUP's specific object for the moment, that object presented the CUP with several fundamental and related problems. They concerned the *what, how,* and *where:*

---

8. Akçam, ASA, p. 72.

9. Akçam, ASA, p. 45. This was clear before 1908. See Göçek, DV, p. 110: "During the Young Turk Congress in 1907 ... Ahmed Riza caused an uproar when he declared that the congress ought to accept the legal principles of the Islamic caliphate and the Ottoman dynasty, principles that would have reproduced the natural Muslim Turkish dominance."

10. Ottoman Turks clung to this belief despite the land losses of the Ottoman Empire in the nineteenth century. See Göçek, DV, p. 117: "Yet the younger generations were often unaware of and therefore unprepared for the degree of imperial loss of lands because what they were taught at school still stressed past imperial glory, not at all acknowledging recent defeats."

11. Akçam, ASA, p. 48.

12. Edib, HW, p. 241. The italics are mine.

1. *What* was the identity around which the "homeland" was to be created?
2. *Where* was the new "homeland" to be?
3. *How* was the CUP to ensure that that identity was adopted by those who lived within the new "homeland"?

Turkish identity and its problems

Despite the fact that the leaders of the CUP thought it obvious that the national cultural identity of their new "modern, centralized state" was to be Turkish, as Halide Edib points out—and unwittingly, perhaps, provides a great deal of evidence for—in 1908 there was no specifically Turkish culture that could serve as the foundation for the culturally homogenous Turkish "modern, centralized state." What is more, those basic elements of the Ottoman Turkish identity that did exist in 1908 were at odds with the foundations of the "modern centralized Turkish state" that the leaders and ideologues of the CUP wanted to create.

a. Superiority, equality, and Halide Edib

The most obvious problem with Turkish identity was that it was incompatible with the CUP's publicly professed political goals: ensuring the survival and prosperity of the multi-ethnic Ottoman Empire and restoring and upholding the Ottoman Constitution. One of the undeniable components of Turkish identity in 1908 was an unquestioning belief in both Turkish superiority and the "sacred Turkish right to dominance."[13] This belief strained the CUP's object of creating a specifically Turkish "modern centralized state"

---

13. See Göçek, DV, p. 99: "After the proclamation of the 1856 edict, many Muslim Turks started to openly complain that such reforms [which abolished the poll tax and allowed non-Muslims to enlist in the army] meant losing that legal dominance, their 'sacred right earned by the blood of their ancestors.'"

predicated on the principles of *liberté, égalité,* and *fraternité* in lands inhabited by a multitude of different autochthonous—and culturally well-defined—peoples. Superiority and equality are mutually exclusive terms. So too are dominance and freedom. It is impossible to create a state that is grounded *both* in the freedom, equality, and brotherhood of all of its citizens and in the dominance, superiority, and mastery of a specific group of its citizens.

The leaders of the CUP were not blind to the incompatibility of their identity and democratic principles.[14] They realized that in order to create their "modern Turkish centralized state" with its presumed liberty, equality, and brotherhood, they had either to

---

14. This is why the CUP hid its agenda, as Erol Köroğlu well describes in his *Ottoman Propaganda and Turkish Identity: Literature in Turkey During World War I* (London/New York: I.B. Tauris & Co. Ltd., 2007), p. 26: "The CUP heroes of the revolution of 1908 may have been in their hearts Islamists, Westernists or Turkists, but when one after the other they came to power, they became Ottomanists so as not to enfeeble the multiethnic Empire. Throughout the Ottoman modernization process until the beginning of the Anatolian based struggle for independence, no political movement ever directly opposed Ottomanism." The incompatibility of the CUP agenda and Turkish identity is also why the CUP hid its agenda by not restricting membership to the Party to Turks, as Hanioğlu points out in LOE, p. 161: "There was a fundamental incompatibility between the aims of the Turkist core of the CUP and those of the non-Turkish populations of the empire. Indeed, the main threat to the survival of the empire came from separatism on the periphery. To win over the separatists, the CUP adopted a prudent policy of inclusiveness." Their inclusivism was nothing more than a public ruse. The leading ranks of the CUP—its Central Committee—was rabidly Turkist and nationalist. The ruse was convincing to some, and was to have terrible consequences for the Armenians. Some Armenians joined the ranks of the CUP. Some were killed despite this. Some had a hand in the destruction of Armenia. See on this, e.g., Aram Andonian, *Exile, Trauma, and Death: On the Road to Chankiri with Komitas Vartabed* (London: Gomidas Institute and Tekeyan Cultural Association, 2010), where Andonian recounts that the Ittihadist Dikran Allahverdi was arrested with the Armenian intellectuals of Constantinople on April 24, 1915 (p. 7). Andonian also touches upon three Ittihadist Armenians who aided the CUP in destroying Armenians. The volume's editor and translator clarifies who they were. On this point see p. 157, n. 10.

relinquish their claim to being the "ruling race" or to ensure that they were the only "race" that lived within that "modern centralized state." As they saw it, there were only two possible ways of building their nation-state: they could either "debase" the Turks (and Turkishness), or they could forcibly assimilate the minorities; they could either equate the "master" and the "inferior," thereby lowering the "master" to the level of the "inferior," or they could ensure that the "inferior" was made like unto the "master."[15] The latter option clearly entailed the cultural (or physical) elimination of the minority peoples.

Edib's highly personal reflections on the Tanzimat[16] are illuminating both on this point and on the path that the leaders of the

---

15. Akçura makes this very point in "Three Kinds of Policy." He implicitly argues against the policies of Ottomanism and Islamism, claiming that they would "put an end" to the Turks' 600-year domination of Christians and other Muslims, and force them to "descend to the level of equality with reayas [or *rayas*, the tax-paying lower classes of the Ottoman Empire, which included the Christians and Jews] whom they had become accustomed over many years to regard as subjugated peoples... [and] be forced to let the reayas enter the government and army positions that they had customarily monopolized up to that time." Also see, on this point, Göçek, DV, p. 163: "How could difference be brought in without segmenting the empire's structure? One could do so around the dominant Muslim Turkish majority, but that would not 'encompass the Christian citizens.' Indeed the eventual failure of this civilian CUP vision turned the CUP into 'the mortal enemy of all naturalist and independence seeking elements ... against all minorities, Albanians, Armenians, the Greek Rum, and Arabs.' ... The new political vision thus started to publicly identify the non-Muslim elements as the other."

16. Tanzimat (which in Turkish means "Reorganization") refers to a series of reforms promulgated in the Ottoman Empire between 1839 and 1876, during the reigns of the sultans Abdul Mecid I and Abdul Aziz. The reforms were meant to ensure the survival of the empire. Ottoman defeats in the Russo-Turkish Wars and in Egypt, coupled with the rise of nationalism in the *millets* (the non-Muslim nations or peoples that existed within the empire) and the successful Greek War of Independence, revealed not just that the Ottomans were militarily—and economically—vastly inferior to Western powers, but also that their grip on the territories of the empire was weak. The reforms addressed the causes of the Ottoman Empire's weakness

CUP chose to pursue in their creation of the *vatan*. Granting equal rights to the minorities during the Tanzimat, she writes, was an ill-conceived move on the part of the sultans.[17] It was not necessary for the internal well-being of the Ottoman Empire. It addressed what she considered (or wanted her readers to believe that she considered) a non-issue, and it resulted in violence.[18]

The "inequality" of the minorities, Edib claims, was only "nominal" in the empire. "I know of no other country," she insists, "where the minorities were so safe and prosperous during the centuries *before* they had so-called equal rights."[19]

---

and attempted to consolidate Ottoman power by centralizing the government, modernizing the army, replacing of the empire's military-theocratic foundations with modern European constitutional foundations, defining an imperial identity that would include all *millets*, transmitting and imposing that identity upon the *millets*. Schools were one of the significant means through which the Tanzimat addressed both military weakness and identity. The government came to include a Ministry of Education. Elementary education was made compulsory and was used to impose Ottoman identity.

17. Equal rights for all citizens was proposed, Edib claims, in response to external pressure and in self-defense. See HW, pp. 240–41: "When the empire became weak, when it became bewildered with internal and external difficulties, greedy eyes from outside turned to Turkey and found a loophole in the nominal inequality of the Christian minorities. Russia's pretext was found in the Orthodox Christians, as England's was the Armenians later on."

18. Edib's claim that the issue of minority rights was a non-issue is simply false. One example suffices to clarify this. In 1836, "By royal decree, many [thousands of] Armenian children [from eight to fifteen years of age] from Sebastia [Sivas] and from other towns in Anatolia were assembled in Erzerum and taken to Constantinople for forced labor.... They were given bread and clothing, but no salary. And this order is renewed year after year and they collect hundreds of Armenian children from every town, depriving them of their parents and their homeland, and during this thirty-day march [journey] in bare feet and rags ... Several die of cold and want," Avedis Perperean, qtd. in Bat Ye'or, *The Decline of Eastern Christianity under Islam: From Jihad to Dhimmitude* (Madison/Teaneck, NJ: Fairleigh Dickinson University Press, 1996), p. 113.

19. Edib, HW, p. 240. The italics are mine.

The equality of non-Moslems appears at first to have been provided for more because of political reasons than of urgent necessity. The non-Moslems had rather enjoyed privileges than suffered from the general social and political disorder of the Moslem communities.[20]

The introduction of universal equality undermined the very foundation of the "safety and prosperity" of the empire's minorities:

the moment the Christians were granted equality by an edict, without sharing responsibility as the soldier citizens of the state, the social order and the old tolerant tradition was upset.[21]

Rather than solve a problem, the Tanzimat created problems.[22]

Edib's point, of course, is that it would have been (and was) best for everyone in the Ottoman Empire if the "ruling race" had retained (and continued to retain) its role as the "ruling race." It was then, and only then she suggests, that Turks could accept living alongside non-Turks. Being "masters" was the condition of the possibility of the "tolerance" of the Turks. That "tolerance,"

---

20. Edib, HW, p. 239.

21. Edib, HW, p. 241. Edib's footnote to her defense of Ottoman magnanimity is enlightening.

22. See, on this point, Akçam, ASA, p. 32: "According to leading Tanzimat reformer Mustafa Reşit Paşa, the full equality promised in the Imperial Rescript would erase the differences between the groups, and thereby end the 600-year dominance of Ottoman Muslims. This was unacceptable to the general Muslim population.... Just as he feared, Muslims created disturbances and these led to massacres. The concessions that Muslims were being asked to make in regard to the principle of fundamental inequality were, as Bernard Lewis states, 'no less great an effort of renunciation than is required of those Westerners who are now called upon to forego the satisfaction of racial superiority.'... While the Muslim population was generally unhappy with the rights granted to non-Muslims, the clergy and lay leadership did their part to incite the masses."

she had explained, "had its roots in the chivalrous attitude of the master to the inferior."

Edib's view implies that if the Turks were to live in peace in a nation-state in which equality was a right of all citizens, that nation-state could only be inhabited by Turks. If the Turks were only tolerant when they were "masters," they could never be tolerant of equals who were not Turks.[23] Her view entails that the only possible way of extending equal rights to all citizens in the CUP's projected "homeland" was for all of the citizens of that homeland to be Turks.[24]

b. Identity, culture, and Halide Edib

But what were the Turks? That was the deeper question that the ideologues of the CUP had to answer. Those who considered themselves the dominant national group, Edib claims, had no distinct identity or culture:

> The Ottoman Turk so far had been a composite being, an Ottoman citizen like any other, his greatest writers writing for all the educated men of the empire, his folk-lore and

---

23. Hanioğlu gives a particularly poignant example of this in LOE, p. 85: "However, Muslim resentment made the immediate and full implementation of the Reform Edict of 1856 impossible. To cite just one revealing example, Christian demands for permission to ring metal church bells in place of the dull wooden ones traditionally allowed were denied in many places to avoid provoking public disorder."

24. As Kévorkian makes the point, p. 191: "For the closed circle of some 30 people who controlled the Ittihad [the CUP], the idea of human rights was an abstraction, as was the motto of the republic. 'Liberty, equality, fraternity' was an archaic 'metaphysical fantasy' that had no other aim than 'to win over various Ottoman ethnic groups to the cause of Ottomanism.' What mattered more than anything else, society included, was the creation of a strong authoritarian state to be at the Committee's beck and call and be capable of realizing the Committee's ends. Nothing was to be allowed to interfere with this historical mission, especially not the opposition."

popular literature passing from one generation to another, unwritten by the educated, but powerful in the minds and memories of all the simple Turkish-speaking Ottomans.[25]

It became crucial for the Turks to define their identity—and to possess their own specific culture—Edib states, "after 1908," when:

> all the non-Turkish elements in Turkey, Christian and Moslem, had political and national clubs. When the Turkish students of the universities saw their fellow-students, whom they had so far identified with themselves, belonging to separate organizations with national names and separate interests, they began to wonder. The non-Turkish youth were passing into feverish activity about their national affairs, as something different from that of the Turk.[26]

That was, she insists, when the Turk, who had "so far identified" with the non-Turk, realized that he was different from him. That was when he began to ask himself crucial questions about himself: "How was he different from the others? Where was he being led in the accumulation of other desires and interests?"

> For the first time reduced to his elements and torn from the ensemble of races in Turkey, he vaguely faced the possibility of searching, analyzing, and discovering himself as something different from the rest. Cast out or isolated in his own country, he not only saw himself different, but he had also the desire to find out wherein lay the difference.[27]

---

25. Edib, HW, p. 323.
26. Edib, HW, pp. 322–23.
27. Edib, HW, p. 323.

This is all a bit romantic. It is deeply political. It is above all revealing. The claims (and especially the inconsistencies) in Edib's attempts to define Turkish identity—which is a *Leitmotiv* in her memoirs—disclose how profoundly problematic the issue was both for her and for the leaders of the CUP. They also point to the reasons why it was so.

A quick analysis of Edib's inconsistencies shows that she (and the CUP) held that the national identity of the Turks had to have two characteristics above all. First, that national identity had to have a distinctive *cultural component* that needed both to be grounded in the oral traditions of the Turks and expressed in the literature of the Turks. Second, that identity had to be genetically and geographically definable. That is, the identity had to be rooted in the geographical location in which the genetics of the *gens Turcica* originated.

c. Composite beings vs. superior ones: The search for new identifying characteristics

An indication of the depth of the issue of Turkish identity for Edib lies in the obvious inconsistency of her claims that the Ottoman Turk was a "composite being," an "Ottoman citizen like any other" who before 1908 "identified" with the non-Turkish Ottoman minorities, and who only then "vaguely faced the possibility of searching, analyzing, and discovering himself as something different from the rest," and the claim she makes seventy or so pages before these that "The Turkish people were used to respecting the lives and the property of a minority, who were almost like religious trusts to them and who went their way without sharing the military burdens of the ruling race."

These claims clearly cannot all be true. The Ottoman Turks cannot *both* have known that they were the "ruling race" and at the same time "identified" with the minorities. Nor could they have "vaguely faced the possibility of searching, analyzing, and discovering" themselves "as something different from the rest," if their conviction that they were the "ruling race" necessarily made them aware of the fact that they were different from those whom they ruled. The Tanzimat could not have been as damaging to the minorities as Edib claims it was, had the Turks not realized that they were "different from the rest" of the peoples living in the empire.

The Ottoman Turks did have a distinct identity before 1908, if by that term one means both a set of characteristics that distinguish one group of persons from another, and the awareness of that set. Edib's account suggests as much. That identity was primarily military. The Turks were, and thought of themselves as, the conquerors and rulers. They were the "race" of "soldier citizens" who bore the "military burdens" of their empire.[28] The key terms that Edib uses to convey this most basic element of Turkish identity are *courageous, chivalrous, honor, prestige, virile*, and *manly*. They are a sort of proud refrain throughout her memoirs. Ottoman Turks were, of course, as Edib herself also mentions, profoundly Muslim. This, too, distinguished them from many of the minorities. The Greeks, the Armenians, the Chaldeans, and the Syriacs were Christian.

Edib hints at one of the reasons why that autonomous Turkish identity was problematic for her (and the CUP) in the passages above. In 1908, she claims, "The non-Turkish youth were passing into feverish activity about their national affairs, as something different from that of the Turk." The mere thought of independent "national affairs" could not but have threatened Turkish identity. One of the conditions of being (and viewing oneself as) a "conqueror and ruler" is having those peoples whom one has subjugated

---

28. As Zürcher claims, the military component of Turkish identity continued to be a significant part of national Turkish identity for the CUP and the Kemalists. The Japanese defeat of the Russians in 1905, coupled with the fact that the vast majority of members of the CUP were soldiers, led the Unionists to believe that "the modern state should be built on a 'nation in arms' and that the strength of the state could only be ensured by creating a nation of soldiers." Their belief became stronger after the Balkan Wars and the Armistice of Mudros. "The idea that the Turks are a nation of soldiers, or even a soldier race later became an integral part of Turkish republican nationalism and it still lives on even today in nationalist circles." See Zürcher, YTL, pp. 117–18.

acknowledge that one is their "conqueror and ruler." Those once-subjugated peoples who begin to belong to "separate organizations with national names and separate interests," and pass "into feverish activity about their national affairs, as something different from that of the Turk," do not and will not acknowledge that role. It is then that the "conqueror and ruler" ceases to be the "conqueror and ruler" and is "reduced to his elements." It is then that he feels "torn from the ensemble of races," "cast out," begins "to wonder" about his own identity, and tries to discover "himself as something different from the rest." A "conqueror and ruler" with no subjugated peoples is a formless and nameless thing. Nothing formless and nameless can define people and turn them into the loyal citizens of a lasting nation-state, as CUP ideologues well knew.[29] Nothing formless and nameless can continue to exist. Gökalp, the leading ideologist of the CUP, states this quite clearly:

> When a nation experiences a great disaster or when it is confronted with grave danger, individual personality disappears and becomes immersed in society. In such times it is only the national personality that lives in the soul of the individual. All souls feel nothing but the great desire to see the continuation of the national personality.... Once a nation creates its own ideals, it never turns its face

---

29. This was the problem that the Ottoman Empire tried repeatedly to solve once Sultan Mustafa III wrote in 1774: "The world is turning upside down, with no hope for better during our reign." The sultans realized that they could no longer rely on brute strength to hold on to their empire, since (1) they no longer had the military strength to do so; (2) Western powers would—often for very self-serving purposes—intervene in their government of subjugated peoples; and (3) the principles of the *Great Democratic Revolution* had taken hold of the world. In response, the sultans began actively to try to define and impose an identity on the peoples of the empire. Shortly after Sultan Mustafa III, they tried with *Ottomanism*—a trans-ethnic identity that would bind the peoples of the empire to the empire itself, thereby sustaining it. *Ottomanism* was a failure. Abdul Hamid tried to bind the peoples of the empire through *Islamism*—a collective religious identity.

towards a dark future; on the contrary a Promised Land,
a heralded Garden of Eden, unfolds itself, day by day, in
an ever-clearer and more inviting prospect. Nations without ideals think that they are doomed to catastrophes;
nations with ideals, on the other hand, are destined for
resurrection even if they are politically dead. A nation
with a resurrecting and creative ideal never dies.[30]

d. Books and peoples

This is especially true when the "conqueror and ruler" is only a
"conqueror and ruler," as Edib suggests the Ottoman Turk was. A
deeper reason why being "torn from the ensemble of races" was profoundly troubling for her (and the CUP) is thus cultural. Throughout the many centuries of his domination, the Ottoman Turk had
not, as she claims in the passages cited above, produced a distinct
Turkish culture.[31]

Educated Ottoman Turks, Edib clarifies, had not produced characteristically Turkish works—works, that is, that both expressed
and defined a specifically Turkish way of being and unified all
classes of Anatolian Turks.[32] Their works, she claims, were written
for "all the educated men of the empire" and were, she apparently

---

30. Gökalp, as cited by Köroğlu, p. 56.
31. Edib was not the only Turkish intellectual to claim so at that time. As
    Köroğlu reports, Hüseyin Cahid claimed in 1916 that the Turks' search for
    a "new national literature had not yet been successful" (p. 8); in 1917, arti-
    cles in *Tanin* criticized Turkish intellectuals for the lack of literary produc-
    tion that would foster true nationalism in the Turkish people and claimed
    that the cause of this lack of production was "that the country's elite had
    no national character" (p. 10). Köroğlu argues that one of the effects of this
    lack of national culture was the CUP's inability to produce coherent and
    effective wartime propaganda, since this requires "simple premises" (p. 16).
    Simple premises were precisely what the CUP did not have, and "all propa-
    ganda efforts ended up being ad hoc affairs" (p. 16).
32. Hanioğlu gives a good summary of the cultural problems at the root of the
    emergence of the CUP in YTO, Ch. 2, pp. 7–32. One of these is precisely

thought, not just indistinguishable from the works produced by other Ottoman *literati*.[33] They were above all disconnected from the "authentic" Turkish people who lived in the empire. Nor, she states, had illiterate Ottoman Turks produced that culture. They could not by definition (she seems to have believed) have done so. Edib adds that those who might have—and should have—written the folklore of the illiterate, and thereby presumably have produced a specifically Turkish culture that was both aimed at Turks and not disconnected from the "authentic" Turkish people of the empire— the "educated"—had not done so.[34]

---

the lack of a culture that met all of what the CUP thought were the requirements of an authentic culture.

33. This is, of course, true. See, e.g., Hanioğlu, LOE, p. 98: "The first Ottoman novels appeared in Turkish written in Armenian script, since both authors were Armenians, Yovsep Vardaneans's *Akabi Hikâyesi* (*The Story of Akabi/Agape*) published in 1851, was the first example of this new genre. It was an Armenian *Romeo and Juliet*, depicting a love affair between two Armenians of different denominations—Armenian Apostolic and Catholic—and touching upon the sensitive question of sectarianism in the Armenian community. In the same year, Yovhannes Hisarean authored the first novel in modern Western Armenian, *Hosrov ew Mak'ruhi*. In Istanbul in 1851, a decade later, Vasil Drumev wrote the first Bulgarian novelette, *Neshtastna familia* (*The Unfortunate Family*). In the 1870s, Ottoman Greeks, inspired by their brethren in Greece and abroad, began to write literature in Karamanli, a central Anatolian Turkish dialect written in Greek script." The first novel written by a Muslim Ottoman was published in 1875. Edib's concerns about the lack of Turkish culture were widespread.

34. The problem to which Edib is alluding concerns the relation between a government and its governed. What concerned her (and the CUP) was that the government of the empire was neither specifically Turkish nor expressly connected to the Turks. This divide could be seen in the culture and language of the Ottomans. High Ottoman Turkish, the written language of the court and of the ruling elite—the language in which laws, novels, and scholarly works were written—was not an oral language. Those who mastered it did not—and could not—use it in their everyday lives. Nor was the language primarily Turkish. It was so filled with Persian, French, Venetian, Greek, and Arabic words that it was unintelligible to the common native Turkish speaker. It was not only spoken by Turks. All of the elites spoke it. As Hanioğlu puts it, High Ottoman Turkish "formed a transnational link

The degree to which the lack of a distinctly Turkish culture was troubling to Edib can be seen in the fact that she is as inconsistent about its non-existence as she is on the matter of the non-existence of an autonomous Turkish identity in 1908. Some two hundred pages before she claimed that Turkish folklore was unwritten, she claims to have been the only *literata* of her generation to have been raised on popular Turkish literature[35] and cites the epic of *Battal Ghazi* and his "Turkish" soldiers as one of the first books that she read.[36] Fifty pages or so before that, she asserts that the Ottoman Turk actually did have an autonomous culture, and that the purest cultural expression of Turkishness is Sinan's architecture:

> Whatever my feelings are toward some parts of the Ottoman past, I am grateful to its conception of beauty as expressed by Sinan in that wonderful dome. The gorgeous coloring of the Byzantines, the magic tracery, and the delicate, lace-like ornament of the Arab influenced him in many ways, but he surely brought that flawless beauty of line and that sober majesty in his Turkish heart from its original home in the wild steppes. There is a manliness and lack of self-consciousness here which I have never seen in any other temple, yet the work is far from being primitive or elemental. It combines genius and science, as well as the personal sense of holy beauty which is characteristic of the Ottoman,

---

bonding elites together within the empire and alienating them collectively from their respective peoples" (LOE, p. 35). Thus, High Ottoman Turkish was not specifically connected to a geographical location or to an ethnicity. This is what bothered Edib and the CUP. One of the first things the intellectual leaders of the CUP did was to "purify" the language. Mustafa Kemal did the same thing for Republican Turkey. On this point see Köroğlu, pp. 40–45.

35. Edib, HW, p. 115.
36. Edib, HW, p. 117.

and it can hold its own with the architectural triumphs of any age.[37]

Nor does she only state that the Ottoman Turks had culturally expressed their Turkishness *before* she claims that they had not. Some fifty pages after she asserts both that the Ottoman Turk had no autonomous culture and that the "educated" Ottoman Turks had not collected the oral culture of the "simple" ones, she states that the great Armenian composer Gomidas Vartabed, whom she considered "an embodiment of Anatolian folk-lore and music," was "probably of Turkish descent, from the Turks who had joined the Gregorian Church" and that "in temperament and heart he was a real Anatolian Turk if unconsciously."[38] In his collection of Anatolian folk music, she claims, he had "simply turned the words into Armenian."[39]

The present inconsistency underscores another reason why a specifically Turkish culture was problematic for Edib. Neither Sinan nor Gomidas was Turkish. The former was a Janissary and most likely Armenian by birth, while the latter was unquestionably Armenian.[40] It is highly unlikely that Edib was ignorant of these

---

37. Edib, HW, p. 73.

38. Edib, HW, p. 372.

39. Edib, HW, p. 371: "As he appeared in the long black coat of the priest, his dark face as naive as any simple Anatolian's, and his eyes full of the pathos and longing which his voice expressed in its pure strong notes, I felt him an embodiment of Anatolian folk-lore and music. The airs were the ones I had often heard our servants from Kemah and Erzeroum sing. He had simply turned the words into Armenian. But I did not pay any attention to the language; I only felt the inner significance of that tender and desolate melody from the lonely wastes of Anatolia."

40. It is particularly odd that Edib claims that Gomidas was Turkish. Gomidas, whose baptismal name was Soghomon Soghomonian, was a fervid Armenian patriot who did everything in his power to record, codify, purify, transmit, and build upon the Armenian musical tradition. He was a formidable man who was at once a scholar, composer, performer, director, and educator. As a scholar, Gomidas was a pioneering musical ethnographer who was convinced that peoples had their own particular musical languages, so to speak. This

facts.⁴¹ That she would call upon these two indubitably great and categorically non-Turkish artists in order to exemplify the identity

---

led him to attempt to define the specific differences of Armenian music. He deciphered Armenian medieval musical notation—the *khaz*, the key to which had been lost by the time he studied music—thereby discovering what he considered the standard through which Armenian sacred music could be cleansed of its foreign influences. He also spent months living alongside Armenian villagers (and working at their sides), getting to know how they lived, transcribing their songs, and attempting to understand the relation between their daily routines and the music they sang and improvised. He collected some 5,000 such songs, part of which he published in Paris (*Hay Qnar*—Armenian lyre) and Leipzig. Gomidas was a meticulous ethnographer. His collection *Hazar ou mi Khagh* (One Thousand and One Songs) took him three years to assemble. In the late nineteenth and early twentieth centuries, there was a tremendous flowering of rural culture in Western Armenia. We have what we do of the musical component of that culture, which was completely destroyed by the genocide, exclusively through Gomidas's transcriptions. Gomidas was also a composer trained primarily in Tiflis and Berlin. As was customary at the time, he composed *lieder*, sacred music, and an opera. He was a lecturer who toured Europe performing and speaking on Armenian music. He was a formidable musical director and performer. Gomidas's choruses were well known throughout Europe and the Middle East.

That Edib would state that such a man is likely Turkish and suggest that the folk songs he claimed for the Armenians were not Armenian is curious indeed. Gomidas himself would have considered the latter statement insulting for at least two reasons. Its insinuation that he could not tell the difference between the folk songs of different peoples went to the heart of his ethnographic capacities and training. Its insinuation that he had to claim as Armenian the music of peoples other than his own suggested that his own people did not have their own musical creativity and language. The truth is that Gomidas was well aware of the differences between the folk music of different peoples and was convinced that his people were so capable of composing their own music that they had no need to claim the music of others. His own publications attest to this. One of them, *Qrdakan Yeghanakner* (Kurdish Songs), which he published in Moscow, is a collection of Kurdish folk songs.

41. Weeks before Gomidas was arrested and sent to the concentration camp at Chankiri, the leaders of the CUP asked him to participate in a gala whose purpose was to promote Turkish nationalism and identity. He was the only Armenian invited to the event. Turkish intellectuals and political leaders were all there. The master of ceremonies, Hamdullah Subhi, gave Gomidas what in hindsight cannot but be seen as an ominous introduction that pub-

and distinct culture of the Ottoman Turk simply corroborates her claim that the Ottoman Turk had no autonomous culture.[42]

e. Books, blood, and land

Like her other inconsistencies, Edib's claims about Sinan and Gomidas point to a deeper reason why Turkish identity was so

---

licly acknowledged the vital importance not just of Gomidas's own work, but that of Armenians in general, whom he clearly stated were the cultural backbone of Anatolia: "This son of Anatolia, and Armenian clergyman, has, with his dedication and hard work, given wings to Armenian music.... He spent his time in the villages collecting folk songs ... and presented those songs as part of the Armenian national heritage.... If only our clergy did the same thing. I wonder what treasures they would find, treasures that would elevate the value of the sensitive heart and the thinking mind of the Turkish nation.... The truth ... is that the Armenian nation remains on the frontier of our cultural life. Wherever you go in Turkey, in any corner of Anatolia, the Armenian mind, the creative Armenian mind and hand will greet you and tell you 'I am here.' If you go to the palaces of the sultans, the architects are Armenians.... The tombstones of your loved ones, which are so finely carved, are the works of Armenian masters.... Armenian masters also make the world-famous jewelry boxes from Van. The founders of the medical school and the writers of scientific books are also Armenians.... These are the people with whom we have lived for centuries." Hamdullah Subhi, qtd. by H.J. Siruni, cited in Rita Soulahian Kuyumjian, *Archaeology of Madness. Komitas: Portrait of an Armenian Icon* (London: Gomidas Institute Books, 2010), p. 115.

42. See Köroğlu, p. 36: "After 1908 there was still an urgent need for scholarly output concerning a common historical memory, cultural/linguistic ties and the creation of a citizen profile since the output created up to that point was far from satisfying the requirements. On the one hand there was the need to develop and spread among all social classes a written language responsive to national requirements and to prepare 'national' history books to be used especially in schools. On the other hand, there was the need to organize 'patriotic agitation' even though the instruments for this did not yet exist. Thus the post-1908 national movement needed both cool-headed people to conduct scientific research and people to organize agitation aiming to create the emotional atmosphere required to transform society into a national community."

profoundly problematic for her (and the leaders of the CUP).[43] In the cases of both men, Edib includes both the man's genetic identity and the geographical location in which it originated in the very definition of his cultural identity. The beauty of the lines of Sinan's architecture, she states, derived from his "Turkish heart" was rooted in "its original home in the wild steppes." Gomidas, on the other hand, was "an embodiment of Anatolian folk-lore and music ... probably of Turkish descent.... [I]n temperament and heart he was a real Anatolian Turk."[44] These descriptions suggest that Edib held more generally that a person's cultural identity—and by extension a *people's* cultural identity— was determined at least in part by the link between his race and the specific geographical domain in which his race originated. This might be the reason why Edib ignores the epic of Battal Ghazi when she claims that Turkish folklore was not written

---

43. There is another emotional reason why the lack of a specifically Turkish culture was problematic for Edib and the CUP. It made them feel inferior and vulnerable. Thus, Ömer Seyfeddin could claim that the lack of a specifically Turkish culture was willed by the other *millets* and part of a more sinister plan to eradicate the Turks: "Terrible dramas were being played out under the guise of Constitutional Rule. Yet the Greeks, Bulgarians, Serbs, Armenians, Albanians had their national ideal, national literature, national language, national purpose, national organizations. And these nations are very shrewd. 'We are sincere Ottomans...they would say to deceive the Turks, and damage the Turks' language, literature, even their scientific books, even erase from their geography and history books the words 'Turks and Turkey.'" Seyfeddin; qtd. in Uğur Ümit Üngör and Mehmet Polatel, *Confiscation and Destruction: The Young Turk Seizure of Armenian Property* (London/New York: Continuum International Publishing Group, 2011), p. 33.

44. I wonder if Edib's reason for claiming that Gomidas was Turkish is not also to insinuate that the Turks were autochthonous to Anatolia. If Gomidas was indeed a real "Anatolian" in the sense that his people were autochthonous to Asia Minor/Armenia, which is a fact beyond doubt, then to claim that he was Turkish would entail that the Turks themselves were autochthonous to Asia Minor/Armenia. Ideologues in Kemalist Turkey attempted to prove this very thing.

down. Neither the original prose epic, nor the historical character on whom it is based, was Turkish.[45]

Herein lies the crux of the problem of Turkish identity. In the
odd lines with which she prefaces her account of the phases and
causes of Turkish nationalism and pan-Turanism, Edib explicitly
states that the origins, historical and racial heritage of the Ottoman Turk could not serve to define him: there was no solid link
between the Ottoman Turk's "genetic identity" and the lands of
the Ottoman Empire.[46] This meant that the Ottoman Turks had
no cultural identity by Edib's own understanding of that term:

> He [the Ottoman Turk] came to the Near East and Eu-
> rope, and there he acquired in his blood and in his lan-
> guage, as well as in every particle of his ego, something
> new, something special. Although one may try to go deep
> into the elemental force and character of his race, one is
> obliged to recognize that things have been added to his
> spirit and physique which have altered him from what he
> was when he had first come to the land which is called
> Turkey today. In short he was the Ottoman Turk and had
> to be considered as such, and everything contrary to his

---

45. The epic was originally composed in Arabic. The character was an Arab
commander, as much as the Turks claimed (and seem to continue to claim)
him as the forebear of one of their dynasties: the Danişmends.

46. See, on this, Kévorkian, p. 192: "It might even be ventured that the slow
erosion of the Ottoman world, which yielded its place to nation-states,
together with the Ittihadists' frequent contact with Albanian, Macedonian, and Armenian revolutionaries endowed with solid national identities, helped catalyze the Young Turk project to found a Turkish nation. As
Bozarslan forcefully points out, the Ittihadists who suggested this project
discovered that there was, properly speaking, no Turkish 'nation.' Living
on its ancestral lands, but a dominant Muslim Ottoman group that had
never wondered about its identity and had long ceased to trace its origins
back to its Central Asian ancestors. Thus, the construction of the Turkish
nation could proceed only by way of opposition to other groups, which for
their part had identities based on a culture and a homeland."

individual development in language and culture could not
be lasting. To force his language back to Chagatay would
be as artificial as forcing it into Persian or into French.
Hence his simplification and nationalization would take
the line of his own national genius.[47]

If, as Edib would implicitly claim, a people's cultural identity
lies in the link between its genetic identity and the geographical
location in which it originated, the Ottoman Turk could have had
no cultural identity.[48] He could have had such an identity, Edib
implies, if he returned to his "original home in the wild steppes."
She discards that possibility without mentioning it explicitly. Just
as one could not "force his language back to Chagatay," one could
not force the Ottoman Turk to return to those lands from which
he "came to the Near East and Europe." She justifies this last claim
genetically. "Although one may try to go deep into the elemental
force and character of his race, one is obliged to recognize that
*things have been added to his spirit and physique which have altered
him from what he was when he had first come to the land which
is called Turkey today.*" These "added things" made the Ottoman

47. Edib, HW, p. 313.

48. The materialism inherent in this view should not be surprising. After the
    Tanzimat, the newly established Imperial Turkish schools instilled mate-
    rialism in their pupils. After a few decades, materialism permeated the
    Turkish intelligentsia. Hanioğlu makes this point repeatedly. See, e.g.,
    LOE, p. 138: "The importance of the acceptance of a hybrid doctrine based
    on eighteenth-century French materialism and nineteenth-century Ger-
    man *Vulgärmaterialismus* by a large segment of the Ottoman intelligentsia
    should not be underestimated. This was one instance where ideas mattered
    a great deal for the winds of materialism continued to blow long after the
    Young Turk Revolution and into Republican times, exerting a profound in-
    fluence on the Weltanschauung of the founders of the Republic and on the
    ideology they fashioned to build modern Turkey." Zürcher also comments
    on this. See YTL, p. 118, where he cites Gustave Le Bon as one of the think-
    ers with the most influence on the military men of the CUP. Hanioğlu also
    comments on this in YTO, pp. 208–12.

Turk, when "nationally analyzed," she claims, "clearly" different "from other Turks in general." They were "something special" that he (and only he among the Turks) had *acquired in his blood* and in his language, as well as in every particle of his ego" from the "Near East and Europe."

Edib does not define the nature of these "added things" and "something special." Nor does she clarify how they were "acquired" in the "blood" of the Ottoman Turks, or how the physical acquisition of these things made any cultural difference at all for the Ottoman Turk. These things were not clear to Edib or to the leaders of the CUP. Explaining them required "searching, analyzing, and discovering himself."

Edib had no doubt that such "discovering" could be done. She relates how fervently that "discovering" was undertaken. "Cultural curiosity as well as the tyranny of external events was throwing most intellectual Turks back into an intense study of the beginnings of the race."[49] Nor did she have any doubt that such "discovering" would produce a nationalist culture. When a nation goes "deep down to the roots of its being" and studies "itself sincerely," she claims, it will "create beauty" and "express its personality." "The process of this deep self-study," she adds, "as well as its results, is nationalism."[50]

Edib herself had participated in the "process." She wrote a wildly successful novel, *The New Turan*. The book, she claims in her memoirs, is an expression of "practically worked out ideals." It "looks forward to a New Turkey ... that is nationalized in its culture and democratic in its politics."[51] Her ideals, she knew, "would

---

49. Edib, HW, p. 312.

50. Edib, HW, p. 325. Edib here sounds very much like Gökalp. In his "Kizilelma" ("Red Apple"), the poem he published in 1913 and that became the title of his first poetry collection, he claims: "Turkish civilization is unique, pure / Until it is born it will a secret remain.... His vision is reaching union / National thought, peace." Gökalk; qtd. in Köroğlu, p. 53.

51. Edib, HW, p. 332.

be at least partly realized."[52] One of her great fans, Cemal Bey, was to become one of the Triumvirs of the Ottoman Empire. She proudly writes that he called on her and "warmly declared himself a New Turanist who would try for the realization of the ideal."[53] He was not alone in his praise. The Turkish nationalist club, *Türk Yurdu* (Turkish Homeland),

> passed a resolution calling me the Mother of the Turk, a tender tribute of the Turkish youth, which not only touched me but has also molded me in the responsibility of a real but humble mother to my people.[54]

Soldiers sent her letters signed "the six officers of the New Turan." The very "name 'New Turan' had become the rage, and some shops already called themselves by it."[55]

Where and how?

Edib's claims concerning the cultural identity of the Turks point to two additional and related problems that the leaders of the CUP had to address in order to create their "homeland." They concerned the *where* and the *how*. Where was the CUP to create the *vatan*? And how was one to make Turks out of the minorities that lived in the lands in which the *vatan* was to be created?

The very categories that Edib (with the leaders and ideologues of the CUP) used to define a people's cultural and national identity made the location of the *vatan* a problem. The racial origins

---

52. Edib did not just write the novel. She was a journalist. In 1912 she, Zika Gökalp, and Yusuf Akçura founded the *Halka Doğru* (Towards the People) movement, whose object was to nationalize the Anatolian masses.

53. Edib, HW, p. 343.

54. Edib, HW, p. 321.

55. Edib, HW, p. 339.

of Ottoman Turks were not geographically linked to any part of the Ottoman Empire. This meant that the *vatan* existed nowhere. It did not, by their definition, exist in the Ottoman Empire. Nor could it exist in lands in which the Ottoman Turks did not live, or over which they did not have dominion.

Some of the CUP's ideologues, most notably Gökalp, tried to solve this problem by claiming that the *vatan* was *Turan*: "an idealized entity that 'would gather all Turks together and reject foreigners' ... the 'entirety of all the countries in which Turks live, in which Turkish is spoken.' The borders of *Turan* would extend as far as the language and political culture of the Turks."[56] It was the place where there would exist no chasm between the racial origins of the Ottoman Turks and their dominion, where there could be a Turkish culture that had the necessary requisites defined by the ideologues of the CUP.

It was the place where there could exist an ethnically and culturally homogenous Turkish nation. *Turan* was the brainchild of Ziya Gökalp, who, as Edib articulates:

> was trying to create a new Turkish mythology which would bridge the abyss between the Ottoman Turks and their Turanian ancestors. He wrote a great many charming stories and poems for children; he tried to popularize his knowledge of the origin of the Turk, and the new ideal of life which he was trying to bring into being.[57]

---

56. Ziya Gökalp; qtd. in Akçam, ASA, pp. 92–93.
57. Edib, HW, p. 316. The word *Turan* is actually Persian and geographical. It referred to the lands inhabited by the tribes that were enemies of the Persians, i.e., the Turks. Gökalp was not the first modern Turk to speak of *Turan* or to use it for political purposes. Hüseyinzâde Ali, another member of the Central Committee of the CUP, had previously used the word—and notion—to refer to the locus where the Turks originated and to attempt to forge some bonds with the Hungarians. Nor were the Turks the first or only people to use it in modern times. Hungarians used the term. See Köroğlu, pp. 51–54.

If *Turan* was ideologically definable, it was, as Edib admitted, geographically impossible to locate. It "never had a clear boundary or a crystallized expression or an explanation. Talaat Pasha pleasantly and humorously remarked at times, if any one criticized it, 'It may lead us to the Yellow Sea.'"[58]

What was certain was that the Ottoman Turks needed both to consolidate their grasp on those lands over which they had dominion and to conquer lands if their *vatan, Turan,* was materially to correspond to the ideological characteristics set forth by the CUP. They had to bridge the chasm that separated them from the geographical location whence they hailed.

This was a problem. Although Enver Pasha fervently believed that he could "clear the path for a powerful Turkish Empire to replace the weak and heterogeneous Ottomans and gather all the Turkish 'race under its mantle,'"[59] and again despite the fact that Turkish society latched on to the "Turan ideal, which seemed to offer a territory even larger than the one the empire had had before the [Balkan] war,"[60] the reality of military defeats and the collapsing borders of the Ottoman Empire quickly proved otherwise. In the defeat at Sarikamish, the Ottoman Army lost nearly half of its Third Army.

This meant that the CUP could only create the *vatan* in those lands that were already under Ottoman control.

How was one to do so?

There was really only one way, given the CUP's object, the categories through which they defined that object, and the array of culturally heterogeneous *millets* (nations) that existed within the borders of what was left of the Ottoman Empire at the turn of the

58. Edib, HW, p. 315.
59. Akçam, ASA, p. 93.
60. Köroğlu, p. 57.

twentieth century: annihilate the *millets*—the often rich and distinct ancient cultures of the autochthonous peoples who inhabited what was left of the Ottoman Empire; destroy all traces of them in those lands in which the *vatan* was to be created; and invent "a new Turkish mythology which would bridge the abyss between the Ottoman Turks," "their Turanian ancestors," and the lands in which the *vatan* was to exist.[61]

The annihilation of the *millets* was a necessary condition of creating the *vatan* not only because the ideologues of the CUP insisted that the *vatan* be exclusively inhabited by people who were homogeneously and culturally Turkish, and the *millets* were not culturally Turkish. It was a necessary condition of creating the *vatan* because the very categories that the CUP used to define homelands demonstrated that at least some of the *millets* possessed and lived in homelands, in *vatans*, of their own: that at least some of the *millets* had a greater claim to the lands in which they lived than the Turks could ever have. Those homelands existed in the very lands in which the CUP wanted to create its Turkish *Lebensraum*. The claims that the *millets* had to the lands in which they lived, to their homelands in the Turkish *Lebensraum*, made the very existence of the *millets* a threat to the CUP and the *vatan* that it wanted to create for the Turks.

Edib's examples of "Ottoman Turkish" culture demonstrate as much for the Armenian *millet*. Gomidas Vartabed was beyond doubt a great artist who had, in his music, expressed and defined the specific way of being of his people. What is more, he was—as Edib herself claims—"in temperament and heart a real Anatolian." His "race" *was* genetically linked to the very lands in which it lived:

---

61. See Köroğlu, p. 63: "Turkish nationalism had two alternatives before it: putting together a patriotic framework to be applied to the lands still controlled by the empire, i.e., Anatolia and the Arab lands, or in addition to this and even before it, putting forward the idea of creating a great Turkish Empire including the Russian lands inhabited by Turks. These two alternatives imply an acceptance of the losses incurred in the Balkans and are thus more realistic, according to Mahmet Ali Tevfik."

the Armenian Highlands, or what the Turks called the "Eastern Provinces." By Edib's (and the CUP's) categories, this meant not just that Armenians had a cultural and national identity. It meant that the Armenian Highlands—the "Eastern Provinces"—were *the homeland of the Armenians*. This was confirmed by all maps and peoples of the time. They called the "Eastern Provinces" of the Ottoman Empire inhabited by Armenians "Armenia."

Armenia also existed within the domains of the Ottoman Empire. It was part of the territory that the CUP came to realize was the only possible territory in which it could create its own *vatan*: Asia Minor, Anatolia, and the Eastern Provinces.[62] It was also on the path that connected Constantinople to Central Asia. That land could not become the Turkish homeland as long as part of it was the homeland of the Armenians. No geographical location can simultaneously be the homeland of two different peoples, especially if one of these peoples believes itself to have the "sacred right" to dominate, and would base its claim to the homeland itself on a bizarre combination of genetic origins and cultural homogeneity. It could also not be part of a future bridge to a genetically proper *vatan* as long as it was Armenian.

Armenia was an obstacle to the creation of the *vatan*. If the *vatan* was to exist, Armenia had to be annihilated. It had to be cleared of Armenians, their history, their culture.

The same thing held for other *millets*. Dr. Nâzim stated this clearly:

---

62. See on this, e.g., Erik Jan Zürcher, "Renewal and Silence," in AQG, p. 307: "There had been a rise in interest in Anatolia since the constitutional revolution, but after 1912 it was embraced as the true homeland of the Turks even, or perhaps primarily, by those [like Mustafa Kemal] who had been born and bred in southeastern Europe and discovered their new homeland when in their thirties.... The combination of resentment against the Ottoman Christian communities and the adoption of Anatolia as the new homeland made it crucial for the Unionists to make sure that Anatolia was and would remain an Ottoman-Muslim land. These sentiments served as the impetus for the policies of ethnic cleansing that started in the summer of 1914 with the expulsion of the Greeks from the coastal areas in the west."

The pretensions of the various nationalities are a capital annoyance for us. We hold linguistic, historical and ethnic aspirations in abhorrence. This and that group will have to disappear. There should be only one nation on our soil, the Ottoman nation, and only one language, Turkish.[63]

The CUP did not immediately pursue the physical annihilation of the *millets* in that part of what was left of the Ottoman Empire on which they wanted to build their *vatan*. Its leaders first attempted to destroy the cultures of the *millets*.[64] They "effected forced-assimilation policies" in "an effort to homogenize society culturally around an Islamic-Turkish identity."[65] They tried to "pound the non-Turkish elements in a Turkish mortar."

---

63. Dr. Nâzim; qtd. in Ronald Grigor Suny, *"They Can Live in the Desert but Nowhere Else": A History of the Armenian Genocide* (Princeton, NJ/Oxford: Princeton University Press, 2015), p. 188. Henceforth, Suny.

64. See Suny for the crescendo of "steady deterioration in the attitudes of Muslims toward Greeks and Armenians, and of Christians toward the dominant *millet*." For example, Suny, p. 179: "The schools set up by the CUP were teaching their students to say they were Turks rather than Ottomans. In Amasia people were boycotting Armenian merchants. In Sivas the situation was particularly tense. Armenians made plans to patrol their neighborhoods and markets, especially at night. Armenians complained about endless shakedowns by Turkish officers and notables. They were often told that 'the Constitution will not suffice to free you from our clutches; you are our merchandise; we will treat you as our needs dictate.... Armenian political leaders protested against the turn toward nationalism among Turks, their cultivation of the Kurds, who had been largely indifferent if not hostile to the reforms of the Young Turks, and their flagrant neglect of their own initial constitutional impulses. Turkish writers referred to the Ottoman territory as 'Turkish land.'"

65. Akçam, ASA, pp. 72–73. There is a popular Armenian song that testifies to the brutality of the CUP attempts to assimilate the Armenians culturally. "They entered the school and caught the school-teacher / Ah, alas! / They opened her mouth and cut her tongue, / Ah, alas!" The teacher had dared to teach Armenian to the Armenian children.

Their attempts met with failure, as Talaat Bey, who was to become one of the Triumvirs, admitted in 1910:

> You are aware that by the terms of the Constitution, equality of Mussulman and Ghiaur [infidel] was affirmed by you. One and all know and feel that this is an unrealizable ideal. The Sheriat [Shari'ah], our whole past history and the sentiments of hundreds of thousands of Mussulmans and even the sentiments of the Ghiaurs themselves, who stubbornly resist every attempt to Ottomanize them, present an impenetrable barrier to the establishment of real equality. We have made unsuccessful attempts to convert the Ghiaur into a loyal Osmanli and all such efforts must inevitably fail.[66]

After the Ottoman defeat in the Balkan Wars, the CUP decided to take a more direct path to clearing the land for their "homeland." As Morgenthau phrases it, they began "to whitewash" Anatolia: to physically annihilate the *millets*. In 1914 they began to clear Anatolia of the Greeks. In 1915 they turned to the Armenians.

Talaat succinctly justified his (and his party's) decision to exterminate the Armenians: "I have the conviction that as long as a nation does the best for its interest, and succeeds, the world admires it and thinks it moral.' In reply, Edib explains to her readers that:

> There are two factors which lead men to the extermination of his kind: principles advocated by the idealists, and the material interest. Talaat was of the idealist kind.[67]

---

66. Akçam, ASA, pp. 75–76.
67. Edib, HW, p. 387.

Chapter 5

THE CAUSES OF
THE CUP OBJECT

In Greece, in 1797, delegates from Athens, Crete, Macedonia and other parts of the Greek world met at a secret conclave in the Morea; they planned an uprising of all Greeks against the Ottoman Empire, if only the French would send weapons, ammunition and a few units of the French army.[1]

Europe was in a frenzy in the latter half of the 1790s. Rebellions broke out in Ireland. Popular uprisings turned the Netherlands into what the French Republic called a *Sister Republic*: the Batavian Republic. Italy became a veritable tapestry of *Sister Republics*: the Cisalpine, Parthenopean, Roman, Cispadane, Subalpine, and so forth. The Cisrhenian Republic ousted the Prince-Bishop of Mainz. Revolution was in the air. Its effects could be felt throughout the continent and across the Atlantic. Edmund Burke was horrified. German intellectuals applauded. His most Catholic Majesty, Charles IV of Spain, "was reported by an eyewitness, in 1799, to wear a white satin vest on which was printed the constitution of the French Republic."[2]

The Greeks wanted a republic of their own.

---

1. R.R. Palmer, "Reflections on the French Revolution, *Political Science Quarterly*, 67 (1952), p. 65.

2. Beatrice Hyslop, "French Jacobin Nationalism and Spain," in *Nationalism and Internationalism: Essays Inscribed to Carlton J.H. Hayes* (New York, 1910), p. 234; qtd. in Palmer, p. 65.

The Great Democratic Revolution

What was happening in Europe was partly a response to the series of revolutions in France in the 1790s. The latter—again, partly—stemmed from the American Revolutionary War of the 1770s. The upheavals were not solely, or even primarily, caused by the American and French Revolutions. The earlier successful revolutions set precedents for later insurrections and revolutions. They had not planted their seeds.

Revolutions were successful when insurrectionists received military support. The Americans won their revolution with the support of the Royal French army and navy. The French got help when they decided to found a republic of their own. The Batavian and Italian Republics were all founded after the intervention of revolutionary French troops. It was not the support that began the revolutions. Nor could the support have fueled the revolutions.

What was happening in Europe was what Palmer calls the "Great Democratic Revolution." It was a vast political paradigm shift. Its "*idée-force*"—which "appeared at all social levels, from rich to poor, and from the most educated to the least"—was the "sovereignty of the people."

> It was new, and revolutionary, in that it really meant Sovereignty, that is absolute lawmaking or norm-setting power, and it really meant People, that is, the whole population considered in its relation to public authority.[3]

No particular form of government was attached to this *idée-force*. It was compatible with monarchy and democracy alike. Nor was the *idée-force* specifically religious or anti-religious. It was as immediately compatible with the American Republic's deep religiosity as it was with the rationalism of France. Pope Pius VII, when he was still Bishop of Imola, claimed that democratic government "was

---

3.   Palmer, p. 69.

not incompatible with the Gospel." He had Aquinas on his side. French Revolutionaries, who were imbued with the same *idée-force*, believed that they had the right (and duty) to abolish faith in God altogether, and replace it with faith in Reason itself.

What was attached to the *idée-force* was a change in the way in which people conceived of their relationship to their governments. The source of a government's power, the new idea claimed, was not might, divine right, or tradition. It was the *consent* of the people. The purpose of government, the *idée-force* insisted, was not the appeasement of a particular human authority, the maintenance of a specific class of persons, or the continuation of a determinate social arrangement, but the *protection* and *flourishing* of the governed. The parameters that were to guide popular consent to a government—and the actions of the government itself—were the *natural rights* of every human being.

American revolutionaries were the first clearly to spell this out in their Declaration of Independence at the very start of the Great Democratic Revolution:

> We hold these truths to be self-evident, that all men are created equal, that they are endowed by their Creator with certain unalienable Rights, that among these are Life, Liberty and the pursuit of Happiness.—That to secure these rights, Governments are instituted among Men, deriving their just powers from the consent of the governed,—That whenever any Form of Government becomes destructive of these ends, it is the Right of the People to alter or to abolish it, and to institute new Government, laying its foundation on such principles and organizing its powers in such form, as to them shall seem most likely to effect their Safety and Happiness.

The success of the American Revolution established the viability of the *idée-force*. It vouchsafed the foundational change inherent in the Great Democratic Revolution. The American

Revolution set the precedent. It established the American people's right to sovereignty: its right to participate in its own government, to "self-rule."

How other peoples were to exercise that right—and what their exercise of that right was specifically to entail—was not determined by the right itself. It could not have been. Every people has its specific history, each its distinctive culture. Its sovereignty, and above all its path to the exercise of its right to "self-rule," is necessarily unique. The American Revolution did not involve—and could not have involved—*la Terreur.* The French constitution did not have the Mayflower Compact or the House of Burgesses as its direct antecedents.

Each of the successive revolutions that swept through the Western world during the Great Democratic Revolution established precedents. Each clarified what natural rights were inherent in sovereignty: in a people's exercise and codification of its natural right to self-rule.

The Greek Revolution was no exception.

Greek Independence and Territorial Claims

The Greeks were historically restless. They had for centuries sporadically rebelled against Ottoman Turkish dominion. At the end of the eighteenth century, they and the rest of Europe had changed. Everyone felt the effects of the Great Democratic Revolution. Its consequences were immediately apparent in the Balkans. The Kočina Krajina rebellion, which was supported by the Hapsburgs, broke out in Serbia in 1788. It was a prelude to the Serbian Revolution that began in 1804. In 1821 it was the Greeks' turn.

The Greek War of Independence was an important revolution. While the Serbian Revolution preceded it, no Western power or people could ignore the revolt of the sons of those same men who had first formulated the very ideas that animated their own quests for sovereignty: Plato, Themistocles, and Sophocles. It was the Greek fight for freedom that inspired Lord Byron to pay for the refitting of a fleet and enter the fray.[4]

The Greek Revolution established that a national property right is implicit in a people's right to "self-rule." This right, which is best described as the *inalienable right of an autochthonous people to the proprietorship of the lands of their forefathers*, established that the lands of an indigenous people—and most especially of those indigenous peoples who had developed and expressed their own cultures—belong to that people by right of descent.

The Declaration of Greek Independence of 1822, which was issued in Epidaurus ten months after the start of the revolution, stated that the Greeks, as "the descendants of the wise and noble peoples of Hellas," were fighting the Ottoman Turks not just so that they might live "under the protection of the impenetrable aegis of the law," but in order "to reconquer the rights of individual liberty, of property and honor": to remove the "yoke" of the "frightful tyrant...who, like an infamous brigand, has come from distant regions to invade our borders," reduced them to "slavery" in their own lands, and "stifled and paralyzed" the "descendants of the wise and noble peoples of Hellas."

---

4. It is difficult to overstate the enormous sway the Greek War of Independence had over Romantic thought. Byron is just the tip of the iceberg, as influential as he was on his times. For a quick overview, see Paul Joannides, "Colin, Delacroix, Byron and the Greek War of Independence," *The Burlington Magazine*, 125.965 (1983), p. 495: "The Greek struggle for Independence united all artistic camps in France, but those most passionately involved belonged to the first generation of Romantic painters;—indeed, the images created by, above all others, Eugene Delacroix, have become part of Greek national memory—a profound testimony to his powers of imaginative and sympathetic projection. Initially, Greece was more a liberal than Royalist cause but, partly as a result of internal pressure, partly in an effort to secure a position in the Eastern Mediterranean, the Government of Charles X intervened decisively in the Battle of Navarino, and guaranteed victory for the Greeks. In 1826, however, after the long siege and heroic defense of Missolonghi and the final immolation of its garrison, the outcome of the war seemed anything but sure."

Are we, then, less reasonable than other peoples, that
we remain deprived of these rights? Are we of a nature
so degraded and abject that we should be viewed as un-
worthy to enjoy them, condemned to remain crushed
under a perpetual slavery and subjected, like beasts of
burden or mere automatons, to the absurd caprice of a
cruel tyrant who, like an infamous brigand, has come
from distant regions to invade our borders? Nature
has deeply graven these rights in the hearts of all men;
laws in harmony with nature have so completely con-
secrated them that neither three nor four centuries—
nor thousands nor millions of centuries—can destroy
them. Force and violence have been able to restrict and
paralyze them for a season, but force may once more re-
suscitate them in all the vigor which they formerly enjoyed during many centuries; nor have we ever ceased
in Hellas to defend these rights by arms whenever opportunity offered.

By winning their war of independence, the Greeks made a principle of their implicit claim that the land that in 1832 officially
became Greece was and always had been Greek land by right of
descent and culture.[5] The Turks were simply invaders, "a cruel tyrant who, like an infamous brigand, has come from distant regions
to invade our borders."

The Greeks had abrogated the principle of conquest that had
informed territorial proprietorship and jurisdiction since time im-
memorial. That right that the Romans had invoked when in A.D. 70

---

5. Suny mentions the principle. See Suny, pp. 49–50: "The discourse of the
    nation that emerged from Europe emphasized most emphatically two ele-
    ments: that a people constituted as a nation has the right to rule itself and
    that it also possesses a right to what it holds to be its homeland, a desig-
    nated territory from which it originated. Such an understanding would
    eventually become the most powerful legitimation for state authority and
    territorial possession."

they destroyed the Temple of Solomon and expelled the Jews from Israel had been overturned.

The Greek Principle

This new national property right was invoked in the eighty-seven years following the Greek Declaration of Independence by each of the nations established in what had been the Ottoman Empire: Serbia, Romania, Montenegro, Bulgaria, and so forth. It was invoked by Crete when, after its many revolts, the island managed first to become semi-autonomous, and then to join the sovereign nation of Greece. Nor was the right invoked only by those peoples who lived within the borders of the Ottoman Empire. Italians called upon the *inalienable right of an autochthonous people to the proprietorship of the lands of their forefathers* when they fought—and, with the help of the French, won—the right to self-rule in and proprietorship of those lands south of the Alps that had been part of the Austro-Hungarian Empire. They later coined the term with which peoples explicitly justify their claims to their ancestral lands: *irredentism*—the movement that would free *unredeemed* lands.

The Poles, whose legions fought under the banner "In the name of God, for our freedom and for yours" alongside the Italians in their irredentist wars against the Austrians, received no military support when they attempted to establish their own nation in the lands of their forefathers. And Austria, Germany, and Russia felt no need spontaneously to give up pieces of their empires, although they did have to contend with the waves of insurrections, revolutions, and upheavals that coursed through Europe throughout the nineteenth century.

As the Austrians (and the Polish case) show, European powers were inconsistent in their application (and recognition) of either a people's right to self-rule or the new national property right, which I shall for the sake of brevity call the *Greek Principle*. They had multi-ethnic empires of their own and every intention of maintaining (and expanding) them.[6] Nevertheless, they invoked the principles—and defended them—often enough to make them impossible to ignore. The Greek Principle was later to become the rule that would inform and justify the dismantling of both the Austro-Hungarian Empire and Germany after World War I.

The Ottoman Response to the Greek Principle

The Greek Principle undermined all imperial land claims. The fact that Ottoman Turks were autochthonous to no part of their dominions—that they had, as the Greeks claimed, "come from distant regions"—made the principle especially threatening to them. Unlike the Austrians, the British, the Germans, the French, the Russians, and the Spaniards, all of whom had empires of their own in the nineteenth century, the Ottomans could not plausibly invoke the Greek Principle to ground their claim to any part of their dominions. This meant that all of their territorial claims could be contested, and not just by the autochthonous peoples who lived in them. European powers might have been hypocritical, but they were not ignorant. They knew some history, and they could read maps.

The Ottomans were well aware of the tenuousness of their land claims:

> The Greek rebellion was the first significant domestic rebellion at the end of which the [Ottoman] empire had to recognize the first independent country (of Greece) formed on imperial lands. Greek independence generated

---

6. As Dominic Lieven remarks in his "Dilemmas of Empire 1850–1918: Power, Territory, Identity," *Journal of Contemporary History*, 34.2 (1999), p. 166, citing Hobsbaum: "Between 1876 and 1915 about one-quarter of the globe's land surface was distributed or re-distributed as colonies among half-a-dozen states."

within the Ottoman governing elite the blueprint of what all non-Muslim demands would lead to if they remained unchecked and not suppressed by force.[7]

Suppress native non-Muslim peoples they did, much to the horror of Europe, whose powers were known to use Ottoman massacres as a pretext for military interventions that were often only nominally meant to help the targeted autochthonous Christian peoples. Suppression did not stop the insurrections. Self-rule was in the air, and the precedent had been set. The Serbs, Bulgarians, Romanians, and Montenegrins all wanted their sovereignty as well. The Russians intervened on their behalf.

The Treaty of Berlin of 1878, in which the victorious Russian Imperial Army forced the Ottoman Empire to cede lands not just to the Tsar and to Austria-Hungary, but also to the new nations of Serbia, Romania, and Montenegro, and to the formally autonomous Bulgaria, shows the deeper Turkish response to the threat that the Greek Principle presented them and their territorial claims. The 61st article of the treaty concerns the Armenians:

> The Sublime Porte undertakes to carry into effect, without delay the improvements and reforms demanded by local requirements in the provinces inhabited by Armenians and to guarantee their security against the Circassians and the Kurds. It will give information periodically of the measures taken for this purpose to the Powers, who will watch over the execution of them.

The prior version of that article—the 16th in the Treaty of San Stefano that the Ottomans signed with the Russians just four months before they signed the Treaty of Berlin—refers to "the provinces inhabited by Armenians" as *Armenia* and qualifies those provinces as a "country":

---

7. Göçek, DV, p. 114.

As the evacuation of the Russian troops of the territory which they occupy in Armenia, and which is to be restored to Turkey, might give rise to conflicts and complications detrimental to the relations between the two countries, the Sublime Porte engaged to carry into effect, without further delay, the improvements and reforms demanded by local requirements in the provinces inhabited by Armenians, and to guarantee their safety from the Kurds and Circassians.

The articles demonstrate four significant things. First, the Armenians were, and felt, mistreated by the Ottoman government: they "demanded" reforms and improvements in the six Armenian *vilayets.*[8] Neither the Russians nor the other European powers challenged their demands. They agreed that the Armenians were oppressed; that the Armenians had the right not to be oppressed, or, put differently, that they had the right to what the Greeks had

---

8.   Armenian claims were justified. See, e.g., Bedross Der Matossian, *Shattered Dreams of Revolution: From Liberty to Violence in the Late Ottoman Empire* (Stanford, CA: Stanford University Press, 2014), p. 12: "Both demographic changes in Anatolia that resulted from the immigration of the Muslim from the Balkans and the Caucasus [that was caused both by Ottoman territorial losses and the Sublime Porte's demographic engineering; see footnote below] and tensions in the Balkans [that led to the establishment of separate nations therein] had an important impact on the deteriorating situation in the eastern provinces. In a span of twenty years, from 1862 to 1882, immigration of the Muslim populations from the Balkans and Russia increased the Ottoman Muslim population of Anatolia by at least 40 percent. A good number of these immigrants moved to the eastern provinces where Armenians lived, the majority of whom were peasants, thus creating a population imbalance and friction between the locals and the immigrants. The overall result was an intensification of agrarian tensions. It is noteworthy that the situation in some parts of the Anatolian provinces had already been deteriorating. Not only these agrarian tensions, but also frequent attacks by Kurdish tribes on Armenian peasants, heavy taxation, friction with the influx of Muslims from the Caucasus, administrative corruption, and failure of Armenian efforts to solve these problems diplomatically led to the emergence of Armenian revolutionary groups."

called "the impenetrable aegis of the law" that defended "the rights of individual liberty, of property and honor"; that the Armenians had the right to expect that their rights be respected; and that they had the right to appeal to the powers to help ensure that their rights were respected. European powers, in other words, acknowledged that the Armenians had the right to sovereignty—that the rightful governance of Armenians rested on the consent of the Armenians.

Second, the articles demonstrate that the Ottomans had begun actively and successfully to respond to the threat of the Greek Principle: they had the word *Armenia* (and the qualification thereof as a "country") stricken from the second treaty.[9]

Third, the articles demonstrate that in 1878 European powers asserted both their leverage and moral authority over the Ottomans.

---

9. See Fuat Dündar, *Crime of Numbers: The Role of Statistics in the Armenian Question (1878–1918)* (New Bruswick, NJ/London: Transaction Publishers, 2010) [henceforth CON], pp. 33–34: "After the Ottoman-Russian War of 1877–8, which is known as the 93 *Harbi*, War of '93, the wave of violence targeting Christians, Armenians in particular, for several years, acquiring a completely different character. The absence of authority created by the War of '93, the increase of desire for revenge against Christians, and *the perception within Muslim society that the San Stefano and Berlin treaties were part of a plan for the establishment of an Armenian state, led to a situation where violence dominated the area. The Hamidiye Regiments attempted to counter the Russian menace, counter the Armenian organizations, and increase central authority over the Kurds, all of which intensified the violence. Finally, the state's efforts to 'settle' the nomads, referring mostly to Kurdish tribes, added to the level of violence.... rather than being part of an Armenia that might be established eventually, they [the Kurdish tribes] preferred to be subject to the authority of the Ottoman state. As it can easily be imagined, the state preferred to settle Kurds in Armenian villages*" [italics mine].

As the passage suggests, the Ottomans' awareness of the applicability of the Greek Principle to Armenia led them to enact a geographical and demographical engineering project in the Eastern Provinces. See Dündar, p. 36: "following the Russian War of 1877–8, the Ottoman State had begun to change administrative borders with the purpose of 'reducing the ratio of the Armenian population to the lowest level'.... Since the Congress of Berlin, the Sublime Porte had wanted to change the demographic composition of the area in question."

They assigned themselves the role of the "defenders" of the sovereign rights of the autochthonous peoples: they insisted on receiving "information periodically of the measures taken" to protect Armenian rights. They also felt entitled to determine who would oversee the "improvements and reforms" in the Eastern Provinces—Armenia.[10]

Fourth, the articles demonstrate that the European powers preferred to subordinate the Armenian right to sovereignty and rule of law to their desire to keep Russian expansion in check: they assigned the supervision of the "improvements and reforms" in "the provinces inhabited by Armenians" to the Ottomans and not to Russian troops, as the prior Treaty of San Stefano had specified. Despite their acknowledgment that Armenian "demands" were well founded and implicit recognition that the "demands" were made necessary because the Ottomans oppressed the Armenians, European powers assigned supervision of the "improvements and reforms" to the very government that oppressed the Armenians. Neither the high-sounding principles of the *Great Democratic Revolution* nor Western logic's insistence that rationality requires coherence had eradicated European self-interest or greed.[11] The British came to regret this.

---

10. This is one of the crucial points upon which Vahakn Dadrian's research has focused. See, e.g., *History of the Armenian Genocide*, Ch. 2.

11. There were two main internal forces at work in the Ottoman Empire in the nineteenth and twentieth centuries: (1) the Great Democratic Revolution, and (2) the Ottoman Turkish desire to maintain dominance. These two forces were contradictory. The Great Democratic Revolution called for both the self-determination and the national self-governance of peoples. The Ottoman Turkish desire to dominate (fueled by the Ottoman Turkish conviction that the Turks were the *Millet-i Hakime*) aimed to deny both popular self-determination and national self-governance for everyone but the Turks. As much as the Ottoman Turks did not want to admit it—and fought to conceal it—they did not have the cultural or military strength to contend with the Great Democratic Revolution. The Ottoman Turks knew this.

  There were also two external forces at work in the Ottoman Empire in the nineteenth and twentieth centuries: (3) Russian expansionism, and (4) the schizophrenic European understanding and implementation of the modern principles of proper governance. The European view of the Ottoman

The first and second points are related and the key elements of the Armenian Genocide. The third and fourth are necessary conditions of the unfolding of history.

Armenia, the Zartonk, and the Greek Principle

Like the Greeks, the Armenians had lived in their native lands for thousands of years. They were autochthonous to them. Like the Greeks, the Armenians had a culture of their own and had expressed it in timeless monuments scattered throughout their

---

Empire was characterized by conflicting aims. Europeans wanted both to uphold the principles of the Great Democratic Revolution and to keep each other in check. What Europe added to the conflict internal to the Ottoman Empire was incoherence. The European Powers alternatively backed those autochthonous peoples who lived within the Ottoman Empire and wanted independence and the Ottoman Turks who wanted to quash national independence movements. On this point see, e.g., Hanioğlu, LOE, pp. 85–86: "The Great Powers of Europe envisioned an Ottoman entity made up of many autonomous provinces, governed by representative assemblies that embodied self-rule for non-Muslims. Such a vision, epigrammatically described by a leading Tanzimat statesman as the *États Désunies de Turquie*, was particularly undesirable from the perspective of the Ottoman leadership. They wished to see a strong, unified state, secured from without by a collective guarantee of territorial integrity and from within by a centralized, efficient administration guided by enlightened laws applicable to all.... After 1856, the quest for centralization clashed with the reality of progressive dissolution. Several regions, provinces, and principalities remained nominally within the Ottoman world, but increasingly loosened their ties to the center. Serbia and Montenegro were now Ottoman in name only. Ottoman influence over Wallachia and Moldavia diminished sharply after 1858, when new organic regulations came into effect there; the unification of the two principalities, followed by Ottoman recognition of the fait accompli in 1861, reduced Ottoman leverage to nil. In Mount Lebanon, massacres and counter-massacres between the Druzes and Maronites, followed by attacks on Christians in Damascus, triggered foreign intervention. The Beyoğlu protocol of 1861 granted Mount Lebanon an organic law. In Crete, a revolt of the local Christians resulted in the conferral of a special administrative status on the island in 1868."

ancestral lands. Like the Greeks, the Armenians had sporadically attempted to throw off the "yoke" of foreign domination, which in their case meant not just the Ottoman Empire, but also Persia and Russia, since Armenia (like Poland) was divided into three parts.[12]

When the Treaties of San Stefano and Berlin were signed, the Armenians were also in the midst of a true renaissance (*zartonk*),[13]

---

12. See Razmik Panossian, *The Armenians: From Kings and Priests to Merchants and Commissars* (New York: Columbia University Press, 2006), p. 110: "Early endeavors took place *before* the 'age of nationalism' had reached Armenia itself, but they nevertheless had an explicit agenda of liberation. All of the attempts were based in eastern (i.e. Persian) Armenia and relied upon the (usually naively) expected support of foreign powers. Hence wider geopolitical dynamics of the region—particularly between the Persian, Russian, and Ottoman empires—were an important dimension of Armenian calculations. In the eighteenth century these three empires clashed over Armenia and Georgia a number of times, vying for control of the South Caucasus."

13. The seeds of the Armenian Renaissance, or national cultural awakening, had been planted over a century before by Mkhitar of Sebaste (1676–1749), who founded an Armenian Catholic religious order—the Mkhitarist Fathers—whose primary abbey was (and still is) on the island of San Lazzaro in the Venetian Lagoon, which the Venetian Republic donated to the order in perpetuity in 1717. Mkhitar was an exceptional man. He wrote the first grammars for vernacular Armenian and classical Armenian, as well as the first comprehensive dictionary of the Armenian language. He understood the importance of enriching, codifying, and using vernacular long before most. He "made considerable headway toward simplifying their classical language, compiling a vernacular grammar and increasing the momentum of national unity through the revival of the Armenian heritage" (Harry Jewell Sarkiss, "The Armenian Renaissance 1500–1863," *Journal of Modern History*, 9.4 (1937), p. 444). His disciples wrote the first modern history of Armenia and collected manuscripts throughout Armenia, which they not only preserved but reprinted. The Mkhitarists "retrieved and researched Armenian history, literature, geography and language and presented it to their contemporary world through their publications. Aware of and in conjunction with the intellectual current of European thought they were very consciously and systematically carrying out an enlightenment project on behalf of the nation. Its motivating force and style were European (and more particularly Catholic ideology), but its content was Armenian. The consequence was the modern intellectual foundation of national identity and consciousness" (Panossian, pp. 102–3). The Mkhitarists trained generations

one of the dominant themes of which was the *Hayrenik* (the fatherland): the Armenian nation. Armenian intellectuals, novelists, poets, journalists, and historians attempted to capture and give a modern definition to what Aristotle would have called the specific difference of the Armenians. Building upon the eighteenth-century retrieval, codification, and renewal of Armenian literature, history, and culture, they began to give a modern frame to their national ideal.[14] Armenians published the Ottoman Empire's first newspaper.[15] Between 1855 and 1876 there were around a hundred different Armenian newspapers in Western Armenia—the *six Armenian vilayets*—through which not only Armenian culture, but also politics and administrative reforms, became part of the everyday lives of Armenians.[16] The Armenian *millet* formed the Armenian

---

of teachers who continued their work. As Suny describes the *zartonk*, it was "the product of hard political and intellectual work by Armenian scholars, teachers, and political activists. The road to emancipation, it was thought, ran through education, the building of schools, and the training of a new generation" (Suny, p. 73). Build schools the Armenians did, throughout the lands in which they lived. When, for instance, in 1885, the Tsar believed that Armenian schools threatened his grasp on the Armenian territories in the Russian Empire, he shut down "five hundred schools, attended by 20,000 pupils and employing 900 teachers" (Suny, p. 81). One of the most famous of the Mkhitarist schools was the Collegio Armeno Moorat-Raphael, which was founded through an enormous bequest by Samuel Moorat and his wife Anna Raphael, who were prominent Armenians living in Madras. The Collegio Moorat opened in 1834 in Padova and moved to Paris in 1846. A second Collegio Raphael was opened in Venice in 1836 and moved to the Palazzo Zenobio, which is still owned by the Mkhitarist fathers, in 1851.

14. See, e.g., Panosssian, p. 107: "Mkhitarists did not create or invent the Armenian nation, but retrieved it—and in the process helped to reshape it for the modern period. By reprinting the generally inaccessible works of the early medieval historians, and writing their own histories based on them, the Catholic monks produced works which 'did nothing less than *lay the foundation for the emergence of secular Armenian nationalism.*' Subsequent writers 'constantly circled back to the themes that had their origin in the classical Armenian texts,' which the Mkhitarists had made available and contributed to."

15. Suny, p. 56.

16. Der Matossian, p. 11.

Educational Council in 1856, which had fourteen members, all of whom had graduated from European institutions.[17] Armenian leaders "speedily founded four cultural associations, which organized elementary schools everywhere throughout the country."[18]

The Armenian Renaissance brought with it not just explicit formulations of Armenian national aspirations.[19] It also engendered comparisons between those aspirations and the real conditions of the Armenians who lived in the Ottoman Empire. Thus, Armenian poets described their people as:

> a people conquered by foreign invaders, made captive in their own ancient land, and oppressed by unjust and cruel rulers, yet all the while maintaining their essential Armenian religious culture and yearning to be free.[20]

The *Great Democratic Revolution*, combined with the Armenian *zartonk* and awareness of the changes in Europe, led the Armenians to demand reforms:

---

17. Johann Strauss, "The Millets and the Ottoman Language: The Contribution of Ottoman Greeks to Ottoman Letters (19th–20th Centuries)," *Die Welt des Islams*, 32.2 (1995), p. 219. Strauss cites Vartan Artinian, *The Armenian Constitutional System in the Ottoman Empire 1839–1863* (Istanbul, 1989), pp. 70–71.

18. Sarkiss, pp. 445–46.

19. See, on this, Richard G. Hovannisian, *Armenia on the Road to Independence, 1918* (Berkley/Los Angeles: University of California Press, 1967), p. 1: "The Armenian people, subjected for centuries to foreign domination, experienced a cultural and political renaissance during the eighteenth and especially the nineteenth centuries. The growth of national consciousness was manifested in literary movements, in the establishment of hundreds of schools throughout the Ottoman and Russian empires, and in the emergence of societies striving for Armenian self-administration. The focus of concern was the great Armenian plateau in eastern Anatolia. On this land the Armenian nation had taken form in the first millennium before the Christian era. It was there that Armenian kings had reigned and a distinctive native culture had developed."

20. Suny, pp. 76–77.

What had been burdensome in the past became intolerable in the present. The arbitrary rule of Islamic conquerors became impossible to justify. In the new paradigm of liberalism and national self-determination the Ottoman Empire was marked by social lawlessness and a predatory state that thwarted the "natural laws" of economic competition.[21]

Armenians dared even to dream of a regional government in Armenia, led by Armenians ("appointed by the Sultan") and with councils "made up of equal numbers of Muslims and Armenians" to "report on conditions in the provinces."[22] In 1860 they drew up a national constitution (*Azgayin sahmanadrutyun*) in order to regulate their affairs. In 1863 the sultan "reluctantly" ratified it, and "authorized the formation of a central assembly for the Armenian *millet*."[23] The Armenian National Assembly—with its twin Political Council and Religious

---

21. Suny, p. 77. See also Sarkiss, p. 444–45: "In the opening years of the nineteenth century another Armenian philologist, Khatchatour Abovian (1804–46), introduced radical changes in the grammatical construction of the cumbersome classical Armenian and modernized it. His first major literary work, *Verk Haiastani* [Wounds of Armenia], written in this new dialect, had a revolutionary effect in learned circles. Before long journals and reviews adopted the new medium and began to pour out a flood of light on the ancient past of Armenia.... Between 1820 and 1860 an illustrious line of talented writers produced many literary works in such important centers as Tiflis, Erivan, and Etchmiadzin. The names of Proshian, Aghanian, Nazarian, and many others are landmarks of literary progress. Literature in their hands attained popularity and—what is more significant—became distinctly nationalistic. By 1860 a veritable literary revival swept over the Armenians both in Russia and in Turkey. In increasing numbers writers in all branches of literature—poetry, novels, drama, satire—produced a number of valuable works, not only to justify the universal use of the new medium of expression but also to add momentum to reviving nationalism. They pictured in colorful words the dignity of their ancestral past and the servility of their present state. Writers delved into the vast field of folk lore and revived ancient melodies and traditions."

22. Suny, p. 91.

23. Suny, p. 59.

Council—was the first of its kind in the Ottoman Empire. The Armenian Constitution was the model not just for the constitutions of the other *millets*, but for the Ottoman Constitution of 1876.

Armenians sent a delegation to the Congress of Berlin, which pleaded with the Western powers to afford their people—a "Christian nation" that had "caused no trouble to the Ottoman government"—the "same protection afforded to other Christian nations": "the right of living its life and of being governed on its ancestral land by Armenian officials."[24] Had they been Greek, the Armenian delegates might have repeated the rhetorical questions of the Greek Declaration of Independence:

> Are we, then, less reasonable than other peoples, that we remain deprived of these rights? Are we of a nature so degraded and abject that we should be viewed as unworthy to enjoy them, condemned to remain crushed under a perpetual slavery and subjected, like beasts of burden or mere automatons, to the absurd caprice of a cruel tyrant who, like an infamous brigand, has come from distant regions to invade our borders?

As it was, Khrimian *Hayrig*, who was to become Catholicos of all Armenians and had been part of the delegation sent to Berlin, explained to his people that the European Powers had served a delicious "dish of liberty," but the Armenians only had a *paper spoon*.

Ottomans and Armenian "demands"

At the Congress of Berlin, the Ottomans snatched a partial victory from the jaws of what had till then been their most humiliating defeat. The price was the island of Cyprus, which they ceded to the British. What they received were the return of parts of their empire

---

24. Suny, p. 96.

in the Balkans and in Armenia, and the reformulation of other terms of the Treaty of San Stefano. Article 16 of that treaty was redacted. The word "Armenia" was stricken, as was the qualification of "Armenia" as a "country."

It was a grave risk for the Ottomans to acknowledge in a formal document signed in the presence of the very powers that could and did (however sporadically and self-servingly) intervene to help a people secure its right to sovereignty and "self-rule," that the "provinces" of the Ottoman Empire "inhabited by Armenians" were *Armenia*—although history, maps, and memories designated them as such. The Greek Principle was being invoked for Romanian, Montenegrin, and Serbian land claims in the very document in which the word "Armenia" was stricken.

The very word *Armenia* was dangerous to the Ottomans. In Berlin, Western Powers turned a blind eye to their maps and histories, to their high-sounding rhetoric, to the Armenian delegation, and even to Lord Byron, who could not, however, in this instance refit a fleet to aid the ancient people for whose language he had written a dictionary, and force their hands. Byron had died in Greece. But blindness of Western Powers was not a certain thing.

The Ottomans never carried out the reforms "demanded by local requirements" in "the provinces inhabited by Armenians" that the Treaty of Berlin had called for and left under their own supervision. Sultan Abdul Hamid II, who had privately exclaimed that he "would rather die than accept reforms that would produce self-government [for the Armenians],"[25] worked publicly to ensure that the Armenians would never again be in a position to make "demands." He promoted the immigration of Muslims from the Caucasus and the Balkans.[26]

[He] shifted provincial boundaries to ensure a Muslim majority in every *vilayet*. Kurdish or Turkish districts

---

25. Akçam, ASA, p. 44.
26. Suny, p. 132.

were attached to Armenian areas so that Christians would not form a majority.[27]

He suspended the Armenian Constitution, "the powers of the Armenian National Assembly," banned "Armenian journals from Russia," and prohibited in Armenia

> all forms of national expression, forbidding the word
> *Hayastan* (Armenia in Armenian) in print as well as the
> sale and possession of pictures of the last Armenian king,
> Levon V, who had lost his throne five centuries earlier.[28]

The Hamidian Massacres broke out in 1894 and claimed the lives of hundreds of thousands of Armenians. The officers who led the slaughter were decorated, even though the sultan had never publicly ordered that they massacre the Armenians.[29] Other Armenians were forcibly converted to Islam.[30] They were

---

27. Suny, p. 101.

28. Suny, p. 68.

29. See Robert Melson, "A Theoretical Inquiry into the Armenian Massacres of 1894–1896," in *Comparative Studies in Society and History*, 24.3 (1982), p. 488: "The vali of Moush, who had called in the troops in the first place, as well as Zeki Pasha, the commandant of the Fourth Army Corps, were decorated for their participation in the massacres while the mutessarif of Moush, who had protested, was dismissed. In protest, the British, French, and Russian consular delegates themselves travelled to Sassoun to hear evidence. Following testimony from the consular delegates, the European powers exerted pressure on the Porte to institute reforms which had been agreed upon in the treaties of San Stefano and Berlin in 1878, but which had never been implemented." Sultan Abdul Hamid's role in the Hamidian Massacres is a contested issue. There are those who argue that the sultan had no hand in the bloodshed. There are those who claim that he was directly responsible for them. The fact that the sultan decorated those responsible for the massacres makes the prior claim doubtful, as do the facts that the sultan could not have been ignorant of the massacres and did not lack the means with which to stop them.

30. See, on this, Selim Deringil: "'The Armenian Question Is Finally Closed': Mass Conversions of Armenians in Anatolia During the Hamidian Mas-

forced off their lands in what Suny calls the "sustained process of alienation of Armenian lands," which he argues took place "from the Hamidian period (1876–1908) through the years of the Young Turk government (after 1908)." Suny quotes G.H. Fitzmaurice, chief dragoman and first secretary at the British embassy, as writing:

> after the Treaty of Berlin [1878], realizing that a sense of nationality cannot easily live without a peasantry, and that if it succeeded in uprooting the Armenian peasantry from the soil and driving them into the towns or out of the country, it would in great part rid itself of the Armenians and the Armenian question, condoned and encouraged Kurdish usurpation of Armenian Lands.[31]

Sultan Abdul Hamid II did everything in his power to erase the existence and very memory of Armenia.

> Even though the grand vizier Said Pasha wept at the Armenian patriarch's complaints and woes and promised everything, he did nothing. Even though it was first decided, then printed and announced many times that a reform delegation was to be sent to the Eastern

---

sacres of 1895–1897," *Comparative Studies in Society and History*, 51.2 (2009), pp. 344–71.

31. Suny, p. 55. Suny outlines some of the figures of the case on pp. 176–77: "The Armenian National Assembly set up a Commission of Usurped Lands, which analyzed 135 reports presented to the Ottoman governments from 1890 to 1910 and found 7,000 cases of illegal land seizures in 35 districts (*sancaks*) of the eastern provinces. This amounted, the commission concluded, to 741,000 hectares of Armenian lands confiscated in 20 years and the estimated emigration in the preceding years of 100,000 Armenians. The percentage of Armenians living in the eastern provinces declined in the three and a half decades from the Treaty of Berlin to World War I. The influx of Muslims from the Caucasus and the Balkans increased the pressure on the poorest and most vulnerable Armenians."

Anatolian provinces under the leadership of the Minister of Foundations Hayri Bey, after a while, this too ceased to be discussed.... In order to deny the existence of the Armenians during the Abdülhamid era, we reduced their population and also invented the formula "Armenia is only a geographical term."[32]

The phrase "only a geographical term" was not original to the Hamidian government. In 1847 Metternich used it to describe Italy.[33] Unlike Metternich, who was likely just expressing a *political fact*, the Ottoman government took the phrase to be a *political program*, a formula through which it could eliminate a problem: Armenia.

In 1895, in the midst of the Hamidian Massacres, European Powers presented Sultan Abdul Hamid II with a new project for the reforms. It was meant to protect Armenians and compensate them for their losses. The sultan "used" (as Dadrian puts it) "various techniques of stalling, temporizing, equivocation and even rejection in order to evade a final, binding commitment."[34] And the massacres continued throughout the Ottoman Empire.[35] The peaceful Armenian protesters, who gathered in Constantinople

---

32. Goçek, DV, p. 149.

33. Metternich's full phrase in a letter of April 1847 is: "The word 'Italy' is a geographical expression, a description which is useful shorthand, but has none of the political significance the efforts of the revolutionary ideologues try to put on it, and which is full of dangers for the very existence of the states which make up the peninsula." Metternich apparently liked the phrase *"L'Italie est un nom géographique."* He repeated it in a letter to Count Dietrichstein on August 2, 1847, and again in a letter to British Foreign Minister Lord Palmerston on August 6, 1847. *Il Nazionale* published the statement the following year. Italians took great offense and used the statement as a rallying call to unite in their *irredentist* wars against Austria.

34. Dadrian, p. 119.

35. Melson, p. 488: "The reforms upon which the Europeans insisted were to go into effect in October of 1895, but this was precluded by the launching

requesting that the reforms promised in Berlin be implemented, triggered a city-wide slaughter of Armenians.[36] "The precedent of autonomy leading to independence in the Balkans loomed like a specter."[37] That specter was large. Ottomans were convinced that in the case of Armenia, independence had to "be prevented at all costs." Anatolia was "the last stronghold" of the empire:

> An Ottoman document generated at this time clearly drew the parallel [with the Balkans]: "However, the Armenian affair is not like the Bulgarian or the Serbian affairs, because it has arisen in Anatolia which is the crucible of Ottoman power."[38]

They developed an elaborate "rhetoric justifying massacres as strategically necessary and as legitimate means to preserve the integrity of the state."[39] A Turkish official made the point clearly: "I assert that the Armenians have brought the calamity on themselves by their ambition for autonomy."[40]

---

of widespread massacres of Armenians throughout the Ottoman Empire." Melson provides an excellent summary of the events.

36. See Stefan Ihrig, *Justifying Genocide: Germany and the Armenians from Bismarck to Hitler* (Cambridge, MA/London: Harvard University Press, 2016), p. 37: "In his report, Ambassador Anton Saurma von der Jeltsch, after having stressed how nonsensical he found both the demonstration and the demands of the Armenians, drew particular attention to the role of the police force. He wrote that the police did not only tolerate 'that the population was slaughtering the Armenians but was cheering them on and took part itself in the slaughtering of already heavily wounded and tied-up Armenians.' He also described how Armenians were then even 'raided and slaughtered' in their own homes."

37. Suny, p. 111.

38. Derengil, p. 349. Derengil is quoting Basbakanhk Osmanh Arsjvi (Prime Ministry, Ottoman Archives, Istanbul) Y.PRK. 32/94, 3 Sept. 1893.

39. Suny, p. 133.

40. Suny, p. 133.

The CUP response to the Greek Principle

Historians have called upon a number of powerful emotions in their accounts of the causes of the Armenian Genocide. Fear is one of these, as are paranoia, rage, resentment, and vindictiveness.[41]

The fear in question, Akçam claims, was "fear of partition," or of territorial losses. The collapse of the Ottoman Empire was stunningly swift. "This week I looked at a map," one deputy claimed around the turn of the twentieth century. "Most of it [Ottoman territories] is gone. This too will go very shortly."[42]

Rage, resentment, and vindictiveness flared up every time the Ottomans lost territories to new nation-states or to other empires. Each territorial loss was both a blow to the Ottoman Turk's pride—his belief in his own superiority—and the source of masses of Muslim refugees, who (especially after the Ottoman-Russian and Balkan Wars) retreated with the Ottoman army from the "lost"

---

41. The same claim is made for the Hamidian Massacres. See Melson, pp. 492–93: "As noted, the Shaws [Stanford Shaw was a well-known genocide negationist who taught at Harvard and UCLA], in their recent influential work, suggest that the massacres were a reaction to Armenian provocation. Theirs is a picture of a strict but beneficent Ottoman order sorely tested by the vagaries and insubordination of the Armenian millet and by the revolutionary activities of the nationalist parties. According to them, these parties pursued a kind of 'the-worst-the-better' strategy. They hoped that by provoking the sultan into mass reprisals against Armenians, they could elicit intervention by the European powers and thus bring about the liberation of Armenia. Thus, the Shaws note that in the period 1890–93, 'Terrorism and counterterrorism went on for three years with the government acting sternly, albeit sometimes harshly to keep order. The Hunchaks were, however, denied the kind of harsh reprisals that they really needed to make their case in Europe. They then organized a major coup at Sasun ... the strongest area of Armenian population, where there were many marauding tribesmen who had caused trouble to the cultivators in the past.' Further, the Shaws claim that the Hnchakists intended to create 'a Socialist Armenian Republic presumably in the six east Anatolian provinces from which all Muslims would be driven out or simply killed.'"

42. Akçam, ASA, p. 54.

territories into Anatolia. The refugees were a wretched lot and told horror stories about the slaughtering that had preceded their escape from the "lost" lands. They thirsted for revenge. They were a powerful reminder of the insubstantiality of the foundations of the Ottoman Turks' pride.

The Young Turk Revolution of 1908, which was a response to the collapse of the empire and had put power into the hands of the CUP—the party that had, among other things, promised to stabilize and strengthen the Ottoman Empire—did not stay its disintegration or remove the causes of its fear. The fragmentation of the empire picked up pace:

> During the first months after the establishment of the new regime in 1908 Austria had broken the feeble thread which bound Bosnia-Herzegovina to Turkey.... It was the first shock to the childish belief that once a New Turkey arose the powers and the aggressive little nations who surrounded her would allow for the difficulties of the reform period, and give her at least a short time to find herself.... Before the sore feeling about Bosnia-Herzegovina had been calmed, the Cretan assembly declared the annexation of the island of Crete by Greece. This aroused another wild outburst.... Then the Italians seized Tripoli, and the burden of the song changed again. So in 1910, Turkey, on top of everything else, was to face the loss of vast lands in Africa. The practical settlement of Bosnia-Herzegovina, the helplessness of the government before the annexation of Crete, had already filled the cup to the brim. Action became inevitable before the outburst of public feeling.[43]

Wounded pride and horror stories breed all sorts of violent emotions. In one of his speeches, Enver Pasha was reported to have protested:

---

43. Edib, HW, pp. 301–3.

How could a person forget the plains, the meadows, watered with the blood of our forefathers; abandon those places where Turkish raiders had hidden their steeds for a full four hundred years, with our mosques, our tombs, our dervish retreats, our bridges and our castles, to leave them to our slaves, to be driven out of Rumelia to Anatolia: this was beyond a person's endurance. I am prepared to gladly sacrifice the remaining years of my life to take revenge on the Bulgarians, the Greeks, and the Montenegrans.[44]

When one adds awareness of one's failure to respond to the deep threat to one's existence as the *Millet-i Hakime*—the inability to stop the "slaves" from taking what "Turkish raiders" had made "*our* mosques, *our* tombs, *our* dervish retreats, *our* bridges"—and the belief that one is being treated unjustly to the mix, the violent emotions fester and erupt in slaughter. Such was Edib's explanation of the CUP's violent response to the disintegration of the Ottoman Empire:

I believe that the two different measures meted out by Europe to the Moslem Turks and to the Christian peoples in Turkey keenly intensified nationalism in Turkey. They also aroused the feeling that in order to avoid being exterminated the Turks must exterminate others. As the Bulgarian victory made the world overlook the crimes of her revolutionaries—crimes of which the Bulgarians themselves surely did not approve, for they are a kindly race—so any other nation in the East could hope to have all her massacres forgotten, so long as she could impose respect with her victorious force.[45]

---

44. Akçam, ASA, p. 115.
45. Edib, HW, p. 333.

Turkish fear, rage, resentment and vindictiveness were not just directed at Western powers, who both held the fate of the Ottoman Empire in their hands and "took advantage" of Turkish weakness by breaking "the feeble thread which bound Bosnia-Herzegovina to Turkey" and by taking Tripoli and the Dodecanese. Nor were they solely aimed at the empire's autochthonous Christian populations who had successfully invoked "the right of living their lives and of being governed on their ancestral lands" and declared independence, or their "annexation" to Greece. CUP leaders—who on this point "were of one mind" with Sultan Abdul Hamid II— publicly, at least, *linked* the actions of the empire's native Christian peoples and the European powers, and *placed the blame* for both Ottoman massacres of the empire's native Christian peoples and the dismemberment of the empire squarely and solely on the shoulders of the autochthonous Christian peoples themselves.[46] As Şurayı Ümmet, one of these leaders, made the case:

> Because the Armenian and Macedonian revolutionary committees know that the only way to get the attention of world opinion and to cause their intervention is to [provoke the] massacre [of] Christians in our country, they have never refrained from provoking the anger and fury of the Muslims, which pave the way for [such massacres].[47]

The consequence of the morass of Turkish emotions and Christian provocation, or so the account contends, was the extermination of the autochthonous Christian peoples of Anatolia. It was,

---

46. This technique was developed by Sultan Abdul Hamid II, who, Suny claims, developed the view "that not Turks or Kurds but the Armenians themselves were responsible for the disaster [the Hamidian Massacres] that befell them." He points out that this "explanation would be repeated in the 1909 massacres in Adana and again in the Genocide of 1915." See Suny, p. 133.

47. Şurayı Ümmet; qtd. in Akçam, ASA, p. 62.

Edib explicitly claims, the cause of the horrendous massacres of the
Armenians of Adana in 1909:

> But some, indeed even the majority of the Armenian
> leaders, still kept their separatist tendencies, and these
> were anxious and watchful. The Armenian Free State,
> which was a mere political game to Russia and England,
> was a real political ideal to some leading Armenians; and
> they needed continual trouble and a martyred Armenian
> nation in Turkey as a pretext to attract the attention and
> the sympathy of the European public and to induce
> European interference in the internal administration of
> Turkey.[48]

The fever pitch of emotions that coursed through the Turks in
1909, the account continues, escalated when the Balkan Wars—
which the Turks entered believing they would easily and soundly
defeat their *küçük komşumuz* ("our small neighbors"), the independent Balkan nations—ended in a resounding defeat for the Ottoman Empire and stripped it of all of its European possessions:

> A defeat of this magnitude at the hands of former sub-
> jects was a very difficult pill to swallow. Reducing an
> empire of three continents to an Asiatic state, it shat-
> tered Ottoman pride and self-confidence. In addition
> to the humiliation, the Ottoman government had to
> deal with an immense financial drain resulting from
> the losses of territory and materiel, and the difficulty of
> resettling hundreds of thousands of refugees pouring
> in from the lost regions. The renunciation of territo-
> ries with large non-Turkish populations, and the ensu-
> ing atrocities against Muslims in those lands, dealt the
> Ottomanist ideal a shattering blow, giving the upper

---

48. Edib, HW, pp. 283–84.

hand to the Turkists in the internal debate over the basis of loyalty in the empire. Inevitably, the loss of the European lands prompted an innovative view of the geographical character of the empire among the Ottoman ruling elite. For centuries, the empire had rested on two central pillars, Rumelia and Anatolia, between which nested the imperial capital. Suddenly the Arab periphery became the only significant extension of the empire outside its new Anatolian heartland. Some influential thinkers went so far as to propose the removal of the capital from Istanbul to a major town in central Anatolia or northern Syria.[49]

The result of these violent emotions, or so the account would have it, was the extermination of the Armenians that took place a mere two years after the Balkan Wars in World War I. The Turkish people, it is claimed, were so filled with fear, rage, resentment and vindictiveness after the loss of the Balkans, the treatment of fellow Muslim Turks in the Balkans, and the "treachery" of the Christians—both the European Christian powers, who had "meted" "different measures" for "the Moslem Turks" and "the Christian peoples in Turkey," and the Christian natives of the Balkans, who had defeated the Ottomans and slaughtered the Turks who lived there—that they exterminated the Armenians.

This violent Turkish response was, the account would add, not just unintended by the central government. It was "provoked." Like their Balkan co-religionists, those who would so frame the events claim, the Armenians had been "treacherous." In response to their treachery, the government in Constantinople ordered that the Armenians be "relocated." During their "relocation," it is said,

---

49. Hanioğlu, LOE, p. 173. An excellent study of the emotional and political effects of the Ottoman defeat in the First Balkan War is Eyal Ginio, *The Ottoman Culture of Defeat: The Balkan Wars and Their Aftermath* (London: Hurst and Company, 2016).

the rabid Turks, who thirsted for revenge, assaulted them and
exterminated them.[50]

---

50. Salt's account of the Armenian Genocide is an excellent example of the sort
of account that I have been describing. See Jeremy Salt, "The Narrative
Gap in Ottoman Armenian History," *Middle Eastern Studies,* 39.1 (2003).
The crucial passage in that account is on pp. 20–21: "The decision to 'relocate' the Armenians was taken after a year in which Armenian guerilla
bands incited and armed by the Russians and organized by the Dashnaks
had thrown themselves into the war effort against their own government.
Not for the first time in late Ottoman history, some Armenians saw collaboration with the Russians as their best chance of carving an independent
state out of the historical Armenian homeland straddling the Ottoman-
Russian border. By the Ottoman government they were naturally regarded
as traitors. At a time when the Ottomans were fighting a war on several
fronts, Armenian guerilla bands were attacking government offices, killing
gendarmes and massacring Muslim civilians and burning their villages.
Thousands of Armenians were involved in these activities. The fighting
between the Russian and Ottoman armies in the eastern provinces was
accompanied by ruthless conflict between the local Muslim and Christian
population which can be seen as the culmination of decades of simmer-
ing tension punctuated by explosions of savage communal conflict. As a
matter of military necessity the decision was taken on 27 May to move the
Armenian population away from the fighting to districts south of Diyarbakir. The details of how this was to be effected were left to the local authorities. The decision was published in the Provisional Law of Relocations
(*tehcir kanunu*). Ottoman documents on the relocations—sent in secret
and seized by British intelligence in the 1920s, after the occupation of Istanbul—included 'strict and explicit rules' on the protection of Armenian
lives and property. Yet on the convoys moving south in the direction of the
Arab provinces Armenians were set upon and massacred. Wartime deaths
through armed conflict, massacre, disease, famine at makeshift camps in
Syria (where there was general famine during the war), along with relocation or emigration to other countries reduced the Armenian community in
the Anatolian heartland of the Ottoman empire to a mere remnant. The
explanation put out by the Ottoman government in 1916 was that infuriated by Armenian treachery and massacres, the Muslim population 'at last
took the law into their own hands.'"
    Salt furnishes no evidence for the crucial claims in his account—namely,
that thousands of Armenians in guerilla bands were running wild attacking government offices, massacring civilians, burning Muslim villages, and
becoming involved in "savage communal conflict." He gives no sources

As Edib made the point, the Balkan Wars

aroused the feeling that in order to avoid being exterminated the Turks must exterminate others ... any other
nation in the East could hope to have all her massacres
forgotten, so long as she could impose respect with her
victorious force.

Emotions, violence, and plans

There is surely much that can be said for this account of the CUP's—
and Ottoman Turkey's—reaction to the wave of revolutions that
swept through Europe and the domains of the Ottoman Empire,
especially by those who believe that emotions are the sole cause of
human actions. To be sure, impotence and blind pride make for an
incendiary combination.

The account is still part of the official histories of the Republic
of Turkey today.[51] Its implicit twin claims are that the Armenian

---

for these claims. Nor does he specify where and when the Armenian guerilla war took place, or the names of the "thousands of Armenians who
were involved in these activities." This is not surprising. The timing of the
events in his account is outlandish. His opening statement makes this clear.
Had the "decision to 'relocate' the Armenians" been taken a year after the
"Dashnaks had thrown themselves into the War effort"—by which one
surmises he means a year after the Ottoman Empire's entry into World
War I—it would have been issued in November 1915. This is absurd. By
November, the Armenians had long been deported. The Tehcir Law was
passed, as Salt himself mentions in the passage, in May 1915.

Robert Melson's fine analysis in "Theoretical Inquiry into the Armenian
Massacres" of what made the Armenians a threat to the Turks points out a
number of deeper flaws inherent in the accounts of the Salts—and Shaws.

51. The account, Akçam points out, is one that "contemporary Turkish histories of the period favor," claiming that "All of the Christian communities played the game of causing bloody slaughter and inciting the Muslim
population to respond with even bloodier actions, and then they embarked
upon a campaign of 'Let's rescue the poor oppressed Christians!' in Euro-

Genocide was not a genocide at all, but a violent (and unplanned) and eminently justifiable reaction to provocation; and that the massacre of the Armenians—and the other autochthonous Christian peoples of Anatolia—was the visceral act of self-defense by the Turkish masses and not the Young Turkish government. Salt makes both of these points explicitly. Citing an official in the Young Turkish government, he claims that it was the Turkish masses that solved the Armenian problem: "infuriated by Armenian treachery and massacres the Muslim population 'at last took the law into their own hands.'"[52]

The primary flaw in the account is that it presupposes that the leaders of the CUP did not think as well as feel strongly. It presupposes that the leaders and ideologues of the CUP had not truly understood the nature and effects of either the Great Democratic Revolution or the Greek Principle, despite the fact that they were the primary causes of the dismemberment of the Ottoman Empire in the Balkans. It presupposes that CUP strategists had not been able to understand how to contrast both the Great Democratic Revolution and the Greek Principle. It presupposes that they had not thought that Armenian independence had to "be prevented at all costs," because Anatolia was "the last stronghold" of the Turks, "the crucible of Ottoman power."[53] It presupposes that they were incapable of planning and acting to save their own *Millet-i Hakime.* It presupposes, in other words, that CUP ideologists, strategists, and leaders were a thoroughly incompetent lot who should never have been at the helm of the Ottoman Empire in the first place.[54]

---

pean public opinion" and again that "All Christian minorities acted in this way: armed actions, undertaking revolts, and, when either the government or the Muslim population itself reacted to this, to raise the cry of 'massacre'... [and] to impel the great powers to action." See Akçam, ASA, p. 63.

52. Salt, p. 21.

53. Derengil, p. 349.

54. Edib suggests this. See HW, p. 266: "The Young Turks stepped into power without having studied the strength of the separatist tendencies, or the way to deal with them in case the constitution of 1876, which they were

The account would have us believe that the fact that the CUP managed a systematic eradication of all of the autochthonous Christian
peoples of Anatolia was a matter of sheer dumb luck.

All of these presuppositions are simply false.

Whatever the account might try to pass off as plausible assumptions, the leaders of the CUP—just as Abdul Hamid II before
them—had understood the nature and effects of both the *Great
Democratic Revolution* and the Greek Principle all too well.[55] They
said as much to Armenian leaders at a meeting in 1906. When the
Armenians asked that the reforms that had been promised for the
Armenian provinces be extended to Cilicia, they recounted:

> The Young Turks became grieved, struck dumb with
> surprise. Our arguments had brought them to a moral
> crisis. Even the color of their faces changed…. The ad-
> dition of Cilicia to Armenia would split the empire in
> two. We said that self-rule would preserve the unity of
> these parts of the empire, that it didn't mean total sepa-
> ration or independence. Dr. Nazim, in replying to our

---

restoring, should fail to solve the fearfully complicated Ottoman dilemma.
Turkey was an empire; the new leaders were at heart unconsciously empire
men with a moderate constitutional ideal which accorded representation
to all; and they did not realize their responsibility in any other important
issue. The fixed idea, that once representative government is established all
the old evils will be cured, blinded them to a clear study of the political
situation in Europe and in their own country."

55.   They criticized the sultans for having been too soft. Joseph Pomiankowski,
military attaché at the Austrian Embassy in Constantinople between 1909
and 1919, claimed that "A great number of Turkish intellectuals have sincerely expressed the sentiment that the reason for the Ottoman Empire's
loss…over the last two centuries…of its provinces…lies first and foremost
in the excessively humanistic behavior of the previous sultans. What should
have been done was either the forcible conversion to Islam of the population in the provinces…or their utter and total extirpation." Pomiankowski;
qtd. in Akçam, ASA, p. 120.

demands, said that this division was merely a precedent for independence, if not today, then in 5–10 years.[56]

The sultan had responded to the modern principles by openly and directly challenging them. He violently and systematically fought to reestablish the rights of the conqueror over the conquered: to "promote the traditional Islamic aspects" of governmental rule and suppress "the disruptive forces of liberalism, nationalism, and constitutionalism."[57] The blood of the hundreds of thousands of Armenians who were slaughtered during his reign earned him the charming soubriquet *The Red Sultan*. His goal was to extinguish the hope of freedom and justice in the very hearts and minds of the conquered autochthonous Christian peoples of the empire. He even tried to force them to forget the names of their nations.[58]

The CUP, whose strength lay in the loyalty of the army, responded to the modern Western nationalist principles that had been the cause of Ottoman undoing by openly embracing them; applying them exclusively to themselves and that *vatan* that they intended to create; and ensuring that no people (autochthonous or

---

56. Sabuh Külian; qtd. in Akçam, ASA, p. 64.

57. Suny, p. 100.

58. As Ihrig points out, Friederich Naumann's *Asia*, written in the aftermath of the Hamidian Massacres, actually defended massacres themselves precisely because an independent Armenia meant the death of the Ottoman Empire. See Ihrig, p. 65: "The chain of thought went like this: Naumann conceded that the massacring of 80,000 or even 100,000 Armenians was something that, 'looked at by itself,' left one with no choice but to condemn it in the harshest terms.... Yet, there was one thing that hindered the Germans from criticizing the sultan and from demanding his overthrow: 'it is the fact that the Turk answers: I am fighting for my life as well—and the fact that we believe him.' This 'barbarity' was the 'last bloody attempt' of an old great empire to save itself, of an empire that did not want to be killed off.... The Armenians were somewhat comparable to the Greeks, Bulgarians, Serbs, and Romanians—all former subjects of the Ottoman Empire that gained independence in the course of the nineteenth century. However, if now the Armenians, too, were to leave the empire, this would mean, 'as a glance at the map of the Turkish Empire will show everybody easily, the end, death.'"

otherwise) could invoke the Greek Principle and challenge their claims to the lands in which they created their *vatan*. Dr. Nâzim clearly stated this before the Balkan Wars:

> The pretensions of the various nationalities are a capital source of annoyance for us. We hold linguistic, histori-cal and ethnic aspirations in abhorrence. This and that group will have to disappoint. There should be only one nation on our soil, the Ottoman nation, and only one language, Turkish. It will not be easy for the Greeks and Bulgarians to accept this, although it is a vital necessity for us. To bring them to swallow the pill, we shall start with the Albanians. Once we have gotten the better of these mountaineers, who think they are invincible, the rest will take care of itself. After we have turned our can-nons on the Albanians, shedding Muslim blood, let the *gâvurs* beware. The first Christian to move a muscle will see his family, house and village smashed to smithereens. Europe will not dare raise its voice in protest or accuse us of torturing the Christians because our first bullets will have been expended on Muslim Albanians.[59]

Any "nation in the East could hope to have all her massacres forgot-ten, so long as she could impose respect with her victorious force."

CUP violence was not just informed by Sultan Abdul Hamid II's failure to eradicate that "nationalism and constitutionalism" from the autochthonous peoples of the Ottoman Empire that led to the disastrous defeat of the empire in the Balkans. Massacres, as Melson has pointed out, are not the proper means by which to snuff out an ideological revolution, let alone a *zartonk* (renaissance):

> Police repression as such could be used effectively against individuals or parties, but it could not be used

---

59. Dr. Nâzim; qtd. in Kévorkian, pp. 120–21.

to prevent the renaissance of a major communal group. For renaissance implies a whole population on the move in the economic, cultural, social, and political spheres. To abort such a broad-based social mobilization what is needed is a broad-based policy designed to prevent change not only in one sphere of progress but in all of them.[60]

The CUP wanted a permanent solution to the threats of the Great Democratic Revolution and the Greek Principle. That permanent solution entailed eliminating the very possibility of land claims by anyone other than the Turks. It entailed wiping the lands of the *vatan* clean of its ancient autochthonous Christian peoples.[61] The CUP could only create a permanent "Turkey for the Turks," their ethnically and culturally homogenous Turkish homeland, with its modern centralized state grounded in the principles of *liberté*, *égalité*, and *fraternité*, in a land cleansed of its natives.[62]

---

60. Melson, pp. 506–7.

61. The CUP had already experimented with the techniques it would later use in Anatolia and Armenia. It had forcefully tried to clean Macedonia of its native Christian peoples and replace them with Muslims. As Dadrian describes it: "The severity with which the Young Turk Ittihadist regime began to forcibly denude Macedonia of its indigenous Christian population and repopulate it with Muslim immigrants [the *muhadjers*] was such as to alarm and agitate these three nationalities [the Greek, Serbian, and Bulgarian], which all began exploring the possibility of an alliance against Turkey primarily. As described in n. 7 of Ch. 10 herein, during the secret meetings of their 1910 annual congress, the Ittihadists had already resolved to resort to massacre, if necessary, in order to cleanse Macedonia of Christians," Dadrian, p. 188. See also Dündar, CON, pp. 43–44.

62. Count Wolff-Metternich, the German Ambassador in Constantinople, wrote as much in 1916: "Turkey is set on fulfilling, in its own way, a policy that will solve the Armenian question by destroying the Armenian people. Neither our intercession, nor the protests of the American ambassador, nor even the threat of enemy force…have succeeded in turning Turkey from this path, nor will they at a later date," Wolff-Metternich; qtd. in Akçam, ASA, p. 177.

By 1913, the only land upon which they could create their *vatan* was (or included) Anatolia: their "last stronghold ... the crucible of Ottoman power." They had no intention of losing it:

> The streets were deserted except for the refugees shivering in the mud, and sick or wounded soldiers who had arrived late, staggering, or leaning against the walls or each other for support. I realized then the extent of my affection for my people and for my land. I cannot make out which I loved best, but I felt my love was personal and incurable and had nothing to do with ideas, thoughts, or politics, that in fact it was physical and elemental. Very often I was the only woman crossing Sultan Ahmed Square. I had on my loosest and oldest charshaf, and often I would stand in the middle of the square and think with infinite sadness of an alien army marching toward it. I had a foolish desire to stoop and kiss the very stones of the place, so passionately did I love it. No force could have dragged me away from Constantinople. I belonged to the place, and whatever its fate, I meant to share it.[63]

The CUP knew that it was in danger of losing its "last stronghold." It organized boycotts of Armenian products, stores, and merchants. It placed its men in positions of power.[64] While it was fighting the Balkan League, it moved Bosnian refugees to Armenian villages. It fostered systematic violence in the Armenian *vilayets*.[65] In response

---

63. Edib, HW, pp. 335–36.

64. One example suffices to show the ruthlessness of the CUP's actions. In 1911 Mezifun, which had a large Armenian population, elected an Armenian mayor. The election was contested. The resulting inquiry confirmed that the Armenian had won. Nevertheless, the *vali* of Sivas invalidated it on orders from the CUP's Central Committee. See Kévorkian, p. 127.

65. Western Armenia—and not just Cilicia, where the 1909 massacres took place—was plagued with problems even after the Constitutional Revolution of 1908. Kurds had seized Armenian properties that they later refused to re-

to the violence, the Armenians attempted to convince the European Powers finally to address the matter of the reforms promised them by the Treaties of San Stefano and Berlin.[66] They drew up an eleven-point plan, which André Mandelstam—the chief dragoman of the Russian Embassy—presented to the Turkish government. It called for the

creation of a single Armenian province in the Ottoman Empire which would be administered by a Governor

---

turn to their rightful owners. They plundered Armenian villages. They assassinated and kidnapped Armenians in the Eastern Provinces. Armenians had no proper means with which to defend themselves against the Kurds, who were not just often supported by the central Ottoman government, but were favored by the Turkish courts, which supported their co-religionists and not Christian Armenians. For a quick overview, see Roderic H. Davison, "The Armenian Crisis 1912–14," *American Historical Review*, 53.3 (1948), pp. 481–505.

The attacks on Armenians in the Eastern Provinces intensified during the Balkan Wars. Alarmed reports written by Armenian political and religious leaders stated that the attacks were systematic and targeted Armenian leaders. Kévorkian quotes several of these reports written in 1912: "Constitutional Turkey has…with greater deceitfulness and methodicalness… been sucking the blood of the Armenian people…for the past four years… and we, naïve as we were and blinded by illusion, insensibly drew closer, a step at a time, to this abyss…. The hellish plot that is being forged against the Armenian people in the dark is no longer a secret. The Turkish government—the Young Turks—no longer feel the need to hide the crime they are meditating" (p. 151). And again: "According to information received in the past few days from absolutely trustworthy individuals…the persecution of the Armenians in the six vilayets is proceeding in a systematic fashion. It is not hidden, but takes place in broad daylight. Everything and anything now serves as a pretext for imputing subversive ideas to the Armenians and pursuing them before the law." This caused what Kévorkian calls a "massive emigration of the exhausted Armenian peasantry" (p. 154). In 1912 the Armenian Patriarch issued a circular demanding that the Ottoman government address the problem. The official response of the grand vizier was to claim that Armenians were making nuisances of themselves.

66. The Armenians sent a delegation to the London Conference of 1912–13 requesting that the European Powers attend to them. Bryce claims that Russia was the one power willing to step up and attempt to deal with the issue. For a detailed account, see Kévorkian, pp. 153–65.

General who was either to be an Ottoman citizen, adhering to the Christian faith, or preferably "a European," to be nominated by the Sultan with the assent of the European powers. This Governor General would have had wide-ranging powers to administer the Armenian province in independence from the general politics of the Ottoman Empire. A legislative assembly, which was to represent both Muslims and Christians living in the Armenian province, would have had lawmaking powers for local matters.[67]

After a great deal of negotiating and a lot of patience, Russia—the head of whose delegation was the Egyptian-Armenian Boghos Nubar Pasha, who had spent a year in Europe discussing the reform—was able to get the Western Powers and Germany to agree with at least some of Mandelstam's plan. On February 8, 1914, the CUP signed the variant of the plan that came to be known as the *Vilayat-i Şarkiyye Islahati* (The Reform of the Ottoman Provinces agreement), or more simply as the Yeniköy Accord. It combined the Eastern Provinces into two large ones and assigned each a foreign inspector invested with complete authority. The accord became official Ottoman policy on July 14, 1914.

For the Unionist leaders this was a fateful, perhaps fatal step, for Serbia, Greece, Romania, and Bulgaria had been lost to the empire through just such a process. The Armenians, as the intended beneficiaries of these reforms, were thereafter viewed as a serious and *permanent threat to the empire's continued existence.*[68]

---

67. Helmut Philipp Aust, "From Diplomat to Academic Activist: André Mandelstam and the History of Human Rights," *European Journal of International Law*, 25 (2014), p. 1106.

68. Akçam, CAH, p. 131. The italics are mine. Akçam cites an official note of May 26, 1915, from the Ottoman Interior Ministry to the grand vizirate to back up this claim. See p. 133.

Thus was the fate of the autochthonous Christian peoples of Anatolia and Armenia sealed. Their crime was not just that they were Christian. Nor was it just that they—especially the Armenians—were in the midst of a national renaissance that had not just produced schools, newspapers, and literary masterpieces, but had catapulted them to the forefront of the Ottoman economy.[69] Nor was it just that the Christian peoples were not Turkish. It was that they were *indigenous* to the lands on which the Turks wanted to build their *vatan*. They had the prior claim to the lands. Armenian leaders could claim all they wanted, as solemnly as they wanted, that they would preserve "the sacred Ottoman fatherland from separation and division."[70] The CUP did not believe them. Armenians were "'microbes,' or 'tumors' endangering the health and survival of the Ottoman body."[71]

The foreign inspectors called for by the Yeniköy Accord had been chosen: Norwegian Major Nicolas Hoff for the Van-Bitlis-Harput and Diyarbekir regions, and Westenenk from the Dutch Eastern India colony for the Trabzon-Erzurum and Sivas regions. They arrived in Constantinople on May 14, 1914. Their work was obstructed from the start by the CUP.[72] The inspectors were immediately to carry out a census of the two Armenian Provinces in order to determine the "true ratio of the various religions, nations, and languages."[73] This was something that the statistics-conscious leaders of the CUP did not want.

The accord was suspended in August 1914 and abrogated when the Ottoman Empire entered World War I on November 11, 1914.[74]

---

69. On this subject see, e.g., Zürcher, YTL, pp. 110–12; Hanioğlu, LOE, p. 190.

70. CUP-Dashnak agreement of August 10, 1909; qtd. in Suny, p. 175.

71. Zürcher, HMT, p. 117.

72. See, e.g., Dadrian, pp, 212–14.

73. Dündar, CON, p. 53.

74. The official date of the abrogation was December 16, 1914. See Akçam, CAH, p. 132.

The sultan declared *jihad* on November 23, 1914.[75] Talaat Pasha later informed his German allies that he was

> intent on taking advantage of the war in order to thoroughly liquidate its [Turkey's] internal foes, i.e. the indigenous Christians, without being thereby subject to foreign intervention.[76]

Cleansing the Homeland

After the Balkan Wars, and to forestall the loss of Anatolia to its native Christian peoples, whose right to sovereignty had been recognized (but not sustained) by European powers—to "save Anatolia from the fate of Rumelia"—they began to "homogenize," to "Turkify," Anatolia.[77] For "Turkey to survive in possession of its

---

75. The *jihad fatwa* was written by a member of the CUP and close friend of Talaat, Mustafa Hayri Effendi. See Hans-Lukas Kieser, "The Ottoman Road to Total War (1913–15)," in Hans-Lukas Kieser, Kerem Öktem, and Maurus Reinkowski (eds.), *World War I and the End of the Ottomans: From the Balkan Wars to the Armenian Genocide* (London/New York: I.B. Taurus, 1915), p. 33. I shall henceforth refer to the volume as Kieser/Öktem/Reinknowski.

76. Wagenheim report of June 17, 1915; qtd. in Dadrian, p. 207.

77. See, on this, Michael A. Reynolds, *Shattering Empires: The Clash and the Collapse of the Ottoman and Russian Empires 1908–1918* (Cambridge/New York: Cambridge University Press, 2011), p 150: "The state-guided demographic transformation of Eastern Anatolia had begun under Abdulhammid II, who boosted the numbers of Muslims in the region by resettling Muslim refugees there. However, the losses of North Africa, Egypt, and then Muslim Albania and Macedonia, as well as the creeping emergence of the Kurdish question into the interstate sphere, all underscored the reality that the Ottoman state no longer had a privileged claim on territories populated predominantly by Muslims. Ethnicity was the critical criterion. Unionists such as Ziya Gökalp prior to the war had begun to think about the need to transform Anatolia into a more ethnically homogenous Turkish territory, but these ideas remained in the realm of conjecture. Istanbul's acceptance of the 1914 reform plan signaled that they would stay there. The war, however, presented an opportunity to remaster Anatolia's demographics and thereby block future partition."

territories," those territories would have to be "free of foreign peoples." Talaat Pasha made the point very clearly:

> These different blocs in the Turkish Empire…always conspired against Turkey; because of the *hostility of these native peoples*, Turkey has lost province after province—Greece, Serbia, Rumania, Bulgaria, Bosnia, Herzegovina, Egypt, and Tripoli. In this way, the Turkish Empire has dwindled almost to nothing.[78]

As Akçam claims, commenting on Talaat's statement: "As Turkish nationalism evolved, its primary goal—to rid the empire of its non-Muslim populations—became clear." After the Massacre of Adana, Dr. Nâzim stated that "The Ottoman Empire must be Turkish alone. The existence of foreign citizenship is a tool for European intervention. The empire must be Turkified by force of arms."[79] In a letter to Zionist leaders he had been even more explicit. The CUP, he claimed, wants

> no nationalities in Turkey. It does not want Turkey to become the new Austria-Hungary. It wants a unitary Turkish nation state, with Turkish schools, a Turkish administration, and a Turkish legal system.[80]

The empire had to "be rebuilt on Muslim and Pan-Turkist foundations…. Non-Muslim communities have to be Islamized by force or, failing that, eliminated."[81]

---

78. Talaat Pasha; qtd. in Akçam, ASA, p. 92. The italics are mine.
79. Akçam, ASA, p. 70. Foreign citizenship here refers even to those Armenians who were Ottoman citizens.
80. Dr. Nâzim; qtd. in Uğur Ümit Üngör, *The Making of Modern Turkey: Nation and State in Eastern Anatolia, 1913–1950* (Oxford/New York: Oxford University Press, 2012), p. 33.
81. Scheubner-Richter, quoting CUP officials. See Akçam, ASA, p. 156.

The CUP began its systematic cleansing of Anatolia in the West. "The 'cleansing' operation in the Aegean basin began in 1914."[82] It targeted the Greeks. More than one hundred thousand Greeks were deported from the coasts and moved to inland Anatolia. In 1915 the CUP began to deport Armenians and arrest their leaders, passed the "Tehcir" law, and unleashed genocide on the Armenians. It was especially important for the CUP (and their *vatan*) that Anatolia and Armenia be "free" of Armenians. For the Turks, "the Armenian movement was the deadliest of all threats":

From the conquered lands of the Serbs, Bulgars, Albanians, and Greeks, they could, however reluctantly, withdraw, abandoning distant provinces and bringing the Imperial frontier nearer home. But the Armenians, stretching across Turkey-in-Asia from the Caucasian frontier to the Mediterranean coast, lay in the very heart of the Turkish homeland—and to renounce these lands would have meant not the truncation, but the dissolution of the Turkish state.[83]

---

82. Akçam, ASA, p. 104.

83. Lewis, *The Emergence of Modern Turkey*, 3rd ed. (Oxford/New York: Oxford University Press, 2002), p. 356. This passage and the lines that immediately follow it are worth analyzing: "Turkish and Armenian villages, inextricably mixed, had for centuries lived in neighbourly association. Now a desperate struggle between them began—a struggle between two nations for the possession of a single homeland, that ended with the terrible slaughter of 1915, when, according to estimates, more than a million Armenians perished, as well as an unknown number of Turks." The purpose of the passage is evident: Lewis wants his reader to view the CUP's slaughter of Armenians not as genocide, but as an act of self-defense. It is also clear that Lewis does not articulate a clear and rational defense of this view. He guides his reader to this conclusion: *the Armenian matter was really just an awful and unavoidable affair for which no one was really responsible and we should leave it at that.*

It is instructive to track Lewis's steps. In the first part of the passage he makes four claims: (1) the Turks could withdraw from the lands belonging to the Serbs, etc., because they had other imperial holdings; (2) the Armenians were in lands that stretched from the Caucasus to the Mediterranean;

The Turks had no intention of "renouncing" Anatolia, giving up

(3) those lands were the "heart of the Turkish homeland"; and (4) Turkish renunciation of those lands would have been "not the truncation but the dissolution of the Turkish state." The argument embedded in these claims seems trite: an empire—i.e., the Ottoman Empire—can lose some of its conquered domains—i.e., the Balkans—and continue to exist; it cannot lose all of its domains—i.e., Armenia—and continue to exist.

The argument thus read would be sound if Armenia had been the only imperial holding in the Ottomans' possession after the Balkan Wars. In 1453 *the Byzantine Empire could not continue to exist if it lost Constantinople*. But, of course, it is not true that in 1913 Armenia was the Ottomans' only imperial holding. The Ottoman Empire stretched over Anatolia and much of the Middle East at that time. Thus, Lewis's argument begs the question: How could the loss of Armenia have entailed "the dissolution of the Turkish state"? Surely it did not involve the loss of Syria, Palestine, Anatolia, etc. Why, then, would the loss of Armenia for the Ottomans not have been an ulterior "truncation" of their empire?

Part of what makes this section of the passage perplexing is Lewis's sleight of hand on the proprietorship of lands in (2) and (3). Rather than claiming, as he did in (1), for the lands of the Serbs, etc., that (2) the lands on which the Armenians lived were "the conquered lands of the Armenians," Lewis avoids attributing ownership of these lands to the Armenians by substituting the noun "land" with the name "Turkey-in-Asia." The extraordinarily odd sentence with which he articulates (2) and (3) states that *the Armenians stretched* "across *Turkey-in-Asia* from the Caucasian frontier to the Mediterranean"—conjuring images of Procrustes in any reader with a decent imagination—and "*lay* in the very heart of the Turkish homeland"—conjuring less appropriate images. Replacing the noun "land" with the name "Turkey-in-Asia" allows Lewis to imply that the lands across which the Armenians "stretched" self-evidently belonged to the Turks. At that point, it was a small step for him to add explicitly that those lands were "the very heart of the Turkish homeland," and implicitly to claim that (5) the Turks had the right to sovereignty in those lands because every people has the right to self-rule in its homeland.

What justifies Lewis's stealthy attribution of the proprietorship of Armenia to the Turks and his claim that Armenia was the *heart of the Turkish homeland*? Surely Lewis did not mean to claim that the Armenian *vilayets* were either the capital, or the seat, of Ottoman power. That capital and seat was Constantinople, and Constantinople is not, and never was, in Armenia. Nor could Lewis have meant to make the absurd claim that Armenia was the birthplace of the Ottoman Turks. What, then, did he mean by stating that Armenia lay at "the heart of the Turkish homeland"? Why were

"Turkey-in-Asia," or renouncing claims on Armenia. "No force

---

the Balkans not that heart? Lewis cannot not have known that many of the members of the CUP's Central Committee—including Talaat Pasha—were born in the Balkans.

Obversely, on what grounds did (or could) Lewis justify his surreptitious denial of the Armenians' claim to their native lands? Why did he in (1) claim that the lands on which the Serbs lived were the "conquered lands of the Serbs" and not make the parallel move in (2) for the "lands on which the Armenians lived"? Why does he call the former and not the latter *the conquered lands of* this or that conquered people?

Lewis's implicit claims that Armenia was both *Turkey-in-Asia* and the *heart of the Turkish homeland* clarify the argument embedded in his first four claims. That argument is not that *the Ottoman Empire could continue to exist after it lost the Balkans, since it had other conquered territories; it could not continue to exist if it lost Armenia.* It is that *the Ottoman Empire could continue to exist after it lost the Balkans, since the Balkans were only conquered territories and not the heart of the Turkish homeland; it could not continue to exist if it lost Armenia, since Armenia was not really Armenia but Turkey-in-Asia and the heart of the Turkish homeland.* This argument is demonstrably false and misleading.

It also provides important premises for the four claims Lewis makes in the next lines: (6) "Turkish and Armenian villages, inextricably mixed, had for centuries lived in neighbourly association"; (7) "Now a desperate struggle between them began"; (8) "a struggle between two nations for the possession of a single homeland"; (9) "it ended with the terrible slaughter of 1915, when, according to estimates, more than a million Armenians perished, as well as an unknown number of Turks."

These claims are oddly articulated and combined. (6) is unintelligible. How can villages be both "Turkish" or "Armenian" and "inextricably mixed"? (8) introduces a version of the claim that Armenia was the homeland of the Armenians and allows Lewis to equate (7), the "struggle between Armenian and Turkish villages," with a "struggle between two nations." (9) would both make "the struggle" in (7) the cause of the "terrible slaughter" of "more than a million Armenians" and attempt to balance the "terrible slaughter" with the claim that some Turks also died. Taking into account the slippery language of these lines, their point seems to be: *both Turks and Armenians lived in "Turkey-in-Asia"; both could claim that the lands were their "homeland"; a war over ownership of these lands erupted in the villages; that war was spontaneous and local; in it more than a million Armenians were slaughtered; some Turks also died.*

Combining this point with the previous argument we get: *the Ottoman Empire could continue to exist after it lost the Balkans, which were only conquered territories; it could not continue to exist if it lost Armenia, which*

could have dragged me away from Constantinople," Edib claims, "so passionately did I love it."[84]

Talaat had drawn up a map of the cleansed *vatan* in his *Black Book* in order "to draw the ethnographic borders" of that *vatan*.[85]

---

was the "Turkish homeland"; both Turks and Armenians lived in the "Turkish homeland"; both could claim it was their "homeland"; a war over proprietorship erupted in the villages; that war was spontaneous and local; in it more than a million Armenians were slaughtered; some Turks also died.

This argument is a morass of mutually defeating claims. If, for example, the Armenian claim to the land was at least equal to that of the Turks, as (8) states, then what (2) and (3) suggest—that those lands were not Armenia—is false. Without (2) and (3), one cannot call on (5) or defend (4). As for the attempt to lay the blame of (9) on the villages, it is not worth addressing.

84. Edib, HW, p. 336.

85. Dündar, CON, p. 76. Dündar adds that "apart from Hatay," the map "corresponds to the present day borders of Turkey." See also Appendix 16 in his book. Dündar argues in CON that the crux of the CUP's solution to the Armenian Question concerned statistics and population census. See, e.g., p. 55: "statistics compiled in the preceding decades would prove to be the reason—as well as the vehicle—for Young Turks' policy on how to resolve the Armenian Questions"; p. 45: "The ethnic maps and statistics prepared according to this order [by Talaat on July 20, 1915] were to serve a very important function in both the reengineering of the Anatolian population and deciding how to distribute the non-Turkish and non-Muslim population amongst Turks and Muslims according to ratios of ten, five, and two percent." The percentage game is also used to explain the slaughter at Deir-es-Zor in 1916. See also, on this point, Akçam, ASA, pp. 178ff. Dündar claims that the cause of this statistically driven social engineering program is the "positivist ideology of the Unionists" and the CUP's odd belief that theoretical sociological studies were concrete medical prescriptions with which to cure the ills of a people. There is no doubt in my mind that Dündar is right and that statistics were a part of both the "reason" and "vehicle" of the CUP's genocidal policies. They are not, I would submit, the only or even the primary cause of the problem that the *indigenous* Christian populations posed for the CUP. They do not explain *why* the Armenians—and the other Christian peoples who were native to the lands on which the Republic of Turkey was built—were a problem for the CUP: i.e., why the CUP viewed the Armenians and other native Christians as a threat. For instance, that 55% of the population living in territory T is Christian, 45% Muslim, and 5% Zoroastrian only becomes problematic under specific conditions. Dündar calls upon control to respond to the deeper

When on May 29, 1915, in a joint declaration, the Allied Powers (France, Britain, and Russia) stated their intent to hold the leaders of the CUP criminally responsible for the extermination of the Armenians—their "crimes against humanity and civilization" [86]—the Sublime Porte responded that:

> Far from having condoned or organized mass murders... it had merely exercised *its sovereign right of self-defense against a revolutionary movement.*[87]

That "self-defense" in the minds of the leaders of the CUP substantially meant eliminating any and all peoples—and the Armenian *millet* most especially—who could lay claim to the lands on which they wanted to build their *vatan*.[88] Talaat made this clear in a circular he sent to all of the Ottoman provinces on August 29, 1915:

---

question of *why* the native Christians were a threat: statistics became important because they determined the representation of the Ottoman peoples in Parliament. This leads to the deeper question of why the Christians (and the Armenians specifically) threatened Turkish control. Why were the Christians an *existential threat* for the Turks? This is the question Melson asks when he discusses the Hamidian Massacres. I expand that question and respond to it not just by looking at the CUP's massive social engineering project—and genocidal policies—but by looking at its toponymical policies, its destruction of Armenian churches, schools, cemeteries, etc. My point in this book is that, in looking at the entire array of actions of the CUP, one sees that the response to Melson's question—"Why were Armenians a threat?"— must invoke what I have been calling the Greek Principle.

86. R.G. 59, 867.4016/67.

87. Ulrich Trumpener, *Germany and the Ottoman Empire, 1914–1918* (Princeton, NJ: Princeton University Press, 1968), p. 210. The italics are mine.

88. Taner Akçam makes a similar point in response to the official Turkish claim that the cause of the deaths of the Armenians were the Van uprisings. Akçam, ASA, pp. 203–4: "The problem for the Unionists was not the Armenian gangs or an Armenian rebellion, but the fact that Armenians lived in the eastern provinces at all. As we have seen, the Treaty of Yeniköy with Russia on 8 February 1914 was considered the beginning of the loss of Anatolia for the Ottomans. Numerous statements by foreign diplomats

The objective that the government expects to achieve by the expelling of the Armenians from the areas in which they live and their transportation to other appointed areas is to ensure that *this community will no longer be able to undertake initiatives and actions against the government, and that they will be brought to a state in which they will be unable to pursue their national aspirations related to advocating a[n independent] government of Armenia.*[89]

By the end of 1916, Suny claims, "The radical ethnic homogenization of the Ottoman East was approaching completion":

The principal threat to the Turkish Nation and the Ottoman state, the Armenians, had effectively been eliminated.[90]

The Destruction of the Armenians

The eradication and slaughter of the Armenians was a well-coordinated operation. The leaders of the CUP took their first concrete steps toward definitively "solving" the Armenian Question on the very day they signed the secret pact with the Germans and promised to fight alongside the Central Powers in the event that Russia entered the War. It was August 2, 1914. They set up the *Teşkilât-ı Mahsusa* (Special Organization forces).[91] The *çete*, as the forces were more commonly known, were bands of terrorists, or assassination

---

deemed the reform plan a step towards partition.... Official Ottoman correspondence clearly shows that the authorities also understood this, and that the purpose of the deportations was to prevent the emergence of an Armenian state."

89. Akçam, CAH, pp. 134–35. The italics are mine.

90. Suny, p. 327.

91. It is not exactly clear how and when the *Teşkilât-ı Mahsusa* was founded. What we know is that some version of the corps was at work during the Balkan Wars and that testimony at the postwar court-martials claimed that

units, composed of Kurds, jailed convicts, immigrants from the Caucasus, and refugees from the Balkans. Their official purpose was to promote "Islamic unity and Turkish nationalism."[92] Their methods were direct. They plundered, terrorized, and slaughtered people. They were deployed in September 1914 and operated primarily in the Eastern Provinces, where they looted, raped, tortured, and massacred Armenians and destroyed their villages. They were also deployed across the Caucasus border and in Anatolia to help the army in its push through Eastern Armenia toward *Turan*.

On September 6, 1914, the Ottoman Public Security Directorate placed Armenian political leaders—and the population more generally—under surveillance.[93] The immediate purpose of the move, as Talaat explained on October 10, 1914, was to intimidate Armenians:

> It is necessary to be content with this for the moment and to abstain from too much pressure or prerequisitions, but at the same time a state of alarm should be kept, so as not to permit provocations and propaganda concerning Armenians.[94]

Armenian political leaders in the provinces were hassled. Foreign (primarily American and French) schools for Armenians were ordered closed. Wartime taxes were raised.

In late September 1914, Armenian soldiers, who had been conscripted into the Ottoman army, began to be disarmed and used in labor battalions, leaving Armenian villages "defenseless before

---

the corps was founded right after the CUP signed the secret pact with the Germans. See Kévorkian, p. 150.

92. Akçam, ASA, p. 131. The full purpose included Turanic aspirations and was to promote "Islamic unity and Turkish nationalism, which related to uniting Turks outside of Turkey." Akçam estimates that there were about 30,000 men in the Special Operations units.

93. See Kévorkian, pp. 152ff.

94. Talaat; qtd. in Dündar, CON, p. 69.

the excesses and attacks of military deserters" and the *Teşkilât-ı Mahsusa*.[95] In October 1914, Armenian goods—including food and livestock—were "requisitioned for the Army." In November, all communication equipment—especially radio transmitters and telegraphic equipment—in Armenian "institutions and houses were confiscated."[96] In December, Talaat ordered that the employment of "all Armenian government officials in the provinces" be terminated.[97] In February 1915, Enver Pasha ordered that all Armenian soldiers be disarmed and placed in labor battalions. Beginning in March 1915, they were murdered. The weapon of choice was the knife. The CUP did not want to waste bullets.

By then the deportation of Armenians had already begun. On February 13, 1915, Cemal Pasha ordered that Armenians be deported from Cilicia. The first town was targeted on March 2. It was Chorq Marzban (Dörtyol), the town that had defended itself during the Adana Massacres of 1909. Shortly thereafter, deportations were ordered in Zeitun.

In April 1915, while it was settling Muslim refugees from the Balkans in the homes of the Armenians of Zeitun, the CUP began

---

95. Wagenheim, relaying complaints from Armenian Patriarchate; qtd. in Akçam, ASA, p. 142. Armenian soldiers were used as pack animals. On this point see Morgenthau, who complains in *Ambassador Morgenthau's Story* (Detroit, MI: Wayne State University Press, 2003) that "instead of serving their country as artillerymen and cavalrymen ... [Armenians] had been transformed into road laborers and pack animals. Army supplies of all kinds were loaded on their backs, and, stumbling under the burden and driven by the whips and bayonets of the Turks, they were forced to drag their weary bodies into the mountains of the Caucasus" (pp. 207–8).

96. Dündar, p. 70.

97. Akçam, CAH, p. 155. The cable specified: "In the event that difficulties arise in the performing of such actions [i.e., the firing of Armenians who held public office in the provinces] the provinc[ial officials] should send [these people] to the far-off areas of the province, force them to resign, and revoke their [official] documents. If this proves unworkable or inconvenient, [local authorities] should send a list of these persons' names so that they can be sent off by [the officials] here to other provinces."

to target the leaders of the Armenian communities: priests, politicians, intellectuals, journalists, and artists. They were first arrested in the provinces and then in Constantinople, where 2,345 of them were rounded up in three days and sent to detention centers in inner Anatolia.[98] The latter arrests took place at night. Those who were arrested were for the most part killed.

At the end of May 1915, the CUP—months after it had unleashed the *Teşkilât-ı Mahsusa*, disarmed Armenian soldiers, worked them to death in labor battalions, "requisitioned" food for the war effort, sent groups to confiscate weapons that it was perfectly legal for the Armenians to possess,[99] seized Armenian communication equipment, publicly executed Armenians, armed the Muslims in the Eastern Provinces, rounded up those who could successfully have organized the anxious Armenian villagers[100]—decided that the Armenians had been weakened enough. It was time for the kill.[101] The

---

98. Andonian gives an idea of the breadth and depth of these arrests in his memoirs. See, e.g., Andonian, pp. 12–15, where he simply lists the names of those fellow prisoners whom he recognized the morning after his arrest.

99. The Constitution gave the Armenians this right. It was restored in 1908.

100. The roundup of leaders was crucial for Talaat. In his memoirs, he wrote: "The beginning of the transfer of Armenians in various places of Anatolia created considerable panic among the Armenians of Istanbul and in particular among committees. The center of management of Armenian committees, or in other words the brain of the foreign organization, was located in Istanbul. This city was at the same time also the command center of all military operations," Talaat; qtd. in Dündar, CON, pp. 74–75.

101. Alma Johansson's testimony relays that in November 1914 they had known that the CUP was planning to "exterminate the Armenian race." She claims: "Already by November we had known that there would be a massacre. The Mutessarif of Moush, who was a very intimate friend of Enver Pasha, declared quite openly that they would massacre the Armenians at the first opportune moment and exterminate the whole race. Before the Russians arrived they intended first to butcher the Armenians, and then fight the Russians afterwards. Towards the beginning of April, in the presence of a Major Lange and several other high officials, including the American and German Consuls, Ekran Bey quite openly declared the Government's intention of exterminating the Armenian race. All these details plainly

command of the Fourth Army was informed whence and whither the Armenians were to be deported.

On May 26, Talaat's office notified the grand vizier that it would commence the deportation of Armenians so that the Armenian Question could be "brought to an end in a comprehensive and absolute way."[102] The next day the Parliament passed the Temporary Law of Deportation—the Tehcir Law. On May 30, the "Directorate of Tribal and Immigrant Settlement" of the Interior Ministry sent around the fifteen articles that regulated the redistribution of Armenian properties to the Muslim refugees from the Balkans.[103] On June 10, 1915, the ministry published a manual with instructions to guide "the registration, administration and transfer to the new Muslim settlers."[104]

Armenian families were evicted from their homes. They were informed that they were being relocated for military reasons and for their own protection. They were told to keep the keys of their homes, since their property would not be touched. For many, the order to leave under the protection of the government must have come as a relief. Armenians in the Eastern Provinces had lived through months and months—if not years and years—of attacks, murders, thefts, kidnappings, and wanton destruction.

---

show that the massacre was deliberately planned." Viscount Bryce, *The Treatment of Armenians in the Ottoman Empire 1915–16*, document 23. The Armenian Patriarch feared the same thing. Realizing just how bad the situation had become for the Armenians in the Eastern Provinces the year before the time Johansson described, he wrote the Grand Vizier (and circulated the letter to the ambassadors of France, Britain, and Russia). He claimed that the "situation suggests that the Armenians no longer have the right to live in the Ottoman Empire. This state of affairs can only lead to the annihilation of the Armenian element." Armenian Patriarch; qtd. in Suny, p. 195. For a more complete summary of the pressure under which the Armenians were put right before the genocide, see Suny, pp. 189–97.

102. Akçam, ASA, p. 155.

103. The Directorate of Tribal and Immigrant Settlement (*Dahiliye Nezareti İskan-i Aşar ve Muhacir'in Müdüriyeti*) or IAMM was set up in 1913 after the Balkan Wars.

104. Akçam, ASA, p. 188.

Armenian men were separated from women, children, and the elderly. They were immediately dispatched. The women were mostly sent off on foot, and with their children, parents, and grandparents. They marched for months at gunpoint toward lands that the Talaat Pasha had previously claimed were unfit for the Muslim refugees from the Balkans, since "all of them would have died of hunger over there."[105] They went to Deir-es-Zor.

Many Armenians were kidnapped along the way, especially if they were young, female, and pretty. Many died of starvation, fatigue, and disease. All were easy prey for the Kurds, the *Teşkilât-ı Mahsusa*, and whoever else was called upon to murder them—or was given free hand to torture them. Some were drowned in the Black Sea. Some were injected with diseased blood. So many were thrown in the Euphrates that the river ran red. There are many ways to kill people. The indescribable tortures that Armenians suffered before they died are best left untold.

> Savagery had become commonplace; indifference to mutilation had become normal; and viciousness spread like spilled blood, covering a wider and wider landscape.[106]

Armenian wealth came in handy. Armenian homes, estates, lands, farms, orchards, industries, businesses, shops, workshops, merchandise, goods, and even livestock were quickly sold and distributed.[107] There were many Muslims—refugees from the Balkans

---

105. Talaat Pasha; qtd. in Dündar, CON, p. 79. See also, on this, Fuad Dündar, "Pouring a People into the Desert. The 'Definitive Solution' of the Unionists to the Armenian Question," in AQG, pp. 276–86.

106. Suny, p. 288.

107. See, e.g., Akçam and Kurt, p. 21: "Two procedures would be applied to goods left behind. First, 'immigrants and tribes' would be settled in the Armenian villages being emptied and, after the value of the land and property there was determined, it would be distributed to the new settlers. In cities and towns, 'immovable property belonging to people who are being transported ... after its type, value, and quantity are determined,' will also

and others—who needed homes and who would Turkify and Islamicize the land simply by living in the confiscated homes.[108] There was a Turkish middle class to construct: Armenian industries, workshops, orchards, and farms were a good place to start. Some Armenian properties were taken over by the Ottoman army. They were useful to the central government, too. Armenian wealth even funded the CUP eradication of the Armenians from their homeland, their slaughter: the genocide.[109]

There had been some minor glitches in the CUP's "solution" to the Armenian Question. Some Armenian communities put up resistance, even after the operation was in full swing. Sometimes the new "owners" of Armenian homes arrived before the rightful owners had been deported.[110] Of course, the Allied Powers blustered about human rights and crimes. But the operation had been successful. The foundation of the *vatan* had been laid.

Those few Armenians who had not died—or been kidnapped—on the horrendous way to Deir-es-Zor were settled in the inhospitable land. By order of Talaat, their villages were to be five or six

---

be distributed to the settlers. Second, 'properties which produce income such as olive, mulberry, grape, and orange orchards, and stores, factories, inns and warehouses, which remain outside of the scope of the work that they know and do…through being sold in public auction or being rented, their equivalent value will be placed temporarily in accounts of local treasury directorates [mal sandiklari] in the names of their owners so that it will be given to the latter.'"

108. The grand vizier openly told the Allies that the decision to deport the Armenians was also made with the refugees in mind: "we have to think of the need to settle the Muslims who have migrated to Anatolia from the provinces that have been lost during the last few years (Macedonia, Western Thrace, and Tripolitana)," grand vizier; qtd. in Dündar, CON, p. 74.

109. See Üngör and Polatel, p. 103: "The assets of these and other Armenians were reused for various purposes: settling refugees and settlers, constructing state buildings, supplying the army and indeed, the deportation program itself. This leads us to the grim conclusion that the Ottoman Armenians have financed their own destruction." See also Akçam, ASA, pp. 189–93.

110. See Akçam, ASA, p. 182.

hours apart from each other. They were expressly forbidden to have Armenian schools.[111]

When Salih Zeki, who had been nominated governor of Deir-es-Zor, saw that Armenians had there "created a veritable Armenia, and the market was largely in their hands,"[112] he liquidated them. Even exiled Armenians were a threat, as Enver told Ambassador Morgenthau:

> If two hundred Turks could overturn the Government, then a few hundred bright, educated Armenians could do the same thing.[113]

Culture and identity, again

Addressing the Greek Principle involved more than massacring and expelling the entirety of the ancient autochthonous peoples of Anatolia and the Eastern Provinces—Armenians chief among them. The very land on which these peoples had for millennia lived also needed to be Turkified. No trace of the presence of these peoples could be left on them. By the Greek Principle, those traces challenged Turkish possession of Anatolia. They demonstrated that the Turks had "come from distant regions to invade our borders." No "invader" could lay permanent claim to invaded lands.

The CUP thus began to impose "a new Turkish mythology which would bridge the abyss between the Ottoman Turks and their Turanian ancestors" on the lands themselves.

It was during the summer of 1913 that the CUP gradually but resolutely launched extensive campaigns of Turkification on practically all domains of Ottoman society. They

---

111. Suny, p. 285.

112. Suny, p. 315.

113. Enver; qtd. in Suny, p. 304.

began with place names, Turkifying them and wiping out all traces of non-Turkish cultures: for instance the Kizilkilize ("Red Church") county in the Dersim district was changed into Nazimiye (after the Ottoman Politician Nâzim Paşa). Although the practise was suspended until the end of the war, this CUP practice continued well into the 1960s and ended up in the alteration of tens of thousands of names.[114]

This would allow them to invoke the Greek Principle for their own *vatan*.

This left the other pesky problem that lay at the heart of Edib's— and Gökalp's—worries for the Turks: culture. It is one thing to deport and slaughter ancient autochthonous peoples, to confiscate their properties and businesses, to change toponyms and zoonyms. It is one thing violently to clear lands for oneself. It is quite another to make what one has taken one's *homeland*. Confiscated properties do not become a *home* because their owners have been killed, their deeds taken over, and their names changed. The new owners of confiscated properties do not become a community because they have been given shiny new buildings and lands. The new owners of confiscated businesses do not suddenly become businessmen because they have acquired buildings and machinery. Warehouses do not make merchants. Workshops do not produce shoes when the cobblers have been slaughtered. Lands and orchards do not flourish in incompetent hands. School buildings do not magically continue to function as schools after the teachers and students have been massacred. Mustafa Abdülhalik Renda, governor of Aleppo, could gleefully write to the Ministry of Trade in 1917, stating that "two years ago eighty percent of the merchants and business owners were Christian; today ninety-five percent are Muslim and five percent Christian."[115] He did not

---

114. Uğur Ümit Üngör, "Turkey for the Turks": Demographic Engineering in Eastern Anatolia," p. 296.

115. Akçam, ASA, p. 273. CUP began to put pressure on the strong Armenian industrial and merchant classes from the start of their tenure. See, e.g., Suny,

thereby create a successful bourgeoisie. Nor did he create a *Turkish* bourgeoisie. A new nation is not made because a violent government has decided to build and impose a new identity on people and lands.

Creating a *vatan* requires a culture, an identity. Culture—and identity—are not easy things to come by. Culture is not a fabric softener that is to be added to the final stages of one's land laundry to make the land (and the people one has left in it) malleable. It is not a dye that will instantly transform land and people. The Armenians flowered in the nineteenth century because in the eighteenth century Abbot Mkhitar retrieved and reprinted Armenian manuscripts (and with them trained scholars and teachers). Mkhitar could retrieve and retransmit Armenian culture because it already existed: it was there for him to retrieve. The "Mkhitarists did not create or invent the Armenian nation, but retrieved it—and in the process helped to reshape it for the modern period."[116] He could make that culture re-flower because the army of scholars and teachers, whom he patiently educated, saw in the manuscripts and faith a truth essential to themselves—each of them individually and all of them collectively.

What culture did those in the CUP have? What manuscripts did they have upon which to base that culture? With which to unify people? Upon what could they base their national identity? This problem was made clear to Talaat Pasha by Karekin Pastermadjian, a deputy of the Ottoman Parliament and member of the

---

p. 180: "Pamphlets in Turkish extolling the idea of the 'National Economy' increasingly referred not to a cosmopolitan Ottoman economy but as one that was Islamicized or Turkified. The tone of the pamphlets was ferocious. Non-Muslims were 'sucking the blood of Muslims,' and as cited in a report by the acting British consul-general in Smyrna, the unsuspecting soporific Muslims were the victims of voracious Christians. 'The Christians, profiting from our ignorance, have for ages been taking our place and taking away our rights. These vipers whom we are nourishing have been sucking out all the life-blood of the nation. They are parasitical worms eating into our flesh whom we must destroy and do away with. It is time we freed ourselves from these individuals, by all means lawful and unlawful.'"

116. Panossian, p. 107.

Armenian Revolutionary Federation whose *nom de guerre* was Armen Garo. Just before the beginning of World War I, the Armenian told the Triumvir:

> Some time ago you told Vramian you would Turkify the Kurds. With what? With which culture? You would not mention these senseless things if you had knowledge about your history. You are forgetting that you have only been on our lands for 500 to 600 years, and that before other nations have passed through these lands: Persians, Romans, Arabs, Byzantines. If they have not been able to assimilate the Kurds, how will you accomplish this? Last summer I went to our three provinces and only saw three bridges in that region: two of them were old Armenian constructions, the third one dates from Tamerlane. I have not even seen any traces of your civilization.[117]

Two years later, Martin Niepage added the following after witnessing column after column of filthy, malnourished, tortured, exiled Armenians approach Aleppo:

> [W]here is there any Turkish trade, Turkish handicraft, Turkish manufacture, Turkish art, Turkish science? Even their law, religion and language...have been borrowed from the conquered Arabs.[118]

---

117. Pastermadjian; qtd. in Üngör, *The Making of Modern Turkey*, p. 41. The Armenian newspaper *Droshak* claimed much the same thing. See editorial of *Droshak*; qtd. in Suny, p. 159: "They [the CUP] think it has suddenly become possible ... for the Ottoman Empire to assimilate, at least, the other ethnic groups, although these groups have centuries-old cultural heritage and are, collectively, at an incomparably higher intellectual level; they think the Empire will at last dissolve them in the predominant Turkish."

118. Martin Niepage; qtd. in Üngör, *The Making of Modern Turkey*, p. 41. Martin Niepage was a high school teacher in the German Technical School in Aleppo in 1915 who wrote an eyewitness account of the brutality of the

The ideologues of the CUP were convinced that they could build this culture and impose it upon the people. The "remedy could hardly be considered outside the context of ... coercion ranging from expulsion to mass murder."[119] But the remedy was possible. It consisted of "redemptive hatred" of the Armenians: "The salvation of the Turkish nation would follow" from the "redemptive final reckoning with Armenians."[120] The abolition of the capitulations, and the elimination of the Greeks and Armenians—who "like the Jews" were "the middlemen and agents of Western capitalism"[121]— would show the world "a nation sprung that is fully conscious of its right and interest, holding its honor and pride."[122] That nation, Gökalp promised in his poem *Vatan* (Homeland), would be:

> *A country where all capital circulating in its markets,*
> *The technology and science guiding its craft, is the Turk's*
> *Its professions always protect each other;*
> *Its shipyards, factories, boats, trains, is the Turk's*
> *O Turk, that is where your homeland [vatan] is.*[123]

Armenian deportations and of the horrendous conditions in Aleppo itself. The report was printed in London in 1917 with the title *The Horrors of Aleppo* (London: T. Fischer Unwin Ltd., 1917) and reprinted on the 60th anniversary of the Armenian Genocide by Plandome (N.Y.: New Age Publishers, 1975).

119. Uğur Ümit Üngör and Mehmet Polatel, p. 39.

120. Üngör and Polatel, p. 39.

121. Yusuf Akçura; qtd. in Üngör and Polatel, p. 32.

122. Munis Tekinalp; qtd. in Üngör and Polatel, p. 34.

123. Gökalp; qtd. in Üngör and Polatel, p. 31.

Chapter 6

WESTERN INCOHERENCE AND THE VATAN: FROM SÈVRES TO LAUSANNE

They had lost the war. And although they had made a lot of progress on the physical foundations of their new *vatan*, it looked like all of their efforts had been for naught. The Turkification project in Anatolia and Armenia had sped along busily for four years, mowing down the Christian peoples autochthonous to those lands.[1]

---

1. The amount of killing the CUP undertook in its Turkification project is simply staggering. It is usually claimed that there were somewhere between 18 and 21 million people living in Anatolia and the Eastern Provinces shortly before World War I, and that these included some 2.5 million Greeks, 2 million Armenians, and 1 million Chaldeans and Assyrians. Thus, the pre-war population of Anatolia and the Eastern Provinces was at least 25% Christian in 1914. The picture changes radically after the Treaty of Lausanne. According to the 1927 census, the population of the Republic of Turkey (i.e., Anatolia and the Eastern Provinces) was approximately 13.65 million people, of whom 2.7% (i.e., approximately 368,500) were not Muslim. Assuming that the birthrates of the Christians and Muslims were comparable at that time, the census reveals that at least 93% of the Christian population of Anatolia and the Eastern Provinces—that is, more than 5 million Christians, or 22% of the total population of those lands—simply "vanished" at some point between 1914 and 1927. We know that roughly 1.3 million Greek Christians—or about 26% of the total Christian population—were sent to Greece in 1923 during the Turkish-Greek population exchange. No such exchange took place for the Armenians, Chaldeans, or Assyrians. This means that about 3.7 million Christians, or 74% of the Christian population of Anatolia and the Eastern Provinces, were disposed

161

The coasts on the Black Sea had been cleared of the Pontic Greeks. Aegean Greeks had been deported from the coasts and sent into central Anatolia, put to work in labor battalions, or simply killed.[2] Chaldeans and Assyrians had been butchered in Tur Abdin (in the *vilayets* of Van, Bitlis, and Diarbekir) and Urmia.[3] The survivors had taken flight. Armenia had been almost completely emptied of Armenians. Muslims—the *muhacirs*, above all—had been settled in their homes.[4] There were pockets of territory that had not been

---

of—killed, deported, or both—in those years. This figure becomes even more horrendous if one bears in mind that Anatolia and the Eastern Provinces were not homogenously populated.

2. See, e.g., Emre Erol, "'Macedonian Question' in Western Anatolia: The Ousting of the Ottoman Greeks Before World War I," in Kieser/Öktem/Reinknowski, pp. 104–5: "In the year immediately after the end of the Balkan wars (1912–13), in 1914 before World War I, some 160,000 Ottoman Greeks, or Romioi (Ρωμιοί, pl.) were ousted or fled by what seems to have been a combination of intercommunal and interethnic tensions of the post-Balkan war climate and the systematic ousting operations of the Unionists. Almost the entire western Anatolian seaboard was ousted of its native Ottoman Greek population, with the exception of the internationally known port city of the eastern Mediterranean, Izmir (Smyrna), and some renowned towns such as Ayvalik, Foçateyn, Çeşme, Edremit, Burkaniye, Kemer, Kinik, Balikesir, Bergama, Karaburun, Menemen, Ödemiş, Uluabad, Eskice, as well as towns and villages on or near the Kasaba-Aydin railway, around Bursa, and around Ayvalik (but not the towns themselves), were all subjected to the violence by Muslim bandits (chetes) who ousted native Christian populations.... The houses and property of the Ottoman Greeks were soon filled by *muhacirs*: the Muslim refugees from the lost Ottoman territories in the Balkans. Western Anatolia, with a reinforced Muslim majority, was now 'safe' from the dangers of Greek irredentism from the CUP leaders' nationalist point of view."

3. On the Assyrian Genocide see David Gaunt, *Massacres, Resistance, Protectors: Muslim-Christian Relations in Eastern Anatolia During World War I* (Piscataway, NJ: Gorgias Press, 2006).

4. The central government in Constantinople kept a careful tally of the deportees, their provenance and holdings. It sent cables requesting detailed information: "the names of the Armenian villages that had been emptied out, their geographic location, the nature and condition of their lands, and their potential for cultivation; the number of persons from the populations

prepared—Smyrna, most notably. But they were few and easily dealt with.

The problem for the CUP had been the Central Powers, or, to be precise, Kaiser Wilhelm II, his generals—such as Liman von Sanders, Colmar Freiherr von der Goltz, and Erich von Falkenhayn—and soldiers. They, Enver first among them, had counted upon the Germans to shore up their military weakness—protect them from their external enemies while they dealt with the internal ones, who were none other than the indigenous peoples who stood in the way of their homogenous *vatan*[5]—and perhaps even help them conquer the corridor that separated their cleansed lands from their Turkish cousins and *Turan*.[6] The Germans had failed. Kaiser Wilhelm II abdicated after the defeat.

---

who have been deported and the quantities and character of the abandoned properties and lands, and the best estimates and opinions about where it would be most beneficial to settle [Muslim] immigrants, as well as what type [of the latter] and from where." In one of the cables it specified that "the central government sees it as extremely necessary that the desired economic, [and] environmental information regarding the Armenian villages be taken into consideration in the [execution of the] general deportations and resettlement, comprehensive information [in this regard] is to be assembled by the state bureaucrats." See Akçam, CAH, p. 231.

5. Talaat Pasha was reported to have made the point explicitly to Dr. Mordtmann, dragoman of the German embassy, when he claimed that: "Turkey is taking advantage of the war in order to thoroughly liquidate its internal foes, i.e., the indigenous Christians, without being thereby disturbed by foreign intervention." See Dadrian, p. 207.

6. As the Balkan League's quick and sound defeat of the Ottoman Empire in 1912 demonstrates, the empire was in no position to defend itself—let alone wage a serious war—in 1914. It was bankrupt and militarily weak. It did not have the industries it needed to arm itself. It did not even have the infrastructure with which to transport troops, munitions, and provisions. This made the German alliance crucial to the CUP, and not primarily because there were those in the party who wanted to conquer *Turan*. The CUP needed the Germans in order to keep the Ottoman Empire from crumbling altogether. The leaders of the CUP admitted this quite frankly. The fourth article of the secret German-Ottoman allegiance was that Germany would protect Ottoman territory. See Zürcher, HMT, p. 111.

What must have made German failure doubly painful for the
leaders of the CUP—Enver especially—was that it came shortly after they had managed to conquer the passageway to their *Turanian
cousins* in Baku, who happened also to have rich oil wells. On December 18, 1917, the Russians had unexpectedly signed an armistice
at Erzincan and officially withdrawn from the war. Even more pro-
pitiously for those ideologues and party leaders who had dreamt of
building a new Turanian Empire, with the Treaty of Brest-Litovsk
signed on March 3, 1918, the Russians gave the *Elviye-i Selâse* (the
three provinces that the Sultan Abdul Hamit II had ceded to the
tsar in the Treaty of Berlin) to the Ottomans: the two Armenian
Provinces of Kars and Ardahan, along with Batum. At that point, all
it took for the CUP to expand its *vatan* so that it encompassed the
lands in which the Azeri Turks lived was to send an army to push
its way through the strip of land that separated Kars from Baku.[7]

---

7. The specific object of the CUP's late push for Baku is somewhat disputed.
    Dadrian argues that it was explicitly genocidal. He cites members of the
    high German military command, a member of Enver's uncle Halil Pa-
    sha's staff, the Austrian ambassador to Germany, and the Austrian mil-
    itary plenitotentiary in Turkey as evidence that that object was "*völlige
    Ausrottung der Armenier auch in Transkaukasien*"; see Dadrian, pp. 349–51.
    Zürcher takes the object of the push to be the CUP's *panturanic* aspirations.
    His evidence is that Enver himself intended to head to Baku when he fled
    Constantinople after the armistice. See Zürcher, HMT, p. 135. Michael
    Reynolds admits that "a secondary objective" of the CUP's late push to
    Baku was, as he euphemistically phrases it, "minimizing Armenian influ-
    ence now and for the future," but against *panturanism* as the main cause.
    The primary goal, he claims, "was to block the re-emergence of Russian
    power in the region." See Michael A. Reynolds, "Buffers, Not Brethren:
    Young Turk Military Policy in the First World War and the Myth of Pan-
    turanism," *Past and Present*, 203 (2009), pp. 137–79. Whatever the spe-
    cific object was, two things are clear: (1) the CUP's push for Baku was
    significant, and (2) its object was informed by the premise that led to the
    genocide, i.e., that Turkish control required the elimination of Armenians.
    Enver sent two different forces on two different routes under the command
    of two different close relatives to conquer the path to Baku. The first force,
    which he placed under the command of his brother Nuri Pasha (an ardent
    Pan-Turanist), was called "the Army of Islam." He placed the second force,

That was accomplished in the spring and summer of 1918. Baku was cleansed of Armenians in September 1918.[8]

One and one-half months later the Ottoman Empire surrendered to the Allied Powers. They had lost the war.

Talaat Pasha and Enver Pasha were not at their wartime posts in the last days of the war. Talaat, who in 1917 had become grand vizier, resigned some weeks before the armistice was signed. Enver had been relieved of the War Ministry shortly before that. The leaders of the CUP assigned the task of signing the Armistice of Mudros to their trusted friend, General Ahmet İzzet Pasha. On November 2, 1918, with İzzet's help, the Triumvirs—along with Dr. Bahaeddin Şakir and Dr. Nâzim of the CUP Central Executive Committee, Bedri Bey, the Chief of Police, and Azmi Bey, the Governor of Trebizond, also known as the "Butcher of Trebizond"—fled like thieves in the night on a ship that their German

---

under the command of his uncle Halil Pasha (Kut), who was another virulently anti-Armenian Turkist. As Bülent Gökay reconstructs the maneuver in "The Battle for Baku (May–September 1918): A Peculiar Episode in the History of the Caucasus," *Middle Eastern Studies*, 34.1 (1998), pp. 41–42: "By the end of June new divisions from the Western front had arrived in the Caucasus, where three Ottoman armies were waiting for the instructions of Enver Pasha. The Third Army (composed of the 3rd, 5th, 36th, and 37th Caucasian divisions) was charged with maintaining order in all territories acquired by the treaties of Brest-Litovsk and Batum. The newly organized Ninth Army (made up of the 9th, 10th, and 11th Caucasian divisions) was bestowed upon Yakub Sevki Pasha, whose temporary headquarters were in Alexandropol. Together, the Ninth Army and the Sixth Army (the latter located in north Persia) constituted the Army Group of the East under the supreme command of Enver's uncle, Halil Pasha. The ambitious task of liberating Baku and expelling the British from Persia and Baghdad rested upon these troops."

8. The massacre of the Armenians of Baku, which took place September 15–17, 1918, is usually called the "September Days." It is estimated that somewhere between 10,000 and 30,000 Armenians were slaughtered. Dadrian cites the fact that Bahaettin Şakir, one of the architects of the extermination of Western Armenians, was "acting as General Director of Police in the ranks of Halil's [Halil Kut] army which in September 1918 captured Baku" as evidence for the genocidal intent of the massacres. See Dadrian, p. 351.

allies had prepared for them in the harbor of Constantinople. They knew that they would be held accountable for their crimes, chief among them the Armenian Genocide. The armistice had been signed on October 30.

The Entente, territories, and irredentism

How history unfolded for the *vatan* and the Armenians cannot but be a reminder of the extraordinary role that modern philosophical theories played in the unfolding of twentieth-century history and geopolitics. Two things *should* have determined the future of Anatolia and the Eastern Provinces: the decisions of the victorious Allied Powers, and their coherent application of the principles that informed their postwar treaties.

After the War, the victorious Entente unilaterally imposed peace terms on the Central Powers: the vanquished empires and kingdoms.[9] The guiding principles of their territorial terms were Wilson's Fourteen Points. The primary underlying territorial assumption of those Points was what I have been calling the Greek Principle: the belief that a people's right to sovereignty includes its right to the proprietorship of its historic homeland.[10]

---

9. The Hungarian delegation's signature under protest of the Treaty of Trianon, as well as the interim German Reichspräsident Scheidermann's resignation over the terms of the Treaty of Versailles, are good measures of the unilaterality of the Entente's postwar treaties.

10. Thus, when, for instance, in the eighth point Wilson demanded that "French Territory" be returned to France by the German conquerors, he presupposed not just that conquest did not determine territorial possession (or else he could not have called it "French Territory"), but that the ownership of Alsace and Lorraine was determined by the identity of its historical inhabitants, and that that identity was French. That is, Wilson was implicitly claiming that the Alsatians' and Lorrainians' natural right to sovereignty included the right of ownership of Alsace and Lorraine. This principle is stated more clearly in Wilson's eleventh point, which claims that in the Balkans the borders should be drawn "along historically established

The Entente's treaties redrew the maps of Europe and the Middle East. They replaced empires with independent nations, republics for the most part: emperors with presidents and prime ministers. They redistributed colonies in Africa and Asia. With the Treaty of Saint-Germain-en-Laye, the Entente parceled out the vast majority of those lands that had been part of the Austrian Empire until the beginning of the War, and fulfilled the (actual or possible) irredentist claims of a multitude of peoples—the Italians, the Poles, the Balkan Slavs, the Bohemians, and the Romanians. They gave Austria's lone miniscule colony at Tianjin to China. With the Treaty of Trianon, Hungarian protests notwithstanding, they assigned parts of the Kingdom of Hungary—the other half of the Austro-Hungarian Empire—to those peoples whom they claimed were their rightful owners: the Balkan Slavs, Slovaks, and Romanians. With the Treaty of Neuilly-sur-Seine, they allocated parts of what had been the Kingdom of Bulgaria to the Balkan Slavs and Romanians. They ascribed other parts to their own protection. With the Treaty of Versailles, the Allies forced the Germans to acknowledge that Alsace and Lorraine were rightfully French; that parts of Posen, Pomerelia, Upper Silesia, and East and West Prussia were rightfully Polish; that Schleswig was rightfully Danish; that part of the Moravian-Silesian territory was rightfully Czech; and that Moresnet, Eupen, Malmédy, and St. Vith were rightfully Belgian. They made Danzig an international city so that Poland could have access to the sea. They assigned the mandate of the Memel Territory in East Prussia to France. In some cases, the Entente was willing to have plebiscites confirm that their new political borders matched

---

lines of allegiance and nationality." Such is presupposed in the thirteenth point, which called for the establishment of Poland.

Wilson formulated this principle in part in his fifth point: "A free, open-minded, and absolutely impartial adjustment of all colonial claims, based upon a strict observance of the principle that in determining all such questions of sovereignty the interests of the populations concerned must have equal weight with the equitable claims of the government whose title is to be determined."

what Wilson called the "historically established lines of allegiance and nationality." They distributed German colonies in Africa and the Pacific to Japan, Belgium, Portugal, France, and the UK.

The Entente dealt with the Ottoman Empire in the Treaty of Sèvres. It ordered the Ottomans to forgo any and all claims to Syria, Mesopotamia, and Palestine, any portion of what had once been part of the Ottoman Empire in Africa (Egypt, Morocco, Sudan, and so forth), and in Europe (the Aegean Islands and Cyprus). It assigned Erzerum, Van, Trebizond, Mush, and Bitlis to the newly sovereign Republic of Armenia,[11] Smyrna to Greece, and other Anatolian lands to a not-yet-formed Kurdistan.[12] Constantinople, like Danzig, was to become an international city. It assigned large parts of the Aegean coast and Cilicia to its own protection. The rest of the Ottoman domains—a large portion of Anatolia—was to become Turkey.

That should have been the end of that, at least with respect to the *vatan* and Armenia. Stability required it. Not to enforce the territorial terms of one of the postwar treaties was implicitly to challenge the territorial principles that informed them all. It was, in other words, to set the precedent that would enable other vanquished empires to challenge the territorial terms of their own treaties. Coherence required it. One cannot defend any principle if one does not universally apply it. Justice required it.[13]

---

11. The republic was formed on May 28, 1918, in what had been part of the Russian Empire. It was formed in time for Armenia to participate in the Paris Peace Congress.

12. The twelfth of Wilson's Fourteen Points is this: "XII. The Turkish portion of the present Ottoman Empire should be assured a secure sovereignty, but the other nationalities which are now under Turkish rule should be assured an undoubted security of life and an absolutely unmolested opportunity of autonomous development, and the Dardanelles should be permanently opened as a free passage to the ships and commerce of all nations under international guarantees."

13. This is not to say that Wilson's Fourteen Points and the Entente's treaties were either above reproach or realistic. As history would prove, international ports are simply a bad idea, as are mandates. It is to point out what Vahakn

The Treaties and Justice

Legislating in the name of justice and the defense of "the rights of the smaller nationalities," to use Asquith's phrase, was not foreign to the Entente, or to its treaties. The Treaty of Versailles imposed harsh punitive terms upon Germany in the name of justice. These comprised not just the vicious reparation payments that the Entente members exacted for the expenses which they had incurred in the war that Germany had "imposed" upon them.[14] They also included "compensation for all damage done to the civilian population"[15] through what we would call "crimes against humanity," committed by Germany or the other Central Powers "in their own territory or in occupied or invaded territory": "acts of cruelty, violence or maltreatment (including injuries to life or health as a consequence of imprisonment, deportation, internment or evacuation, of exposure at sea or of being forced to labor)."[16] There was

---

Dadrian has repeated for years: impunity breeds the repetition of crimes. More basically still, it is to claim what Aquinas indicated in his treatise on laws: the non-enforcement of a law is equivalent to its abrogation.

14. See Treaty of Versailles, Article 231: "The Allied and Associated Governments affirm and Germany accepts the responsibility of Germany and her allies for causing all the loss and damage to which the Allied and Associated Governments and their nationals have been subjected as a consequence of the war imposed upon them by the aggression of Germany and her allies"; and Article 235: "Germany shall pay in such installments and in such manner (whether in gold, commodities, ships, securities or otherwise) as the Reparation Commission may fix, during 1919, 1920 and the first four months of 1921, the equivalent of 20,000,000,000 gold marks." The full amount to be paid is specified in Annex II. This was not all Germany was expected to pay. It had also to give France and Belgium goods and property of all sorts: machinery, livestock, coal, chemicals, pharmaceuticals, and so forth. See Annexes III–VI of the Treaty.

15. See Article 232 of the Treaty of Versailles.

16. Treaty of Versailles, Annex I to Article 232. The full text of the parts quoted is: "(2) Damage caused by Germany or her allies to civilian victims of acts of cruelty, violence or maltreatment (including injuries to life or health as a consequence of imprisonment, deportation, internment or evacuation, of

every reason to believe that the Ottomans and the CUP would be held to the same standard.[17]

The CUP's Turkification venture, or what the rest of the world referred to more simply as the murder of the ancient Christian peoples of the Ottoman Empire, was no secret to any of the Allied Powers. Newspapers in every corner of the globe had reported with horror the unprecedented and systematic atrocities the CUP had perpetrated against the Armenians, Assyrians, and Greeks. Pope Benedict XV had implored the sultan to stop the attacks on the *miserrima Armeniorum gens qui prope ad interitum ducitur*—"the most forsaken Armenian people (*gens*) that is being led to near destruction."[18] Anatole France gave a rousing speech at the *Hommage à l'Arménie* held at the Sorbonne in April 1916, exclaiming:

> Armenia is dying, but it will live again. The little blood that remains is precious, and from it will be born a heroic posterity. A people which does not wish to die does not die. After the victory of our armies, which are fighting for liberty, the Allies will have great obligations to fulfil. And the most sacred of these will be to restore life to the martyred peoples, to Belgium, to Serbia. And then they will ensure the security and independence of Armenia. They will say: "My sister, arise, suffer no longer. Henceforth you are free to live according to your own nature and your own faith."[19]

---

exposure at sea or of being forced to labour), wherever arising, and to the surviving dependents of such victims. (3) Damage caused by Germany or her allies in their own territory or in occupied or invaded territory to civilian victims of all acts injurious to health or capacity to work, or to honour, as well as to the surviving dependents of such victims."

17. Every one of the Entente's treaties contained reparation clauses.

18. After the war, he opened the doors of his summer residence, Castel Gandolfo, to Armenian orphans.

19. Anatole France; qtd. in Richard G. Hovannisian, "The Allies and Armenia, 1915–18," *Journal of Contemporary History*, 3.1 (1968), p. 150.

Lloyd George was especially horrified by the slaughter of Christians and felt personally responsible for the eradication of the Armenians.[20] Ambassador Morgenthau had noisily resigned from his post, returned to the United States, and founded the largest relief organization the world had seen in order to save what could be saved of the "starving Armenians," who had been butchered, ripped from their homeland, and sent in columns marching toward the very "area that had resisted cultivation to remain untamed despite efforts for a half a century."[21]

The Allied Powers had even announced that such terms would be imposed upon the CUP in their joint declaration of May 29, 1915, in which they stated that they would hold the Ottoman government and its agents criminally responsible for the

---

20. David Lloyd George explicitly accepted for Great Britain the blame for having played a key role in the destruction of Armenia: "Had it not been for our sinister intervention, the great majority of the Armenians would have been placed by the Treaty of San Stefano in 1878, under the protection of the Russian flag. The Treaty of San Stefano provided that Russian troops should remain in occupation of the Armenian provinces until satisfactory reforms were carried out. By the Treaty of Berlin (1878)—which was entirely due to our minatory pressure and which was acclaimed by us a great British triumph which brought 'Peace with honour'—that article was superseded. Armenia was sacrificed on the triumphal altar we had erected. The Russians were forced to withdraw. The wretched Armenians were once more placed under the heel of their old masters, subject to a pledge to 'introduce ameliorations and reforms into the provinces inhabited by Armenians.' We all know how these pledges were broken for forty years, in spite of repeated protests from the country that was primarily responsible for restoring Armenia to Turkish rule. The actions of the British Government led inevitably to the terrible massacres of 1895–1897, 1909, and worst of all to the holocausts of 1915. By these atrocities, almost unparalleled in the black record of Turkish misrule, the Armenian population was reduced in numbers by well over a million." For the full citation see Dadrian, *A History of the Armenian Genocide*, p. 62.

21. Dündar, CON, p. 68. Morgenthau's move came after his many meetings with Talaat Pasha convinced him that the only means with which he could help the Christian peoples autochthonous to Anatolia were material: food, shelter, etc.

extermination of the Armenians: their "crimes against humanity and civilization."[22]

What Really Happened

Coherence was not to be. The Entente did not enforce all of the terms of the Treaty of Sèvres. Put differently, although the Entente ensured that six of the seven territorial provisions included in Wilson's Fourteen Points were respected in four of the five treaties that it imposed upon the defeated Central Powers, it did not enforce the territorial terms of the fifth treaty, or ensure that the seventh of Wilson's territorial provisions—the twelfth of the Fourteen Points—was realized. Nor did the Entente's dogged pursuit of justice extend to all of the vanquished empires and kingdoms. The ferocity with which it ensured that Austria and Germany "pay" for wartime crimes did not extend to the Ottoman Empire—or the CUP—despite the genocide.

Two intersecting power struggles determined what would become of the lands that the CUP had prepared for its *vatan* once the War was over. The first was Ottoman Turkish. Its protagonists were the CUP—which quickly transformed into the Turkish Nationalist

---

22. R.G. 59, 867.4016/67: "For about a month the Kurd and Turkish populations of Armenia has been massacring Armenians with the connivance and often assistance of Ottoman authorities. Such massacres took place in middle April (new style) at Erzerum, Dertchun, Eguine, Akn, Bitlis, Mush, Sassun, Zeitun, and throughout Cilicia. Inhabitants of about one hundred villages near Van were all murdered. In that city Armenian quarter is besieged by Kurds. At the same time in Constantinople Ottoman Government ill-treats inoffensive Armenian population. In view of those new crimes of Turkey against humanity and civilization, the Allied governments announce publicly to the Sublime-Porte that they will hold personally responsible [for] these crimes all members of the Ottoman government and those of their agents who are implicated in such massacres." The declaration was wired to the State Department of the then-neutral United States with the request that the American Ambassador transmit it to the Turkish government.

movement—and its enemies, the Ottoman Liberals. The Liberals and the CUP had had opposing plans for the future of the Ottoman Empire before the CUP gained dictatorial control of it.[23] The CUP's defeat gave the Liberals (and the sultan) a chance to take control of the empire and put an end to that homogenization and Turkification of Anatolia and the Eastern Provinces that the CUP considered a necessary requisite of its lasting *vatan*. The CUP—or the Nationalists—had no intention of relinquishing control or abandoning its project. What erupted was a civil war of sorts: a contest between two would-be leaders of (and futures for) the new Turkish nation.

The second power struggle was among the Allied Powers: the Entente. During the War, the Powers were (at least nominally) bound by a common purpose and commitment to principles when it came to Ottoman Christians and the assignment of the Eastern Provinces. The Russian Revolution delivered the first blow to their bond. After the Bolsheviks toppled the tsar, the Russians did everything in their power to sabotage the Entente's postwar plans for the Ottoman Empire. The second blow came at the Paris Peace Conference, where the other members of the Entente remembered that they had national and imperial interests of their own, and that they considered these more important than their common commitment to those principles that had informed not just their promises to the Armenians, but the bulk of their postwar treaties.

These two power struggles overlapped. Both Turkish camps counted on the support of the powerful members of the Entente in their attempts to win control over what was left of the Ottoman

---

23. As Hans-Lukas Kieser points out, one of the great *what ifs* of the history of Anatolia and Armenia concerns the political struggle in the late Ottoman Empire. "While the CUP pursued the empire's 'union and progress' through centralizing policies, opposition parties such as the Liberal Entente (*Hürriyet ve İtilâf Fırkası*) allowed for greater regional participation. Whether the Liberal Entente or any other party would ever have been successful in sidelining the CUP or in solving the empire's very serious problems is an unanswerable question." See Kieser, "The Ottoman Road to Total War (1913–15)," in Kieser/Öktem/Reinkowski, p. 38.

Empire. As for the Allied Powers, they one by one forgot how horrified they had been by what inspired the coining of the word "genocide," Wilson's Fourteen Points, justice, and the Treaty of Sèvres, once the Russians forcefully backed (funded and equipped) the heirs of the CUP—the Turkish Nationalists. One by one they whimpered to the Nationalists, trying to broker the best possible deal for their own nations or empires.

The Crossroads

Turkey was on Wilson's map of Anatolia and Armenia. It was not the Turkey that the CUP had envisioned for its *vatan*. It did not include all of the lands that they had cleared of Christians so that they could construct their ethnically and socially homogeneous modern centralized state thereon. Those lands encompassed all of Anatolia, the Eastern Provinces, and Constantinople. Wilson's Turkey did not include Constantinople, Cilicia, the Aegean coasts, and four of the Eastern Provinces.

The Ottomans were at a crossroads. They could continue on the path chosen by the leaders and ideologues of the CUP, the path that led to the creation of the *vatan* (with its homogeneous national *Turkish* population, economy, and culture) in at least *all* of Anatolia *and* the Eastern Provinces as an unrelinquishable goal.[24] That path equated the death of Armenia with the life of Turkey. Or they

---

24. The crucial question here is: Why did the CUP/Turkish Nationalists insist upon including the Eastern Provinces in their *vatan*? Or, put differently, why had the CUP made thorough preparations to ensure that the *vatan* included the Eastern Provinces? Or to look at the question from a different vantage point: Why was the land that Wilson's Fourteen Points had allotted to the Turks *a priori* not enough for the CUP/Turkish Nationalists? If one looks at the whole issue dispassionately, that land—which objectively included a sizable amount of territory upon which to build a nation—should have sufficed for the defeated government of an empire that had acquired semi-colonial status and relied upon its allies to defend itself, given both the ease with which land was assigned and reassigned

could abandon CUP's path to national and cultural homogeneity: come to terms with the horrendous crimes perpetrated by the CUP, return Armenian properties, attempt to make reparations, accept to live alongside an independent Armenia that included at least part of the ancient Armenian homeland that the CUP had wanted to incorporate in the *vatan*, and define a new path.

The immediate reaction

In the weeks before the Armistice of Mudros, the Ottomans gave every sign of having opted for the latter path. The CUP government had resigned. In a flurry of activity, the new government reversed the CUP laws that had targeted the Armenians. On October 18, 1918, it ordered that Armenians be allowed to return to their homes.[25] On October 19, İzzet Pasha announced that Armenian

---

after World War I and the principles which purportedly regulated that assignment. It did suffice for the sultan.

This question becomes especially intriguing if one bears in mind that none of the leaders or ideologues of the CUP or the Turkish Nationalist movement—excepting the Ziya Gökalp—hailed from the Eastern Provinces, and none actually was familiar with Anatolia or the Eastern Provinces. So why the *a priori* insistence on including the Eastern Provinces? The question clearly points to the fact that there was something ideological driving the CUP and Turkish Nationalists and that this ideological component had something to do the Armenians. One cannot respond to the real question behind the CUP/Nationalists' land demands, in other words, without responding to Melson's question: Why did the Ottoman Turks consider the Armenians an existential threat? See Melson, "A Theoretical Inquiry into the Armenian Massacres of 1894–1896."

25. The exact wording of the order is that it gave "permission for the return to their places of all people removed from one place and deported to others due to conditions of war by military decision." It specified that "evasion and delay in the application of the order not being allowed to happen in the least." See Akçam and Kurt, p. 36. The authors add that Armenians were the last people to be allowed to return from their deportation. In April and May 1918, deported Muslims were allowed to return to their homes. Deported Greeks were given permission to return home at the end of that summer.

properties would be returned to their rightful owners. On October 20, the government added that Christians who had forcibly been converted to Islam be allowed to return to their former religion. On October 21, it informed the authorities in the provinces that the Armenians could return:

> [Government] orders continued to be sent to the provinces for the precise and orderly realization of the return process. These orders asked that Armenians and Greeks be allowed to travel without travel documents; the assignment of special trains to them; the provision of their needs including food, drink, and travel expenses; and their secure arrival in the places to which they were going. According to figures reported on 20 November 1918, 7,138 Armenians, and a total of 10,601 people returned. On 21 December 1918, it was announced that 2,552 Muslims, 19,695 Greeks, and 23,420 Armenians returned. The minister, who made the announcement in the parliament, also said that these people had been resettled.[26]

On November 4, 1918, the Deportation Law (the *Tehcir Kanunu*) of May 27, 1915 was declared unconstitutional. A circular of December 18, 1918, was sent to the provinces asking for the return of "confiscated properties of the Armenians and the most rapid evacuation of their homes by officials, police, and other individuals who might be living in them."[27]

The government established commissions to oversee the repatriation of Armenians and Greeks and the restoration of their properties. It attempted to find those Armenian women and children who had been kidnapped during the genocide and forcibly converted. It

---

26. Akçam and Kurt, p. 37. Official Ottoman documents claim that by June 7, 1919, 276,015 Armenians and Greeks had returned to their homes. See Akçam, ASA, p. 277.

27. Akçam and Kurt, p. 37.

confiscated the properties of the CUP leaders. On January 12, 1920, it issued the Vahdeddin Regulation, which formalized its practice of overturning and revoking those CUP laws and regulations that had sanctioned the seizure of Armenian properties.[28] It launched a thorough investigation of the war crimes. It organized court-martials against those who had organized and overseen the perpetration of the genocide.[29] Many of those responsible for the "crimes against humanity and civilization" were arrested.

Some members of the Ottoman Parliament insisted that the CUP's wartime crimes needed to be addressed.[30] It was not just the Armenian and Greek deputies who did so.[31] Claiming that he

---

28. The Vahdeddin Regulation of January 20, 1920, was comprehensive. It not only revoked the Liquidation Law of September 26, 1915, and the regulation of November 8, 1915. It spelled out in great detail how Armenian properties were to be returned; how Armenians were to be compensated for lost revenues; how quickly the squatters were to be evicted; and so forth. See Akçam and Kurt, pp. 38–40.

29. The trials took place over a period of nearly three years: 1919–1922. Some of the transcripts of the trials have been recovered and printed. See Vahakn Dadrian and Taner Akçam, *Judgment at Istanbul: The Armenian Genocide Trials* (New York/Oxford: Berghahn, 2011).

30. See, on this topic, Ayhan Aktar, "Debating the Armenian Massacres in the Last Ottoman Parliament, November–December 1918," *History Workshop Journal*, 64 (2007), pp. 240–70.

31. The Armenians and Greeks did, however, give very good reasons for doing so. Matyos Nalbantyan, the deputy from Sis, was particularly convincing. He pointed out that "For a long time, in this country...sovereignty has meant sovereignty of the Turks. The true Turks may well be opposed to the persecutions that were repeated again and again.... It is spoken of three to five people who did this.... Three to five could not have done this.... Those who did shouted: 'We do this for Turkish sovereignty!' and 'Our strength is Turkish bayonets!'... Those who did this are individuals who belong to the Turkish nation.... Both world opinion and the victims will demand an accounting and compensation, and the Turks will have to provide it. The Turks who claim that their hands are clean, must give an accounting, they must punish those who deserve punishment.... Redemption is possible, but we must find every person who committed these crimes and punish them, and we must return and restore those rights that were trampled and abused.

wished "the conscience of humanity be satisfied," Ahmet Riza, one of the founding members of the original CUP, demanded that "the Imperial Government establish a trial venue in the name of the public ... that the murderers are identified as soon as possible and delivered to the hands of justice."[32] Damat Ferid Pasha claimed that the word "deportation," which was being used to describe what happened to the Armenians, was not the correct one. Armenians, he claimed, had been "expelled." He added that "neither humanity, nor civilization, nor the Islamic world" could accept the reasons that the CUP government adduced for its crimes against the Armenians.[33] Even the CUP deputy from Trebizond, Mehmet Emin, complained that the "guilty parties were still driving around in their cars, in public, and that the situation was unbearable." He claimed to want the real culprits punished so that all Turks would not suffer for their crimes.[34]

The crimes committed against the Armenians were condemned in the Turkish press as "the greatest and most unpardonable act in history." Articles calling for the heads of those responsible for the crimes were published: "no lesser punishment than death is right for these people."[35] There were formal protests against the CUP.

And after this we will go before the civilized world as a delegation and declare that we are going to do this ... this is the soundest and most righteous path." Nalbantyan; qtd. in Akçam, ASA, pp. 259–60.

32. Akçam, ASA, p. 269.

33. Akçam, ASA, p. 267–69 *passim.*

34. Akçam, ASA, pp. 248–49. The matter of guilt was not just morally and historically significant. Just who was responsible for the Ottoman "crimes against humanity and civilization" seemed at that time to be crucial. The Paris Peace Congress wanted not just to make the Central Powers pay reparations for the war. It wanted collectively to punish the peoples who had perpetrated the war crimes. Thus the German nation, whose armies had devastated France, were made to pay exorbitant reparations. The gravity of Ottoman war crimes far exceeded that of the Germans. It was logical to deduce that the Ottomans as a whole would be punished for the Armenian Genocide.

35. Akçam, ASA, p. 247.

At Sultan Mehmed VI Vahdeddin's court-martials—whose organization fell first to Tevfik Pasha, who became grand vizier shortly after İzzet Pasha was hurriedly dismissed, and then to Damat Ferid Pasha—hundreds of members of the CUP were put on trial. The Triumvirs and other leading members of the CUP were sentenced to death *in absentia*. Evidence was presented that demonstrated that not everyone in power in Ottoman Turkey during the war had been complicit in the CUP's crimes. There had been "the opposition of broad sections of society to the campaign against the Armenians."[36] There had been governors who had not complied with the CUP's orders to exterminate the Armenians.[37] That they had been removed from their posts and replaced spoke to the criminality of the CUP itself, not that of all Turks.

As for Sultan Mehmed VI Vahdeddin, his primary concerns were Islam, the caliphate, and his dynasty. He had no taste for either the CUP or its ideology. He considered both devastating. The CUP had actively undermined everything for which the sultanate and caliphate stood.[38] They had made a puppet of his brother, Sultan Mehmet V Reşat. Vahdeddin also "cared little for the complete independence of Anatolia or any other region."[39]

But for every person who condemned the actions of the CUP, there were many still in power who condoned, and even justified, them. In the short time that he was grand vizier, İzzet Pasha destroyed crucial documents that would incriminate the CUP. He had the archives of the *Teşkilât-ı Mahsusa* destroyed. He actively sabotaged all attempts to have members of the CUP held responsible for

---

36. Akçam, ASA, p. 179.
37. Other governors such as Hilmi Bey, the *mutasarrif* of Mardin, were murdered on the *vali*'s orders for not obeying the orders to deport the Armenians. See Suny, p. 329, for more information.
38. This was made obvious by the counter-revolution of 1909, when Turkish conservatives wrested control of the government from the CUP. See, e.g., Zürcher, HMT, pp. 96–103.
39. Zürcher, HMT, p. 137.

their crimes. He assisted in the escape of more than just the seven people who had fled on the German ship that November 2. On November 8, 1918, the sultan forced him to resign. The official reason he gave the English press was that İzzet Pasha was slowing down the criminal proceedings against those responsible for the genocide.[40]

After having attempted to skirt the matter altogether, Halil Menteşe, the president of the chamber, successfully curbed parliamentary discussions of the responsibility of CUP's wartime "crimes against humanity and civilization" despite calls for him to step down and for the parliament, the majority of whose members belonged to the CUP, to be dissolved. The frustrated sultan, who was also being pressured by the Allied Powers to arrest and try those responsible for the genocide, decided to dissolve parliament altogether.

CUP postwar preparations

Halil Menteşe and İzzet Pasha were not lone wolves. The Central Committee of the CUP had made thorough resistance plans long before the Armistice. It had constructed a vast network, above all in the Eastern Provinces, that was fully operational in 1918.[41] Although

---

40. Akçam, ASA, pp. 281–82.

41. In November 1918, Midhat Şükrü, the minister of education, claimed that "The government has previously thought about this angle and already taken measures. Weapons, ammunition and organization: all is ready for the struggle in the mountains as well as armed militias. We will hold out for 50 years." M. Şükrü; qtd. in Akçam, ASA, p. 127.

In the paragraphs in which he quotes Midhat Şükrü, Akçam suggests that the CUP's resistance plans had been both (a) prepared shortly after the Yeniköy Accord had been signed, and (b) prepared alongside the "broad Unionist plans for Turkification" of Anatolia. Kuşçubaşı Eşref's account, he claims, is evidence for the first point, and allows us to assume that the plans were first discussed sometime between May and August 1914. As for the second point, he simply cites the documents: "The [resistance] plan generated much discussion and correspondence between various military commanders over such issues as where to place the army's headquarters. And this documentation

Talaat, Enver, Dr. Nazim, and Dr. Şakir had left Constantinople, the CUP still controlled the post-armistice parliament—until the sultan dismissed it. It controlled the army, the police force, and communications (the telegraph and post offices).

That was the tip of the iceberg. The CUP still had the terrorist bands of the *Teşkilât-ı Mahsusa*, which were renamed the *Umum Alem-i İslam İhtilâl Teşkilâti* (General Revolutionary Organization of the Islamic World) instead of being disbanded.[42] The Central Committee had set up a guard—the *Karakol* (Guardians)—to protect those who had had a hand in the genocide and had not fled, and to arm the resistance war in Anatolia and the Eastern Provinces. It had left caches of weapons for the *Karakol* and the new *Teşkilât* forces throughout Anatolia.[43] It founded societies for the "defense of

---

provides some important clues as to the immediate background to the Armenian genocide. The Turkification of Anatolia was not the only objective; Unionists had also planned for a drawn-out war of resistance in Anatolia."

Akçam then asks if there is a connection between the resistance plans and the genocide. He claims that "there is no document that shows a clear connection between the long-term resistance plan in Anatolia and the Armenian genocide. But it is certain that the decisions to enact the two events were made during the same period and their simultaneous start is significant," Akçam, ASA, p. 128.

42. Enver ordered Colonel Hiisamettin Ertiirk, who was to be in charge of the guerilla bands: "Officially you will dissolve the Special Organization but in reality, this organization will never cease to exist. It will in this form confront the victorious powers. We have spoken to Ahmet Izzet Pasha and we are unanimously agreed. Whatever you need in the way of assistance they will give you, they will provide money from secret funds," Enver; qtd. in Cruickshank, in A.A. Cruickshank, "The Young Turk Challenge in Postwar Turkey," *Middle East Journal*, 22.1 (1968), p. 20.

43. Zürcher, HMT, p. 141: "Between November 1918 and March 1920, *Karakol* managed to smuggle a considerable number of Unionist officers—many of them wanted men—to Anatolia. In addition, it supplied the emerging resistance movement in Anatolia with large quantities of arms, supplies and ammunition stolen from Ottoman stores under Entente control. Some 56,000 gun locks, 320 machine guns, 1500 rifles, 2000 boxes of ammunition and 10,000 uniforms are reported to have been smuggled to Anatolia in this way."

national rights" (*müdafaa-i hukuk-u milliye*) in provincial capitals.[44]
It set up a new political party, the *Teceddüt Firkasi* (Reform Party),
and left it with sufficient funds to operate for a long time.[45]

> Finally, the crack Caucasian division (*Maveray-i Kafkas*)
> and a division stationed in Erzerum, in Eastern Anatolia,
> were brought up to full strength and prepared to return
> to the offensive.[46]

That there was a Turkey on Wilson's map was not remotely
enough for the leaders of the CUP. That a host of new nation
states (and an *international* Danzig) were going to be carved out
of the dominions of their allies meant nothing to them. That
they had murdered millions of people and stolen their property
left them stone-faced and more determined to see their *vatan*
completed:

> Why should we call ourselves murderers? Why have we
> taken on this vast and difficult matter? These things
> were done to secure the future of our homeland, which
> we know is greater and holier than even our own lives.[47]

---

44. Zürcher, HMT, p. 147.

45. Zürcher, HMT, p. 135.

46. Cruickshank, p. 20. The Eastern Provinces were the only place where a siz-
    able and well-equipped and well-led Ottoman force was concentrated. See
    Zürcher, HMT, p. 149: "The only place where sizable Ottoman forces were
    concentrated was the east. The troops that had been ordered back from
    Azerbaijan after the armistice were not also garrisoned here and their total
    strength (when mobilized) was about 30,000. These troops, now called
    the XVth Army Corps, were also much better equipped than those in the
    west and they operated in an inaccessible area. Militarily speaking, their
    commander, Kâzim Pasha (Karabekir), was the key figure in Anatolia,
    followed by Ali Fuat Pasha (Cebesoy), the commander of the XXth Army
    Corps in Ankara, who moved back from Cilicia to central Anatolia in the
    end of 1918."

47. Ottoman Parliamentarian; qtd. in Akçam, ASA, p. 129.

They held that if they had not perpetrated the genocide, they would not be in a position to create the *vatan*.[48] Halil Menteşe said as much:

> Had we not cleansed out the Eastern Provinces of Armenian revolutionaries…there would have been no possibility of establishing our national state.[49]

Bahaettin Şakir had, too, once the first deportations had started: "The Committee is ever ready to rescue the homeland from the blemish of this accursed nation [i.e., the Armenians]."[50] He knew that "rescuing the homeland" entailed "to act contrary to the laws of nations and humanity." Şakir declared himself

> ready to pay the price for this with my own life. Whether I achieve the goal or not, there will be many who will castigate me. This I know, but there will also be those who in the distant future will understand that I sacrificed myself in the name of serving my country.[51]

Western Brawls and Brute Force

For the leaders of the CUP, the Armistice of Mudros was nothing more than a temporary setback. Enver Pasha told those who attended the last pre-exile meeting of the Central Committee of the CUP that was held at his house in Kuruçesme the night before he left on the German ship:

---

48. Edib clearly claims as much. Edib, HW, p. 387: "There are two factors which lead men to the extermination of his kind: principles advocated by the idealists, and the material interest. Talaat was of the idealist kind."

49. Akçam, ASA, p. 122.

50. Bahaettin Şakir, letter to Cemal Bey of March 25, 1914; qtd. in Akçam, ASA, p. 129.

51. Bahaettin Şakir; qtd. in Akçam, ASA, p. 129

[T]he world war is about to start on its second phase. Don't forget in the past we won the Balkan War in its second phase.[52]

Enver's reference to the "second phase" of the Balkan War was apt. The Balkan Wars confirmed the two things that the Central Committee of the CUP had learned in its short tenure in power. The first was that brute force could quash Turkish resistance. The second was that it could diplomatically defeat Western powers and nations, even after it had been militarily crushed.[53]

The second lesson taught the Young Turks nothing that the preceding Ottoman governments did not already know. By the late nineteenth century, the Ottomans were well aware of Western squabbling and had mastered the art of provoking and taking advantage of it. The Armenian Reforms clearly demonstrate this. Despite being a "semi-colony," the Ottomans managed through a combination of promising and blustering to avoid altogether the implementation of the Reforms that Western Powers insisted upon—vociferously at times—for thirty-seven years.

The first lesson was also not new to the members of the Central Committee of the CUP. In their ten years in power, they had survived a counter-revolution in 1909 and fierce opposition between

---

52. Enver; qtd. in Cruickshank, p. 18.

53. After having been trounced by the Balkan League (Greece, Serbia, Montenegro, and Bulgaria) in 1912, the Ottomans agreed in December to an armistice. The terms of the peace treaty were discussed in London, where the powers decided to give Edirne to the Bulgarians. The prospective loss of Edirne—the first capital of the Ottoman Empire—was enough of an emotional blow to the CUP for it to seize control of the government. The CUP then did some saber rattling, was again defeated, and accepted the very terms for which it had stormed the Porte. But Greeks, Serbians, Montenegrins, and Bulgarians could not get along for long. After their victory, the nations who had formed the Balkan League began to fight over who got what. When the Bulgarians attacked Serbia, Enver decided to recapture Edirne. The Constantinople peace agreement with which the Second Balkan War ended forced the Bulgarians to give the city back to the Ottomans.

1910 and 1913. They had held onto power through brute force. The elections of 1912

> are known in Turkish history as the *sopali seçim* (elections with the stick) because of the violence and intimidation with which the CUP made sure of its majority.[54]

In their second *coup d'état* after the first Balkan War, high-ranking members of the CUP stormed the Sublime Porte, shot the war minister, took prisoner a few members of the cabinet, and forced the grand vizier to resign. After they had grabbed power the second time, the Central Committee of the CUP ruled the empire with an iron fist.

Enver's point at the meeting in Kuruçesme was that the Balkan Wars had taught the leaders of the CUP all they needed to know to win the "second phase" of their battle to construct the *vatan*. They needed only to force their internal enemies to submit to their plans and wait for Western Powers to fight among themselves. He added that

> This phase will be perhaps longer and more trying, but they will never be able to wipe out this nation since the Turkish nation and especially the Anatolian Turk, cannot give up his independence easily.[55]

Damat Ferid Pasha, the sultan, and the soul of the empire

Damat Ferid Pasha, his liberal party, and Sultan Mehmet VI Vahdeddin could not have won the internal struggle for the soul and direction of the empire without the help of the Allied Powers. The

---

54. Zürcher, HMT, p. 103.
55. Enver; qtd. in Cruickshank, p. 20.

amount of devastation that the CUP had left behind in Anatolia and Armenia was too much—and the number of accomplices on the ground too many—for the grand vizier and sultan alone to steer the Ottoman Empire off the path carved by the CUP.

Their attempts to return confiscated Armenian properties to their rightful owners quickly became a nightmare. The refugees and other Muslims, whom the CUP had settled in the houses from which it had torn the Armenians, simply did not want to give them up.[56] The new "Turkish bourgeoisie," the landowners and traders, whom Armenian (and Greek) land and businesses had made wealthy, did not dream of giving up the sources of their newfound wealth.

> A new class of "notables" had been created through their acquisition of Armenian property, having become wealthy as a result of the genocide and the attendant looting. To return the looted property was unthinkable to them.[57]

The refugees and the new "notables" did not and would not side with Ferid Pasha and the sultan. The CUP easily recruited them for its "defense of national rights" committees. With the help of the men whom the CUP had left in their posts throughout Anatolia and the Eastern Provinces, the committees would organize congresses that

---

56. See, on this, e.g., Akçam, ASA, pp. 274–76. See also Akçam and Kurt, p. 38: "Reports in the newspapers of the period make it evident that the removal of those who had settled in Armenian homes was a serious issue. According to a report of 27 March 1919, Muslims who had settled in vacant Armenian and Greek houses established an organization called the Society of Refugees. In a statement, they explained that 'upon their [the Armenians and Greeks'] return, Muslim refugees who had settled in their places, being taken out from those places, [became] utterly homeless.' The Society estimated that there were 'approximately 150 thousand' Muslims left without homes."

57. Akçam, ASA, p. 280.

would then pronounce on the Turkish and Muslim character of the area and its determination to stay united to
the motherland.[58]

The sultan's attempts to call upon the conscience of the Turks fared
no better than his attempt to return stolen Armenian property. As
horrified as Ferid Pasha and the sultan were at the CUP's wanton
destruction of the autochthonous Christian peoples, much to the dis-
gust of both—and the British—the Nationalists managed to whip up
the Turkish population, which rose up to defend those who had perpetrated that destruction. In April 1919, the funeral of Kemal Bey, the
first man to be condemned to death by the sultan's court-martials—at
the Yozgat trial—and executed for the atrocities committed against
the Armenians, "quickly turned into an anti-occupation demonstration. Wreaths bore inscriptions such as 'Kemal Bey, the Great Martyr
of the Turks,' and 'to the innocent Muslim martyr.' Anti-British, anti-
occupation and nationalist speeches were made."[59]

The British Foreign Office quipped:

not one Turk in a thousand can conceive that there
might be a Turk who deserves to be hanged for the killing of Christians.[60]

The sultan warned that the trials would end in massacres, retalia-
tion, or worse.

As for Damat Ferid Pasha's promise as the newly appointed grand
vizier to eliminate "persons loyal to the CUP from bureaucracy," it
was one he could not keep. The network of people that the CUP had
left in power was simply too vast. Ferid's government was not even

---

58. Zürcher, HMT, p. 148. Twenty-eight such congresses were held between
    December 1918 and October 1920.

59. Akçam, ASA, p. 293.

60. British Foreign Office; qtd. in Akçam, ASA, p. 294.

able to arrest many of those whom it suspected of "crimes against humanity and civilization." The men were tipped off before the arresting officers arrived. As a leading member of the CUP described it:

> No matter how hard they tried, they couldn't staff the Chief of Police's office with just their own people. There were always some kids there who loved us and kept us informed...by telephone, three or four times a day if necessary.[61]

The truth is that the sultan and grand vizier were not just outnumbered. They had been outmaneuvered. They were hopelessly out of touch with the reality of the CUP's postwar preparations. Nothing proves this more than the grand vizier's appointment of Mustafa Kemal as the inspector of the Third Army in the Eastern Provinces. As resistance to the restitution of Armenian property, "national defense committees," and the aftermath of the Yozgat trials show, there was a great deal of unrest in the Eastern Provinces in 1919. Fighting also erupted between Greeks and Muslims on the Black Sea. This concerned Damat Ferid Pasha. By the terms of the armistice, it could lead to the Entente's intervention in the area. This was something he wanted desperately to avoid. He needed a trusted man to take control of the area for him: to disperse and disarm the nationalist committees. The sultan's interior minister, Mehmet Ali Bey, suggested Mustafa Kemal for the position, and, after a brief meeting, the grand vizier appointed the brigadier general inspector of the Third Army in the east.[62] Had Ferid understood the nature of his internal enemy, he would have seen that appointing Kemal

---

61. Yunus Nadi; qtd. in Akçam, ASA, p. 292.
62. This event also shows how deeply the CUP had infiltrated the sultan's government in 1918. Mehmet Ali Bey was a cousin of the nationalist Ali Fuad Pasha (Cebesoy), who was one of Mustafa Kemal's closest officer friends. When the meeting between the Ferid Pasha and Kemal took place, Ali Fuad was already in Anatolia. See Zürcher, HMT, p. 142.

as the person to disperse and disarm the nationalists was playing straight into the hands of those who had organized and armed them in the first place: he was giving them the leader they needed to carry their plans through to their completion. By the time he found out, it was too late.

Mustafa Kemal set sail for Samsun on May 16, 1919:

> He arrived on May 19, 1919—a day later generations of Turks would celebrate as Youth and Sports Day and eventually Atatürk Commemoration Day. He immediately began acting as a resistance leader, attending meetings organized by the nationalists, backing Muslim bandit activity, and issuing subtle but strong statements criticizing the very government that had dispatched him to suppress nationalist activities.[63]

He worked with energy, refused to obey the summons to return to Constantinople, and resigned from his post "in open defiance of the imperial government." He organized congresses (regional and national ones), formed a parallel government in Anatolia, and had the imperial government accept the resolutions of the Erzerum and Sivas Congresses—all this in four months' time. Such were the circles that Mustafa Kemal and the nationalists ran around the sultan and Liberals that they won a landslide election in December 1919. Kemal himself won a seat in Parliament. He was elected deputy for Erzerum. He decided not to accept, lest he be arrested.

Italy, Lloyd George, and the megali idea

The Allied Powers seemed to have every intention of enforcing the terms of the Treaty of Sèvres, sustaining the sultan and Damat

---

63. M. Şükrü Hanioğlu, *Atatürk: An Intellectual Biography* (Princeton/Oxford: Princeton University Press, 2011), p. 97.

Ferid Pasha, containing the Turkish Nationalists, and ensuring that justice be done for the Armenians. Aristide Briand, while prime minister of France, wrote Senator Louis Martin in 1916, promising:

> When the hour for legitimate reparation shall have struck, France will not forget the terrible trials of the Armenians, and in accord with her Allies, she will take the necessary measures to ensure for Armenia a life of peace and progress.[64]

Clemenceau promised the same thing to Boghos Nubar Pasha in 1918. Britain made similar promises. Lloyd George, Balfour, and Lord Cecil were adamant that Armenia would be established and protected. Lord Cecil stated:

> I recognize fully the strength of the observations that we must not allow the misdeeds of the Turks to diminish the patrimony of the Armenians. That is the general principle. I recognize the great force of what the hon. Member said—that there ought to be no division of Armenia and that it ought to be treated as one whole.... As far as I am concerned—and I believe in this matter I am speaking for the Government—I should be deeply disappointed if any shred or shadow of Turkish government were left in Armenia.[65]

A few months after the Armistice of Mudros, the British began to arrest those it deemed responsible for the Armenian Genocide. It also ordered commanders to consider the Ottoman army's food supplies Armenian property.[66] The Senate of the United States resolved that:

---

64. Aristide Briand; qtd. in Hovannisian, "The Allies and Armenia," p. 150.
65. Lord Cecil; qtd. in Hovannisian, "The Allies and Armenia," pp. 149–50.
66. Akçam, ASA, p. 236.

Armenia, including the six *vilayets* of Turkish Armenia and Cilicia, Russian Armenia, and the northern part of the Province of Azerbaijan, Persian Armenia, should be independent and that it is the hope of the Senate that the peace conference will make arrangements for helping Armenia to establish an independent republic.[67]

Intentions are not concrete help. When the time came for the Allied Powers to guarantee that no "shred or shadow of Turkish government were left in Armenia," "to ensure for Armenia a life of peace and progress," and to "make arrangements for helping Armenia to establish an independent republic," they simply did not. They had waited too long. It took the Entente nearly two years to present the Ottoman Empire with terms of the Treaty of Sèvres. Many things happened in those two years—not the least of which were the Powers' demobilization of its own troops and Mustafa Kemal's alliance with the Soviets. When the sultan accepted the treaty in August 1920, the Allied Powers were no longer in a position to enforce the terms of their treaty and did not have the will to muster the strength to do so.

The problem was to a great degree the problem of old. Despite their high-sounding words, the Allied Powers were incapable of acting coherently, or in accordance with anything other than their own immediate benefit. They had promised too many contradictory things to too many nations in order to convince them to join the war. A clamorous example of their dealings was their contradictory promises to Italy and Greece. The Italians were told that they could fulfill their *irredentist* claims on Istria and Dalmatia (with the exception of Fiume) and expand on their Greek holdings with Smyrna. The Greeks had also been promised Smyrna, on which they had *irredentist* claims.

Once the Paris Peace Conference began, the contradictory promises came back to haunt the Allied Powers. Vittorio Emanuele

---

67. *Congressional Record*, December 10, 1918, p. 237; qtd. in Hovannisian, "The Allies and Armenia," pp. 154–55.

Orlando, the Italian representative, left in a rage when the Powers tried to assign the once-Venetian Balkan territories, which were still heavily populated by Italians—Istria and Dalmatia—to the newly formed Kingdom of Serbs, Croatians, and Slovenes. With the Italians still smarting over what they considered *la vittoria mutilata*—"the mutilated victory"—Lloyd George convinced Elephtherios Venizelos of Greece to send his army and fulfill his country's *irredentist* claims in Anatolia. Venizelos presented his people with the *megali idea*—the big idea—and couched it as a mission to reconquer Constantinople and ensure the protection of the Christian Greeks of Smyrna. His army landed in May 1919, seven months after the Armistice.

Bolsheviks, Ittihadists, weapons, and deals: Or on how to use brute force to resolve territorial issues

The one true excuse for the Entente's mishandling of the Treaty of Sèvres—and the Nationalists' defeat of the sultan—was Russia. The problem was not that Russia, which was one of the original members of the Entente, was in the midst of a civil war of its own, did not participate in the Paris Peace Conference, and did not help its former allies actuate their plans. The problem was that the revolutionary Russian government *sabotaged* the treaty. The Sovnarkom had territorial plans of its own, and these did not allow for a Caucasian, Armenian, or Turkish foothold at or near the Russian borders from which the "imperialist powers" could threaten it. Its response to the Treaty of Sèvres was to strengthen the strategic *rapprochement* with the Turkish Nationalists for which it had laid the groundwork at Brest-Litovsk.

The Russians and the Ottomans were neighbors and historical enemies; or, rather, the Ottoman Empire in the last century or so of its existence was an irresistible quarry of lands for the ever-expansionist Russia.[68] That changed—or at least seemed to—after

---

68. It was Russia's nineteenth-century military advances—most especially that of 1877–88—that turned the Ottoman Empire into a European

the tsar and the subsequent provisional government were toppled. Once the Bolsheviks took over the government in Petrograd, they issued the decree *On Peace*, calling for an immediate cessation of hostilities and declaring Russian readiness to negotiate for

> immediate peace without annexations (i.e., without the seizure of foreign lands, without the forcible incorporation of foreign nations) and without indemnities to be concluded within a period of "not less than three months."

The decree could not have come at a better time for the CUP. The Ottoman army was by then in deplorable condition.[69] The Third Army, which had directly engaged the Russians in the Eastern Provinces, had suffered enormous casualties and been forced to withdraw from Erzerum and Trebizond in 1916. Only the long and difficult winter of 1916 had kept it from being completely destroyed. Nor did the CUP have any way of replacing the soldiers that it had lost, let alone pay or feed them. Even Constantinople was by that time grappling with inflation and hunger.

"semi-colony" by the turn of the twentieth century. It was Russia's intervention that forced the Ottomans time and time again to promise reforms for the Eastern Provinces, most notably the Yeniköy Accord of 1914. Russia's interest in the Eastern Provinces was not humanitarian or religious, though it was often presented as such. After the Treaty of Berlin, the Russo-Ottoman border ran through Armenia. Russia had every reason to want a say in the Eastern Provinces. Eastern Armenians were in constant touch with their cousins across the border and could make life difficult for the Russians.

69. Cf. Zürcher, HMT: "By 1917, the soldiers were dressed in rags and they often went barefoot. Conditions were so bad that soldiers deserted in droves. It was not unusual for divisions to lose half their strength or more on the way from Istanbul to the front (often a journey of a month and a half) and by the end of the war there were more than half a million deserters. The army reached a maximum strength of 800,000 in 1916. By 1917 its strength was halved and by October 1918 only 100,000 men remained in the field."

Soviet intentions were not immediately clear.[70] After *On Peace,*
the Sovnarkom issued more (incompatible) appeals and decrees
concerning Armenia and the Ottomans. In late November, much
to the embarrassment of the Entente, it published and denounced
the Sykes-Picot Agreement. In early December, it issued an *Appeal to the Muslims of Russia and the East,* bearing the signatures of
Lenin and Stalin, in which it claimed that Armenia both belonged
and did not belong to the Turks:

> The treaty for the partition of Turkey, which was to despoil it of Armenia, is null and void. Immediately after
> the cessation of military operations, the Armenians will
> be guaranteed the right freely to determine their political
> destiny.

In late December, after it had signed the Armistice of Erzincan, it released the decree *On Turkish Armenia,* which had
Stalin's signature. It defended Russia's intervention in Armenia,[71]

---

70. Part of what obscured the strategy were the contradictory claims Lenin
himself published on Armenia. See, e.g., V.I. Lenin, *Collected Works, September 1917–February 1918,* Vol. 26, ed. George Hanna, trans. Yuris Dobnikov and George Hanna (Moscow: Progress Publishers, 1964), p. 62: "In
offering the peace terms, the Soviet Government must itself immediately
take steps towards their fulfilment, i.e., it must publish and repudiate the
secret treaties by which we have been bound up to the present time, those
which were concluded by the tsar and which give Russian capitalists the
promise of the pillaging of Turkey, Austria, etc. Then we must immediately
satisfy the demands of the Ukrainians and the Finns, ensure them, as well
as all other non-Russian nationalities in Russia, full freedom, including
freedom of secession, applying the same to all Armenia, undertaking to
evacuate that country as well as the Turkish lands occupied by us, etc.";
and pp. 175–76: "When we win power, we shall immediately and unconditionally recognise this right for Finland, the Ukraine, Armenia, and any
other nationality oppressed by tsarism (and the Great-Russian bourgeoisie).
On the other hand, we do not at all favour secession."

71. The first paragraph of the decree issued on December 31, 1917, reads: "So-
called 'Turkish Armenia' is the only country, I believe, that Russia occupied

denounced both Turkey's treatment of Armenians and its intentions, and again proclaimed that Armenia had the right to free self-determination:

> the Council of People's Commissars has decided to issue a special decree on the free self-determination of "Turkish Armenia." This is particularly necessary today, when the German and Turkish authorities, true to their imperialist nature, make no secret of their desire forcibly to retain the occupied regions under their sway. Let the peoples of Russia know that the striving for conquest is alien to the Russian revolution and its government. Let everyone know that the Council of People's Commissars counters the imperialist policy of national oppression by the policy of complete liberation of the oppressed peoples.

The Soviets' intentions became clearer when, with the Treaty of Brest-Litovsk, they gave the CUP the coveted *Elviye-i Selassie* (three provinces), opened the path for the CUP to reconquer the Armenian Highlands, and made its way through Caucasian Armenia to Baku. At the signing, they even "pledged to disperse the Armenian 'bands' operating in the Caucasus and the 'occupied provinces' of eastern Anatolia."[72] The "Armenian bands" were none other than

---

'by right of war.' This is that 'bit of paradise' which for many years has been (and still is) the object of the voracious diplomatic appetites of the West and of the bloody administrative exercises of the East. Pogroms and massacres of Armenians, on the one hand, and the hypocritical 'intercession' of the diplomats of all countries as a screen for fresh massacres, on the other, and a blood-soaked, deceived and enslaved Armenia as a result—who is not familiar with these 'commonplace' pictures of the diplomatic 'handiwork' of the 'civilized' Powers?" https://www.marxists.org/reference/archive/stalin/works/1917/12/31.htm

72. Hovannisian, "Armenia and the Caucasus in the Genesis of the Soviet-Turkish Entente," *International Journal of Middle East Studies* 4.2 (1973), p. 131.

the irregular forces who had held the front for five months after the Russian Army had abandoned it.[73]

Soviet intentions became unmistakable after the Armistice of Mudros, during what cannot but be thought of as the Turkish civil war, when the Soviets offered money and weapons to support the Nationalists in their "struggle for national liberation" in exchange for Turkish help in securing a mutually beneficial redrawing of the borders in the Caucasus.[74]

A Soviet-Turkish Nationalist alliance was beneficial to both parties, and both knew it. The Soviets made no secret of the benefits that they would reap from the alliance. Their newspapers announced that it would clean up "Armenia and the Caucasus, where counter-revolutionary 'so-called governments' had been set up by

---

73. As Walker puts it, "Armenian irregular forces had held the front for five months in 1917 after the defection of Russia," Christopher J. Walker, "Between Turkey and Russia. Armenia's Predicament," *The World Today*, 44.8/9 (1988), p. 141. See also Artin Arslanian, "British Wartime Pledges, 1917–18: The Armenian Case," *Journal of Contemporary History*, 13.3 (1978), p. 520: "To bolster its defense [of the weakening Caucasus front], the British government attempted to fill the depleted and unstable Russian ranks with local, especially Armenian, levies. They had every reason to fight to the bitter end. About 35,000 of them were already attempting to hold the Caucasus front, and thousands more were serving in other Russian theatres. The War Cabinet began pressing the Russian Provisional Government to transfer Armenian soldiers to Transcaucasia. Meanwhile, Britain requested the American government to enlist Armenians living in the United States for service in the Caucasus. After the Bolshevik Revolution, the British depended on the Armenians to block the Turkish offensive."

74. See Hovannisian, "Armenia and the Caucasus in the Genesis of the Soviet-Turkish Entente," p. 131: "According to a rather detailed description of the rendezvous [that apparently took place between Mustafa Kemal and a Soviet Officer in 1919], Budenny gave assurances that Soviet Russia would help Turkey scuttle all efforts to carve from Ottoman territory separate Armenian, Pontic Greek, and Kurdish states. The Armenians, said Budenny, had become particularly annoying, their opportunistic Hnchakist and Dashnakist parties serving as nothing more than lackeys of imperialism. Budenny pledged money, weapons, and even direct armed intercession in return for Turkish defiance of the common enemies in the West."

the German and then by the Anglo-French imperialists."[75] Turkish Nationalists did not make a show of announcing why they pursued an alliance with the Soviets. They had no need to. The CUP's and Nationalists' abhorrence and fear of an independent Armenia was not a secret.[76] Nor was its aggressive defiance of the Entente and its territorial plans.

---

75. See, e.g., Hovannisian, "Armenia and the Caucasus in the Genesis of the Soviet-Turkish Entente," p. 133: "The featured article [in *Izvestiia* in early April 1919] elaborated on the ramifications of the Turkish revolution. First and foremost was its impact upon Armenia and the Caucasus, where counter-revolutionary 'so-called governments' had been set up by the German and then by the Anglo-French imperialists. These hostile states were standing between the 'Russian and Turkish Soviet Republics, which are inspired by mutual sentiments.' The Turkish revolution would make it impossible for those counter-revolutionary creations to trouble any longer 'either of the Soviet Republics.' And it would eventually deprive the Entente nations of the bases from which they were attempting to strangle Soviet Russia. The ripples the revolution had stirred would send waves into the Balkans, Central Europe, Africa, and, in particular, all Asia, where the oppressed peoples were at last awakening from centuries of indifference. 'The Turkish revolution has given us an important ally,' concluded the front-page article in the Sovnarkom's official organ. With similar expressions, *Zhizn' natsional' nostei*, a publication of the Commissariat for Nationalities, declared that 'the revolution is moving to the south, and if in Turkey the government actually passes to the workers, then the fate of the Caucasus can be regarded as predetermined.'"

76. See, e.g., Michael A. Reynolds, "Buffers not Brethren," pp. 165–66, in which he cites Talaat's and Enver's fear and loathing of the very notion of an independent Armenia. Talaat remarked: "[I] am absolutely not in favour of the Armenians establishing a government. A small Armenian autonomous [government] will five years later become a five-million-strong Armenian state, it will dominate the Caucasus, and it will become the 'Bulgaria of the East.' All the Armenians in Iran and America will gather there and, as you describe, they will get every form of aid from the English and French, and in the future they will move against us with the Christian Georgians and also with great ease with the Persians. Therefore, were it possible, the best thing would be to lance the boil [*çibani kökiinden temizlemek*]. Since it is not possible, it is necessary that Armenia be formed in an extremely weak and unviable form." Enver retorted: "today in the Caucasus a small Armenia possessing a population of five to six hundred thousand and sufficient territory is formed, in the

In Berlin, Enver and Talaat met with Karl Radek, Lenin's emissary to Germany, whom Talaat knew from his time in Brest-Litovsk.[77] Radek invited them to Moscow. Mustafa Kemal apparently had similar meetings of his own with a Soviet army officer in Havzah.[78] Enver and Cemal went to Russia at the Soviets' invitation. Talaat wrote Mustafa Kemal, whom he acknowledged as the leader of the Nationalists, and informed him of the Soviet offer.[79] The CUP in

---

future this government, together with the Armenians that will come mainly from America and from elsewhere, will have a population of millions. And in the east we will have another Bulgaria and it will be a worse enemy than Russia because all the Armenians' interests and ambitions are in our country. Consequently, in order to remove this danger, the formation of even the smallest Armenian government must be prevented. Land from the Muslims must not be given to the Armenians, rather to the contrary I prefer that the Muslims occupy provinces such as Erivan."

77. Radek himself gives an interesting account of the meetings. See, e.g., E.H. Carr, Karl Radek, and M. Philips Price, "Radek's 'Political Salon' in Berlin 1919," *Soviet Studies*, 3.4 (1952), p. 419: "Two of my first guests were the former Grand Vizier Talaat Pasha, the Head of the Young Turk Government, and his War Minister Enver Pasha, the hero of the defence of Tripoli. After the rout of Turkey, they lived semi-illegally in Berlin—the Entente was demanding their extradition—and they were planning how to conduct the further defense of Turkey. Enver, having fled after the rout through Soviet Russia illegally to Germany, was the first to bring home to the German militarists that Soviet Russia was a new and growing world force with which they would have to count, if they in fact meant to struggle against the Entente."

78. See Hovannisian, "Armenia and the Caucasus in the Genesis of the Soviet-Turkish Entente," p. 137: "Meanwhile, Mustafa Kemal may have shown himself receptive to other feelers extended from Moscow. Several sources corroborate an account that during his stay in Havza, 25 May to 12 June 1919, the military inspector general conferred with a Soviet army officer, most frequently identified as Colonel Semen M. Budenny. Traveling incognito on an exploratory mission, Budenny is supposed to have broached the possibility of Soviet-Turkish collaboration against the Allied powers and Caucasian republics. An air of mystery shrouds the particulars of the meeting, the authenticity of which has been challenged."

79. See Hovannisian, "Armenia and the Caucasus in the Genesis of the Soviet-Turkish Entente," p. 135: "Late in 1919 Talat Paşa wrote Mustafa Kemal

exile and the Nationalists in Anatolia coordinated their efforts on the matter:

In exile Talât Pasha, Azmi Bey (ex-Chief of Police under the Young Turk régime) and Rüsuhi Bey remained centered on Berlin, an area which was to be a focal point of the Committee in exile. Enver and Dr. Nâzim moved between Berlin and Moscow, Cavid in Lausanne and Berne, Cemal Pasha and Bedri Bey in Kabul, Berlin and Moscow, Vehbi Pasha in Rome and Halil Pasha and Nuri Pasha in Moscow and the Caucasus. Not only was there a constant passage between these centers but, in an attempt to dispel suspicions in Ankara, the closest contact was maintained and a special courier service functioned uninterruptedly from the earliest days between the exiles and Mustafa Kemal.[80]

Formal negotiations between the Bolsheviks and Nationalists began in April 1920:

In addition to settling the northeastern boundaries of Turkey, the Russians secretly pledged to provide ten million gold rubles, as well as sufficient weaponry and ammunition to arm two divisions in order to help the nationalist government fight Western imperialism.[81]

---

that Radek had pledged Soviet support to the movement in Anatolia and that Enver and Cemal were among those who had already set out for Russia. The Ittihadists, Talat insisted, were striving toward a goal in no way contradictory to the aims of Kemal and would apply all their resources to engender a favorable foreign opinion toward the Turkish revolution. The former minister of interior and grand vizer now offered to submit to Kemal's direction."

80. Cruickshank, p. 21.

81. Hanioğlu, *Atatürk*, p. 120.

A first draft of their alliance was completed by the fall. It was not until the following March that they signed the Treaty of Moscow, which articulated the terms and principles of their alliance, and defined the borders of Turkey—and consequently also Armenia and Batum.[82] Its mention of "the right of people's self-determination" notwithstanding, no principle other than brute force lay at the foundation of the treaty's definition of Turkey's—and Armenia's—borders.[83]

---

82. The treaty was actually between the "Government of the Socialist Federative Republic of Russia and the Government of Grand National Assembly of Turkey"—i.e., the Nationalists and the Bolsheviks. It was signed on March 16, 1921, when neither the Republic of Turkey nor the Soviet Union formally existed. By Article I, "Turkey" was "the sum of the territories included in the National Turkish Pact of January 28th, 1336 (1920), formulated and proclaimed by the Ottoman House of Delegates in Constantinople and communicated to the press and to all foreign nations." By the territorial assignments of the subsequent articles, Kars and Ardahan were to be parts of Turkey; Nakhichevan an Azerbaijani protectorate; Batum and the land north of the village of Sarp were to be parts of Georgia; "the final elaboration of the status of the Black Sea and the Straits" were to be determined by "a future conference of delegates of the littoral states" and would be accepted, provided that neither the "sovereignty" nor "Turkey's security and the security of its capital city of Constantinople were not injured."

83. The treaty's use of the right of self-determination is fascinating especially in light of (1) its prohibition of any future claims to the territories whose ownership it purported to establish, and (2) its claim that the Soviets were establishing a new social order. See Article VII: "Both contracting Parties hereby promise never to allow the formation or presence of organizations of groups that lay claim to the government of the other Contracting Party or of a *portion of its territories*, as well as of any group that exist with the purpose of struggle against the other nation, within their territories." Since the Armenians were the most significant of the "groups" that could "lay claim" to "a portion of" the territories assigned by the treaty to Turkey and the Soviet, this clause represents a contractual guarantee to Turkey that the Soviets would never allow the Armenians "to lay claim to" their historic homeland. That is, it ensured that the Armenian right of self-determination would never be recognized. For the second point see Article IV: "In acknowledgement of the common interests of the national freedom of the Eastern peoples and the Russian peoples' struggle to bring about a new social order, both Contracting Parties do hereby solemnly recognize these

On September 13, 1920, one month after the Treaty of Sèvres was finally signed by the Ottomans and most of the Allied Powers including Armenia,[84] and two months after the British had withdrawn the last of their troops from the Caucasus,[85] Mustafa Kemal gave the order for Nationalist forces to invade the Republic of Armenia. They took Kars, Ardahan, and more.[86] They had

---

peoples' right to freedom and independence and, consequently, their right to choose the form of government that is in keeping with their desire." It is unclear how one can both respect a people's right of self-determination while claiming to "struggle to bring about a new social order."

84. The United States and Greece did not sign the treaty.

85. As Hovannisian points out, British forces in the Caucasus "always had to be taken into account in the formation of Turkish Nationalist policy and strategy." See "Armenia and the Caucasus in the Genesis of the Soviet-Turkish Entente," p. 146, n. 2: "The British 39th Infantry Brigade had occupied strategic points in Baku in November 1918 and the 27th Division, disembarking at Batum in December, had spread out along the Transcaucasian railway system and established headquarters in Tiflis. Because of strong domestic pressures and international considerations, most of these forces were withdrawn in the summer of 1919, and only at the last moment, with the entreaties of the United States government and the urgings of the British Foreign Office, did the Cabinet order the British command at Constantinople to hold Batum for a time longer. The Batum garrison, which always had to be taken into account in the formation of Turkish Nationalist policy and strategy, was finally withdrawn in July of 1920." See also Arslanian, "British Wartime Pledges" pp. 524–25: "British postwar intervention in Transcaucasia was not undertaken for the purpose of redeeming British pledges to Armenians, although the British presence did provide them a measure of protection. Britain obtained control of the region in order to force the evacuation of the Turks, defend India from a future German or Turkish threat, and assist the anti-Bolshevik forces in South Russia. The British intervention was virtually terminated in the summer of 1919 because of the accelerated demobilization of troops, increasing criticism at home, and the need to concentrate dwindling military resources in areas considered more crucial for the protection of British imperial or national interests: India, Egypt, and Ireland."

86. The Turkish XV Army was led by General Kâzım Karabekir. Its explicit objective, Dadrian claims, citing a cipher telegram from Ahmet Muhtar, Ankara's Minister of Foreign Affairs, to General Kâzım Karabekir sent on November 8, 1920, was that "Armenia be annihilated politically and

already received a considerable amount of money (and weapons) from the Bolsheviks, who were in part simply repaying a favor.[87] In late April, Mustafa Kemal's Nationalists gave the Soviets substantial help when they decided that it was time for Baku (and its oil), which had been taken over by the White Russians after the CUP withdrew, to enter into the Soviet fold.[88]

---

physically," because "By virtue of the provisions of the Sèvres Treaty Armenia will be enabled to cut off Turkey from the East. Together with Greece she will impede Turkey's general growth. Further, being situated in the midst of a great Islamic periphery, she will never voluntarily relinquish her assigned role of a despotic gendarme, and will never try to integrate her destiny with the general conditions of Turkey and Islam." "Under 'the pretext' (*vesile*) of protecting the rights of Azerbaijanis, who are related to the Turks by ethnic and religious ties, the General was advised to: militarily occupy the entire territory of Armenia; temporarily arrange the frontiers of Armenia in such a way that 'under the pretext of protecting the rights of Muslim minorities there is ground for constant intervention [on our part]' (*hukuku muhafaza vesilesiyle daimi müdahaleye zemin*)," Dadrian, pp. 358, 359, and 371, n. 4. Dadrian adds that "the genocidal design of that Turkish government to deliver a final blow to the rest of the Armenian people was foiled, however, by the last-minute intervention of the 11th Red Army that was stationed nearby" and concludes that the salvation of Armenia from "all-but-certain extinction" was the Sovietizing of Armenia itself. See Dadrian, p. 360. The Soviets reported that Karabekir's army killed 60,000 Armenians (of whom 30,000 were men), wounded 38,000 (of whom 20,000 were men), took 18,000 male prisoners, and that only 2,000 of the prisoners survived. They later claimed that the number of dead caused by the Turco-Armenian war was around 198,000 and that the value of the properties appropriated or destroyed by the Turks was estimated at 18 million gold rubles. See Dadrian, p. 361.

87. In 1920 the Lenin government gave Mustafa Kemal 200.6 kilograms of gold bullion, 6,000 rifles, more than five million rifle cartridges, and 17,600 projectiles.

88. See Reynolds, "Buffers not Brethren," pp. 177–78: "When Mustafa Kemal and his nationalists turned to the Bolsheviks in 1919 for assistance in the fight for Anatolia they were able to use their influence in the Caucasus to facilitate the Bolshevik conquest and thereby secure Bolshevik material aid in exchange. Ottoman officers now assisted the Bolsheviks. The reversal in the geopolitical dynamics could not have been any more stunning. In less than a year Russia had metamorphosed from being the single greatest

The haste with which Mustafa Kemal's Nationalists and Lenin's Soviets partitioned Armenia technically invalidated the seal of their Caucasus deal. Foreign Minister Alexander Khatisyan of the First Republic of Armenia signed the Treaty of Alexandropol, which ceded all of Ottoman Armenia to the Nationalists and Nakhichevan to Azerbaijan, on December 3, 1920, a day after his government had been replaced by a Soviet-backed one. The Nationalists and Soviets corrected their sloppiness with the Treaties of Moscow and Kars.

From brute force to diplomacy

With the borders redrawn, Lenin's Soviet money and weapons flowed freely into Mustafa Kemal's Nationalist coffers and armories. And as Hanioğlu admits:

> It was the reliable flow of Russian gold and armaments that made possible the prosecution of the war against the Greeks and thus secured the independence of Turkey.[89]

Brute strength was only half of the equation. The Allied Powers had also to be dealt with. Even as they allowed Armenia to collapse, they had troops in Anatolia. Here is where Mustafa Kemal

> [t]urned for insight to the centuries-old Ottoman tradition of playing off one power against another in order to create a space for diplomatic maneuvering. He had also

---

existential threat to the Ottoman Empire to becoming the best hope for Muslim sovereignty in Anatolia. Where in 1918 the Ottomans had rejoiced at Russia's weakness and sent their army to bolt across the Caucasus in a race to bolster anti-Russian states before Russia's resurgence, the Kemalists now fervently wished for the Bolsheviks' success and scrambled to hand those same lands over to the Bolsheviks, causing Azeris to charge the Turks with selling Azerbaijan out to save themselves."

89. Hanioğlu, *Atatürk*, p. 120.

learned from his Ottoman predecessors that dealing with
the liberal democracies of Europe was easier than grappling with Russian despotism or Austrian autocracy.[90]

The first of the Allied Powers to jump ship were the Italians,
whose *vittoria mutilata* still smarted in 1921. In the person of
Carlo Sforza, they came to terms with the Nationalists in March
1921 and withdrew their troops in exchange for economic concessions that were not honored by Mustafa Kemal. Then came the
French, who in October 1921 abandoned weapons and their claim
to Cilicia to Mustafa Kemal's Nationalists. They had, as Hanioğlu
bluntly puts it, "Lost their appetite for protecting Armenians."[91]
The last of the Allies to cave were the British, who held out until after the Greeks were routed and the Christian quarters of
Smyrna burned to the ground in 1922. The Americans never even
attended the show.

"Armenia" is not mentioned once in the Treaty of Lausanne,
which marked the end of the Turkish Civil War and the Allied attempt to safeguard the Greek Principle.

Back to the vatan's culture and identity: The Sun Language, Hittites, and the world's "cultural debt" to the Turks

Once he had—with a masterful combination of brute force, di-
plomacy, and genuine military prowess—dealt with the external
threat to the *vatan*, Mustafa Kemal turned his attention to ensuring that he was the person who oversaw its actual construction.
In 1923 he moved the capital to Ankara. In 1924 he abolished the
caliphate and millet system. He literally eliminated his political
rivals—and erased all traces of his indebtedness to them—with

---

90. Hanioğlu, *Atatürk*, p. 120.
91. Hanioğlu, *Atatürk*, p. 121.

the trial and execution of the high-ranking members of the CUP in 1926.[92] With his *Nutuk*, the thirty-six-and-a-half-hour speech he delivered to the Congress of the Republican People's Party—which he had founded and made the only legal political party in Turkey—over six days in October 1927, he dictated how the Republic of Turkey was to frame its own immediate history.[93]

Kemal also took upon himself the task of defining the entire history of the Turks. It was his crucial contribution to solving the problem that had most haunted the last century of the Ottoman Empire: the matter of culture and identity. Like his immediate CUP predecessors, Kemal was convinced that the necessary condition of a lasting nation was an ethnically and culturally homogenous people: that a lasting Turkey needed to be grounded in a national Turkish culture that would both bind its citizens to each other and to the state. Like his immediate CUP predecessors, he believed that that culture had to be defined and imposed upon the people of the *vatan*. Also, like his immediate CUP predecessors, he was keenly mindful of the fact that Turkey's new national culture needed to preclude the possibility of territorial claims by the many peoples autochthonous to Anatolia and the Eastern Provinces. His own native Thessaloniki had been lost to the Greeks.

Once the Nationalists had firmly taken control of Anatolia, Kemal began to assemble a motley team of intellectuals to help him define the *vatan*'s national culture. It included two of the CUP's leading *Turanist* ideologues (Ziya Gökalp and Yusuf Akçura[94]),

---

92. See Cruickshank's summary in "The Young Turk Challenge."

93. See, on this subject, Zürcher, YTL, pp. 6–16.

94. Gökalp, who after a brief stint in Malta had settled in Diyarbakir, was invited to join the Ministry of Education and then the Grand National Assembly's Education Committee, which reformed the school system, its curriculum, and textbooks. Unlike Gökalp, Akçura had not been a member of the Central Committee of the CUP. Having avoided arrest and exile to Malta, he was actively involved in the Nationalist cause from its very start and moved to Ankara, where he was considered one of the Nationalists' intellectual leaders. He became a member of the Grand National

historians and linguists. Above all, Kemal hired archaeologists, biologists, and physical anthropologists "employing ethnic and racial concepts to describe the special qualities of the Turkish nation."[95] He wanted "evidence" that would allow him to "prove" the trustworthiness of his cultural claims, and thought that he would get it by physically "investigating the Turk."[96] This was a "national goal" from the moment in which the Turkish school of anthropology was founded.[97] Kemal then:

[c]harged the Turkish History section of the Turkish Hearths (a Turkist society that had helped the CUP advance the cause of Turkism during the last years of the empire) with producing a new nationalist and scientistic interpretation of Turkish History. He placed a premium on findings that highlighted Turkish involvement in the origins and evolution of Turkish Civilization.[98]

Assembly. He was appointed the first president of the Turkish Historical Society, where he played a key role in the formulation of the official history of the Republic of Turkey.

95. Nazan Maksudyan, "The *Turkish Review of Anthropology* and the Racist Face of Turkish Nationalism," *Cultural Dynamics*, 17.3 (2005), p. 292.

96. Like most of the leading members of the CUP, especially those who had been educated in Ottoman Royal Military Academies, Mustafa Kemal was a firm believer in that curious mix of positivism, materialism, scientism, and genetics that fascinated a good number of nineteenth-century European intellectuals.

97. The biologists/anthropologists primarily compared physical measurements of different peoples in order to determine their characteristics and strength: the Turks, the Armenians, the Greeks, the Jews, and the French. Their methods were eerily similar to those used in World War II. "Basically three measurement methods were widely used: somatometry or anthropometry (measurement and study of the human body and its parts), cephalometry (the measurement of the bones in the head of the living), and craniometry (measurement of dry skulls after removal of their soft parts). The measuring techniques adopted were usually designed to determine unchanging racial characteristics." See Maksudyan, p. 295.

98. Hanioğlu, *Atatürk*, p. 163.

The result of Kemal's cross-disciplinary team's effort was a grand new cultural history of the world, which is now called the *Turkish History Thesis*. Its central claim was simple: the Turks are the *founders of all world civilizations*.

The articulation of the thesis was what de Gaulle would have dubbed a *vaste programme*. With the "evidence" provided by theories like the mythically grounded *Sun Language Theory*—which claimed that the Turks were the "white" race that was the first to transform grunts into phonemes, and consequently that proto-Turkic was the progenitor of all languages—the Turkish History Thesis claimed that the Turkish homeland, Central Asia, was the cradle of all human culture; that the Turks, who wore clothes "5000 years" before the Europeans did, had in Neolithic times embarked on a civilizing mission throughout the world:

> Establishing major states, such as the Sumerian and Hittite empires, and helping "backward" human groups such as the Chinese and Indians to produce impressive civilizations. Similarly, the Turks could take substantial credit for the achievements of Greco-Roman civilization, which was the product of Turkic peoples who had migrated to Crete and Italy...all people owed their civilization to Turkish immigration, which had been prompted by environmental changes.[99]

The Turkish History Thesis became the cultural backbone of the new Republic of Turkey. It was taught in schools. The 1932 textbook *Tarih I* proudly answered the question, "Who created Mediterranean civilization?" with:

---

99. Hanioğlu, *Atatürk*, pp. 164–65. For an excellent introduction to the Turkish History Thesis, see Can Erimtan, "Hittites, Ottomans and Turks: Ağaoğlu Ahmed Bey and the Kemalist Construction of Turkish Nationhood in Anatolia," *Anatolian Studies*, 58 (2008), pp. 141–71.

the Turks who had been driven out of the Turkish motherland of Central Asia.... Until not so long ago, people
were so misinformed that they imagined and assumed
an autonomous Greek civilization in the entire Mediterranean basin.... The first inhabitants of the Aegean
Sea, just like those of the land west of the Aegean and
of those of Thrace, belonged to the same root and race
(they were Turkish).[100]

The *History Thesis* was used to name banks.[101] It served to prove to the
Turks that the collapse of the Ottoman Empire, poverty, and Western
progress notwithstanding, they were the true leaders of the world.
    Above all, it served to provide the Republic of Turkey with

a central metaphor of a national myth of origin, one that
sought to establish that the contemporary Turks were
the autochthonous "race" of the land.[102]

Turkish archaeologists were called upon to find proof of this "myth
of origin," proof of the Turkishness of the ancient civilizations of
Anatolia. They were helped by anthropologists sponsored by the
Turkish Historical Society:
    Afet Inan conducted a vast anthropological survey in Eastern
Thrace and Anatolia, during which she measured the "skeletons,"
"craniums," and "noses" of some sixty-four thousand men and
women. In *L'Anatolie, le pays de la "race" turque*, of 1941, she concluded that a brachycephalic race (*type alpin*) from Central Asia

---

100. S.M. Can Bilsel, "Our Anatolia," *Muquarnas*, 24. *History and Ideology: Ar-
    chitectural Heritage of the "Lands of Rum"* (2007), p. 224.

101. Erimtan, p. 142: "And with regard to the Hittites, the opening of Etibank
    or 'The Hittite Bank,' as a state-run financial enterprise on 2 June 1935
    could be interpreted as an official measure that was meant to ensure that
    Turkish citizens would be aware of their ancient forebears even while con-
    ducting financial transactions."

102. Bilsel, p. 223.

brought Neolithic civilization to Europe, and that the contemporary inhabitants of Anatolia, like the Sumerians, Hittites, Seljuks, and Ottomans before them, were in large proportion the descendants of that prehistoric, civilizing race.[103]

Thus did Mustafa Kemal try solve the problem that neither the sultans nor the CUP were able to solve: invent an identity that would not just unite the Turks, and demonstrate that they were not culturally inferior to the Europeans. It would above all ensure that no autochthonous people could threaten their claims to their land. The new *Turkish History Thesis* allowed him to claim that in its last century, the Ottoman Empire was simply on an *irredentist mission civilisatrice* conquering back the lands that newcomers like the Armenians, Greeks, Assyrians, and Chaldeans had robbed from them. It also allowed him to take care of the Kurdish problem.

Destroying the traces

Mustafa Kemal, it seems, might have believed the outlandish Turkish History Thesis, which informed what historians have called the most significant "sustained and intricate attempt at social engineering outside communism."[104] What is certain is that since 1932, the History Thesis "formed the mainstay of history teaching in schools and universities" in Turkey,[105] and that every scholar and rational person inside and outside of Turkey has taken the History Thesis to be exactly what it is: a myth.

The ridicule with which the History Thesis was greeted outside of Turkey demonstrated that the theory was an insufficient means

---

103. Bilsel, p. 225.

104. David Shankland, "Integrating the Rural: Gellner and the Study of Anatolia," *Middle Eastern Studies*, 2 (1999), p. 132.

105. Zürcher, HMT, p. 191. Zürcher adds that "its more extreme claims were quietly dropped from the late 1940s onwards, but traces remain even in the school books of today."

with which to protect Turkey's irredentist claim to the lands of the *vatan*. Protection required bombs and bulldozers that would ensure that the traces of Armenian culture and civilization in the Eastern Provinces were not left as a reminder that the Turks had destroyed ancient civilizations in order to build their *vatan*. Of the more than 2,500 Armenian churches that dotted the Armenian highlands and Cilicia in 1915, fewer than 40 still stand today. Of the nearly 2,000 schools, fewer than 20 are still functioning. If fairy tales prove to be unconvincing to those who will call you to task for your actions, destroy the evidence.

There were, of course, two more steps to take. The first was to forbid mention of the whole matter:

> The official stand of the Republic was to dismiss the checkerboard structure of Anatolia by passing it under silence. The generations that were socialized into the ideology of the Republic were thus ready to dismiss local religious and ethnic groups as irrelevant survivals from the dark ages of Turkey. Whenever encountered they treated them as such.[106]

The second was to deny it.

---

106. Talin Suciyan, *The Armenians in Modern Turkey: Post-Genocide Society, Politics and History* (London/New York: I.B. Taurus, 2016), p. 38.

CONCLUSION

It is time to attend to the matter that gave rise to this book: to Ambassador Kandemir and the official letter that he commissioned in 1990 from an American academic, sent to Professor Lifton, in which he chided the professor for poor scholarship and denied that the 1915 genocide had taken place.[1]

There is no question that with his letter Ambassador Kandemir—and the Republic of Turkey, in whose name he wrote—committed an act of genocide against the Armenians. That letter—along with countless other instances of genocide denial that continue to be instigated and issued by the government of the Republic of Turkey—was, as Erich Kulka would claim, an undeniable act of "intellectual aggression" against the Armenians. It repeated "in thought" and word "what was enacted earlier as physical deed." It

---

1. The crucial passage in the letter is: "In short, you have simply passed along questionable secondary sources as evidence for a number of contentions which are, to say the least, hotly debated among contemporary scholars writing on the period and events at issue. It is particularly disturbing to see a major scholar on the Holocaust, a tragedy whose enormity and barbarity must never be forgotten, so careless in his references to a field outside his area of expertise. For Turks, who are justifiably proud of our long and continuing role as a haven for minorities (including the Jews evicted from Spain by the Inquisition), it is particularly disquieting to find our own history distorted in works devoted to the Holocaust of World War II. To compare a tragic civil war (initiated by Armenian nationalists) and the human suffering it wrought on both the Muslim and Christian populations with the horrors of a premeditated attempt to systematically eradicate a peaceable people, is, to anyone familiar with the history in question, simply ludicrous," SML, p. 10.

attacked the collective memory of the Armenians, which—as Israel Charny reminds us—lies at the "foundation" of the very identity of the Armenian *genos*. It aimed "to reshape history in order to rehabilitate the perpetrators and demonize the victims," as Lipstadt would claim. It echoed the very inflammatory propaganda that the CUP promulgated in order to incite and justify the genocide and attempted to have it accepted as historical truth. Ambassador Kandemir's letter, in other words, was categorically the product of an act that aimed to eliminate not just a *genos*'s past right to existence, but the foundations of its future existence. That its means were verbal, as opposed to physical, does not alter the act's genocidal nature. The UN Genocide Convention explicitly includes acts like the ambassador's in its classification of genocidal acts. Ambassador Kandemir's letter to Professor Lifton was beyond any reasonable doubt an Armenian genocide.

How should we understand Ambassador Kandemir's—and the Republic of Turkey's—genocide? Was it a *new* act of genocide perpetrated by the Turkish government, an act that is essentially distinct from the 1915 genocide, and whose victims happen once more to be the Armenians? Or was the ambassador's—and the Republic of Turkey's—just one of the many acts that constitute what the Armenians call the *Aghed* (Catastrophe) or *Medz Yeghern* (Great Crime) and what we refer to as the Armenian Genocide: an act that specifically "continues the process" of that genocide into the present time?

To ask this question is to ask to what category of genocide negationism Ambassador Kandemir's—and the Republic of Turkey's—denial belongs. Was it an act of *post-genocidal* negationism similar to David Irving's *ex post facto* ravings concerning the Holocaust: the spewing of hatred meant to exonerate men long dead for their murderous acts and thoughts and perhaps also to ignite in others the passions that might result in a repetition of their crimes? Or was the ambassador's an instance of *intra-genocidal* negationism similar to Eichmann's and Heydrich's horrendous Theresienstadt ruse: a bald-faced lie told by the Nazis while the

Holocaust was taking place so that they could complete their hei-
nous murder?

The key to this question lies in the object of Ambassador Kandemir's letter. Why did the Ambassador send a negationist letter to
a great American Holocaust scholar? For that matter, why does the
Republic of Turkey continue so vehemently to avoid mentioning
that what it now obstinately calls Eastern Anatolia was until very
recently known as Western Armenia and inhabited by Armenians?
Why its systematic destruction of the Armenian monuments that
existed in those lands? Why did it continue the CUP practice of
renaming ancient Armenian towns, cities, and locations? Why
does it still doggedly attempt to change the scientific names of animals and plants when these contain a reference to Armenia? Why
does it spend millions upon millions of dollars in order to sabotage
genuine scholarly research on the Armenian Genocide and public
knowledge thereof? Why does it issue brash threats to governments
that officially acknowledge that the slaughter of Armenians begun
in 1915 was a genocide? What is the *object* of the successive (and
successor) governments of the Republic of Turkey when they deny
the factuality of the genocide perpetrated by the CUP government
of the Ottoman Empire, and do everything in their power to erase
the very memory of the fact that Armenia and Armenians once
existed and lived within the borders of their republic?

Denial and the survival of the Republic

The short answer that scholars give this question is that the governments of the Turkish Republic believe that denying their—and the
Armenian—past is a necessary condition of protecting the existence
of what the CUP would have called the *vatan*: the Republic of Turkey itself. There is, scholars claim, something about Armenians—
their existence, their past, indeed their very memory of both their
hayrenik (homeland) in the Eastern Provinces and Cilicia and of
the genocide that these governments have considered—and still

consider—an existential threat to the *vatan*. The specific way in which they have dealt—and deal—with the "Armenian threat" is to deny and distort both the Armenians' past and their own. This includes denying and distorting the Armenian Genocide.

Thus, after pointing out that neither the "fear of restitution or compensation claims by Armenia diaspora organizations and individuals," nor the besmirching of Turkish "national honor," is a sufficient cause of Turkish negationism, Kieser, Öktem, and Reinkowski claim that:

> The single most important reason for this [the Republic of Turkey's] inability to accept culpability is the centrality of the Armenian massacres for the formation of the Turkish nation-state. The deeper collective psychology within which this sentiment rests assumes that any move toward acknowledging culpability will put the very foundations of the Turkish nation-state at risk and will lead to its steady demise.[2]

This fear, they add, "also explains deep-seated fears of Kurdish autonomy," which the Turkish government also systematically exhibits. Akçam and Kurt claim much the same thing:

> The Turkish Republic is a construction based on the transformation of Christian existence to absence—or, more rightly, on the negation of an existence. This is the reason why the topic, which is called the Armenian Question in Turkey, is basically discussed as a national security issue. Bringing it up, or even just calling for an

---

2. Kieser/Öktem/Reinkowski, p. 5. The reason why the scholars reject restitution or compensation fears as a sufficient cause of negationism is that the Republic of Turkey currently has the means with which to pay compensation. They reject nationalism because they claim that Turkish honor, per se, is not "representative of a deeper collective sentiment."

open discussion, is perceived as a threat to national existence and national security.[3]

This answer naturally begs the question: Why did and do the successive governments of the Turkish Republic consider Armenians—or, more specifically, their memory and their past—a "threat to national existence"? That is, why did and do these governments believe that "any move toward acknowledging culpability," including "bringing up" the very existence of Armenians and their past, will "lead to" the "steady demise" of their nation?

Obversely, why did and do the governments of the Turks think that the denial of Armenians' history—and their own—was (and is) a necessary condition of the existence of the Republic of Turkey itself?

Genocide, Denial, Property, and Survival

Akçam and Kurt point to one of the elements behind the Turks' insistent belief that *oblita Armenia vita mea*: Armenian property. The seizure of Armenian movable and immovable property, they claim, was not just an essential component of both the genocide and the establishment of modern Turkey. It presented a Gordian knot that has both defined and haunted the governments and legal system of the Republic of Turkey since the genocide and the very establishment of the republic itself.

The centrality of the seizure of Armenian movable and immovable property to the genocide should be obvious. It served two crucial functions for the CUP: it deprived Armenians of the means with which to survive, and it allowed the CUP to erase the traces of the presence of the Armenians and their ancient culture and history from the lands from which they had eradicated them. Talaat Pasha made the latter point explicitly with respect to the religious capital of Western Armenians:

---

3. Akçam and Kurt, p. 3.

Essentially the goal of the abolition of the Sis Catholi-
cosate and, at the first opportunity, the expulsion of the
Catholicos from there aimed at *completely eliminating
the existence* of this place which possesses a very great historical and national value in Cilicia for the Armenians
and is presented by them as supposedly the final seat of
an Armenian Government.[4]

The centrality of this seizure to the establishment of the Republic of
Turkey should be equally obvious. Akçam and Kurt state it succinctly:

The Republic of Turkey and its legal system were built, in
a sense, on the seizure of Armenian cultural, social, and
economic wealth, and on the removal of the Armenian
presence.[5]

The construction of the "Turkish bourgeoisie," of Turkish "tech-
nology and science," "shipyards, factories, boats, trains," which
Gökalp promised in his poem *Vatan*, depended upon the seizure of
Armenian properties. The dramatic upheaval of the late Ottoman
Empire's economy through which the Muslims came in 1918 to have
the "upper hand" in the ownership of the empire's industrial and
financial institutions, as Hanioğlu puts it, when over eighty percent
of these institutions had been Christian-owned in 1915, could not
have taken place without the seizure of Armenian properties.[6] Thus,
Akçam's and Kurt's statement that: "Turkey was founded on the
transformation of a presence—Christian in general, Armenian in
particular—into an absence."
    The Gordian knot, Akçam and Kurt claim, stemmed from the
fact that although they were convinced that they needed both forcibly to remove the Armenians and to seize their property for their

---

4. Talat Pasha; qtd. in Akçam and Kurt, p. 5.
5. Akçam and Kurt, p. 2.
6. See Hanioğlu, LOE, p. 190.

vatan, the leaders of the CUP did not want *to appear* to be doing either one of these things.[7] They used the war as a cover for their eradication of the Armenians and assumed control over Armenian properties under the cover of protectionism: through a series of abandoned property laws, the most significant principle of which is that the Turkish government is "administering" these properties "in the name of the original owners."[8] The Republic of Turkey, Akçam and Kurt add, not only adopted the CUP's legal approach

---

7. See also Akçam and Kurt, p. 8: "While the material wealth of the Armenians was being seized, it did not take place in the form of a simple appropriation, or irreversible plunder: that is, it was not said that the goods or their equivalent values would not be returned to their owners. On the contrary, it was stated that the goods, or their value, would be administered by the state in the name of their owners. Everything was organized around the idea that the goods or their equivalent worth would eventually be returned to their true owners—though when this would actually occur was uncertain.... Moreover, the forcible seizure of goods not in the form of appropriation or plunder, but through the preservation of the rights of the Armenians to their ownership, created internal tension and contradiction. Again, the state accepted that the true owners of the properties taken were the Armenians, and adopted the principle that the equivalent values of these properties would be given later. In the post-genocidal period, even the right of restating the ownership was accepted, which created serious and complicated legal problems for the state."

8. The evidence Akçam and Kurt present for the premeditation of the seizure of Armenian properties is the complete absence *ab initio* of a Turkish restitution plan. This fact becomes especially significant because the Turks did have a restitution plan for the Greek properties that they seized during World War I. See Akçam and Kurt, p. 7: "The administration of Armenian goods confiscated as a result of the deportation law of 1915 was treated as a matter distinct from the administration of the aforementioned Greek properties. In government correspondence with the provinces it was specifically requested that authorities pay attention to the difference. The most important one was that the Greek goods were not subject to certain liquidation. Orders to the provinces emphasized this point. The government's aim was to exchange the properties left behind by the Greeks going to Greece with properties of Muslims coming from Greece. Additionally, it was expected that the Greeks deported to internal Ottoman districts for military considerations would eventually return, so their property was not liquidated."

to the seizure of Armenian properties.[9] It codified it. "The majority of the relevant laws and regulations [concerning Armenian property] were issued in the Republican period."[10]

The Republic's peculiar approach to Armenian properties clearly links the conditions of the continued existence of the Republic of Turkey itself and genocide denial. If holding onto Armenian properties is a necessary requisite of the continued existence of the Republic of Turkey, and if both the absence of the "original owners" and the appearance of not having removed them and seized their properties a necessary condition of holding onto them, then perpetrating the deception of not having disposed of the "original owners" and seized their properties cannot *not* be a necessary requisite of the continued existence of the Republic of Turkey. If the means through which the Armenians were liquidated and their properties seized was the genocide, then denying the genocide cannot but be a necessary requisite of the continued existence of the Republic. Finally, if the very legal framework of the Republic of Turkey—its codification of both its identity as a nation and the terms of its existence—incorporates its approach to Armenian property, then the existence itself of the Turkish Republic requires the denial of the genocide. Thus, Akçam and Kurt conclude:

> The primary goal of the laws and decrees, by seizing all the movable and immovable property of the Armenians, was to eliminate the physical foundations of Armenian existence in Anatolia. Thus, the removal of the physical and cultural existence of the Armenians was intrinsic to

---

9. Akçam and Kurt, p. 2. See also p. 8: "The tension or contradiction mentioned is this: on the one hand, there is a state that does not wish to be accused of appropriating goods by force, and the language of the Abandoned Property Laws was set accordingly; however, on the other hand, the same state wished to destroy the bases of existence of the Armenians and institutionalize and render official the appropriation. The present legal system was founded on this tension and contradiction."

10. Akçam and Kurt, p. 2.

the Turkish legal system. This is why we call the system
a genocidal regime.[11]

They note that in 2006, the Turkish National Security Council sealed
the 1915 land records because they endangered national security.[12]

Armenians, the Greek Principle, the vatan, and Halide Edib

There remains the problem of why the CUP, the Nationalists, and
the successor governments of the Republic of Turkey adopted their
peculiar approach to Armenian property. Why their need both
to preserve the fact that the Armenians were (and are) the "original owners" of the properties in their very foundational laws only
to force themselves to hide the fact that they eradicated—murdered—the Armenians and seized their properties? Would it not
have been—and be—simpler to have confiscated, sequestered, or
expropriated the properties and thereby perhaps even spared Armenian lives?

The simple truth is that the CUP believed—as its successors still
believe—that they could not directly seize Armenian property, or,
to be precise, that their seizure of those properties would not make
those properties Turkish. As Akçam and Kurt point out, the reason
for the Turks' peculiar approach to the problem of property is to
be found in:

the way the Genocide was structured and its ideological justifications. This approach made it difficult for the
government to simply confiscate the properties without
addressing ownership rights.[13]

---

11. Akçam and Kurt, p. 13.
12. Akçam and Kurt, p. 3.
13. Akçam and Kurt, p. 8.

The specific element of the CUP's ideology that "made it difficult for" them to "confiscate" Armenian properties "without addressing ownership rights" is that very element that led the CUP both to eradicate the Armenians and to invent the grand Turkish identity that they intended to impose upon the peoples of Anatolia: the conviction that the Armenians *are* the rightful owners of their properties because the territory on which those properties existed, or in some cases still exist, irrevocably belongs to the Armenians. That is, the CUP and its successors firmly believed (and believe) that what was once called Armenia—the Eastern Provinces or six *vilayets* and Cilicia—is and can only be Armenia. The CUP and its successors firmly accepted—and still accept—what I have been calling the Greek Principle.

In 1908 the Ottoman Turks lacked, as Halide Edib so forcefully claimed, not just an authentic culture and national identity. They also lacked the very requisites of what she—and the CUP—considered a *proper* culture and national identity: a link between their genetic origins, history, and the geographical location in which they lived, insisted upon living—as she herself made clear: "No force could have dragged me away from Constantinople. I belonged to the place, and whatever its fate, I meant to share it"—and above all insisted on governing as the *Millet-i Hakime*, the ruling race.

This deficiency was, they were convinced, a fatal one. It did not just make the political building of that *vatan* that they aspired to create difficult: without a national identity and culture, as Akçura argued, the Ottoman government was not in a position to bind the motley peoples who lived in what remained of the Ottoman Empire both to the state that the CUP meant to build and to each other. It made the very existence of the *vatan* impossible. As long as there were autochthonous peoples—peoples, that is, who did have what the ideologues of the CUP and Nationalists considered *national cultures* grounded in the appropriate link between their genetic origins, history, and the geographical locations in which they lived—living on the lands that the Turks had no intention of leaving and not ruling, they could not by their own categories lay permanent claim to those lands. What convinced them of this was Greek independence and the flowering of nationalism in the Balkans. They demonstrated that the age of conquests had passed, that the world believed (and believes) that peoples have the natural right to sovereignty, and that ancient peoples specifically have the right to be sovereign in the lands of their origin. The vast majority of the leaders of the CUP hailed from the Balkans, which the Ottoman Empire lost to autochthonous peoples and their right to sovereignty in their homelands.

The twin actions of the Armenian Genocide and the historical myths were the CUP's and the Nationalists' solution to their national culture and identity problem. They were meant to be the means with which to construct and preserve a permanent Turkish *vatan*: to furnish the lands for the *vatan* and the justification of the proprietorship thereof.

But try as they might to overcome the fatal flaw of the *vatan* ideologically, the Turkish governments and ideologists were simply not able to do so. Neither *Turanian* mythology nor the grand *Turkish History Thesis*, with its ridiculous linguistic, biological, archaeological, and cultural claims, could convince the ideologues themselves, the multitude of peoples living in the Turkish Republic, or the world that the Turks were indigenous to Anatolia and the source of its—and all of the Mediterranean's—ancient cultures. They could not convince the motley autochthonous peoples still living in Turkey that they are Turks.[14] Nor could they convince the Turkish governments, the multitude of peoples still living in the Turkish Republic, the Armenians themselves, and the world that the Armenians are not autochthonous to the six Armenian *vilayets*

---

14. This is most notably true for the Kurds, whom the successive governments of the Republic of Turkey have tried to Turkify since the 1920s and who have refused to be Turkified. For an excellent study of the Kurdish question, see Hamit Bozarslan, *Violence in the Middle East: From Political Struggle to Self-Sacrifice* (Princeton, NJ: Marcus Wiener Publishers, 2004). The Kurds are not the only autochthonous people who have resisted Turkification. There is evidence that the Laz have as well.

and Cilicia. They could not eradicate the Armenian claim to their homeland. They could not make the *hairenik* not Armenia.

Nor need one deduce the facts that the governments of the Turkish Republic are convinced that what was once called "Armenia" is truly Armenian, that the proprietorship of those lands belongs to the Armenians, and that the recognition of this fact would lead to the demise of Turkey itself from the ideological pronouncements of the Halide Edibs, the Ziya Gökalps, and the Yusuf Akçuras. The 2007 official ruling on two Armenian journalists who were condemned under Article 301 of the Turkish Criminal Code of insulting "Turkey, the Turkish ethnicity or Turkish government institutions" for calling what happened to the Armenians "genocide" clearly states that the governments believe as much:

> Talk about genocide, both in Turkey and in other countries, unfavorably affects national security and the national interest.... The acceptance of this claim may lead in future centuries to a questioning of the *sovereignty of rights of the Republic of Turkey over the lands on which it is claimed these events occurred.*[15]

Denialism

So was Ambassador Kandemir's genocide a new genocide, or was it simply part of the original one? If, as should be evident, the objects of the Ottoman Turks' committing genocide on the Armenians and of the Republic of Turkey's denialism are one and the same, then Ambassador Kandemir's—and the Republic of Turkey's—negationism cannot but be *intra-genocidal*. Turkey's genocide denial, in other words, is much like the Nazis' Theresienstadt ruse: a bald-faced lie being told while the enactment of the plans

---

15. Taner Akçam, "Facing History: Denial and the Turkish National Security Concept," *Armenian Weekly* (April 25, 2009), p. 6. Italics are mine.

that led to the genocide can be completed, which in their case means securing the *vatan*.

The Armenian Genocide is not just a historical fact. It is a present crime that continues to be perpetrated by every official act with which the Turkish government denies the truth in order to preserve what the eradication and slaughter of one of the great ancient cultures gave it: Ararat and the lands that once were home to its people.

Hitler and the Armenian Genocide

One person who had a keen understanding of both the Armenian Genocide and Turkish mythology was Adolph Hitler. Much ink has been spilled on the question Hitler posed right before his invasion of Poland: "Wer redet heute noch von der Vernichtung der Armenier?"—*Who today still speaks of the annihilation of the Armenians?* What is not mentioned as frequently, and is not linked to that question or the invasion, are the territorial principles that informed Hitler's invasion of Poland (and Russia): his conquest of *Lebensraum* for his "master race." A quick glance shows that they are the very same ones that informed the CUP's—and its successors'—attempts to secure the *vatan*.

Like Halide Edib, Ziya Gökalp, and Mustafa Kemal, Hitler was convinced that his claims over Poland and Russia could only be firm and lasting if he could demonstrate that the Germans were autochthonous to Poland and Russia. Like Mustafa Kemal, he gathered a vast team of biologists, archaeologists, anthropologists, and historians to "demonstrate" that they were. Hitler's team also measured skulls—and did other horrendous things to those who did not belong to the "master race"—and produced very imaginative biological accounts of peoples. They linked their biological accounts with anthropological ones. Above all:

Nazi archaeologists looked for evidence of ancient German settlements in desired territories (and argued that

the Poles and Russians were occupying the Eastern territories illegally or unnaturally).[16]

Their director, Wolfram Sievers, wrote Himmler a few days after
Hitler's invasion of Poland, asking him to send *Ahnenerbe* ("ancestral inheritance") scholars to seize "all potentially useful ma-
terials—'catalogues, reports of grave excavations, drawings and
photographs'—and ship them back to Germany. Such records,"
Pringle claims:

> would greatly assist scholars in fabricating evidence for
> claims that Germany was merely righting an ancient
> wrong and seizing land that had legitimately belonged
> to it.… the Reich wanted all of Poland, and it intended
> to present criminal acts of mass murder and deportation
> as legitimate policies.[17]

Hitler's disadvantage, when one compares his venture with that of
the CUP and Mustafa Kemal—whom Hitler greatly admired—
was that the autochthonous Poles and Russians whose lands he
wanted to seize for his own *Millet-i-hakime* were not also the scholars and the bankers, the novelists and the professors, the merchants
and the industrialists. He could not in one fell swoop rid his future
vatan—or his homeland—of its enemies and grab economic and
intellectual control of his Reich.

Modern Philosophy and Genocide

In the midst of the controversy that persisted in Germany throughout the Hamidian Massacres and the genocide over the "Armenian
Question" and the kaiser's involvement therein, Heinrich Vierbücher

---

16. Shermer and Grobman, p. 240.
17. Pringle, p. 195.

exclaimed: "metaphysics, you have become the whore of violence."[18] He was responding to the Protestant pastor Friederich Naumann, whose defense in *Asia* of both the sultan's slaughter of the Armenians and the kaiser's indirect responsibility for the same had pinned the culpability of the slaughters primarily on the Armenians themselves, whom he had viciously portrayed as "wicked people," and on the German right to protect its own national interests.[19]

What Vierbücher's phrase points to is not the fact that Naumann—and the political powers he defended—called for political and economic interest to determine the principles of morality, which is bad enough. It points to a deeper concern. Naumann subordinated his definitions of the real people and actions involved in the "Armenian Question"—the Armenians, the sultan, the kaiser, the Germans, the massacre of hundreds of thousands of people—to political and economic interest. His idea of what Germany should be—his ambitions for it—drove what he claimed the Armenians, the sultan, the Germans, and the massacres *were*. This is why he claimed that the Armenians were wicked people: they were a barrier to his project for Germany. It is why he claimed that the massacres were simply acts of self-defense: Germany, he thought, needed the Ottoman Empire to exist in order for an independent greater Germany to exist.

What Vierbücher was pointing to was that reality itself was for Naumann what Naumann himself thought and wanted. He was also pointing to the horror of this fact. Once reality itself is subordinated to our thoughts and wills, all of our actions are violent, because none respects what actually is.

There is no greater example of this than the Armenian Genocide. There is hardly a party involved in it whose actions do not call upon

---

18. Ihrig, p. 69.

19. In his groundbreaking study of the relation between Germany and the Ottoman Empire, Ihrig claims that the kaiser's—and Germany's—understanding and approval of the Ottoman governments actually radicalized their stance toward the Armenians. It is not difficult to see why this is so.

the very principle that Vierbücher accused Naumann of following. The CUP, the Nationalists, and the successor governments of the Republic of Turkey all clearly did and do. But so did the Soviets, the Central Powers, and the Entente, as do the powers of today. They all allowed—and still allow—"expediency and national interests ... rather than moral commitments" to inform their actions and policy toward the "Armenian Question."[20] All do so because they make metaphysics serve their policy instead of informing it.

There is also no greater example of the inefficacy and falsity of Naumann's metaphysics. Over one hundred years have passed since the *Aghet* began. Armenians still exist. They withstood the unspeakable brutality of their eradication. They are withstanding the battering of Turkey's denialism. They will not become what those who do not want them to exist want. They will not bend to the thought of their enemies. Armenians *are*, and I for one salute you. *Zartir lao mernem kezi.*

---

20. For an account of the British betrayal of Armenia, see Arslanian, "British Wartime Pledges, 1917–18: The Armenian Case."

BIBLIOGRAPHY OF CITED TEXTS

Adams, Marilyn, *Horendous Evils and the Goodness of God* (Ithica/London: Cornell University Press, 1999).

Akçam, Taner, *The Young Turks' Crime Against Humanity: The Armenian Genocide and Ethnic Cleansing in the Ottoman Empire* (Princeton/Oxford: Princeton University Press, 2012).

———. "Facing History: Denial and the Turkish National Security Concept," *Armenian Weekly* (April 25, 2009), 1–11.

———. *A Shameful Act: The Armenian Genocide and the Question of Turkish Responsibility* (New York: Metropolitan Books, 2006).

———. *From Empire to Republic: Turkish Nationalism and the Armenian Genocide* (London/New York: Zed Books, 2004)

Akçam, Taner, and Kurt, Umit, *The Spirit of the Laws: The Plunder of Wealth in the Armenian Genocide* (New York/Oxford: Berghahn, 2015).

Akçura, Yusuf, "Üç Tarz-I Siyaset" *Oriente Moderno*, 61.1/12 (1981), 1–20.

Aktar, Ayhan, "Debating the Armenian Massacres in the Last Ottoman Parliament, November–December 1918," *History Workshop Journal*, 64 (2007), 240–70.

Alayarian, Aida, *Consequences of Denial: The Armenian Genocide* (London: Karnac Books, 2008).

Algan, Bülent, "The Brand New Version of Article 301 of Turkish Penal Code and the Future of Freedom of Expression Cases in Turkey," *German Law Journal* 9.12 (2008), 2237–2251.

Alpago-Novello, Adriano, *The Armenians* (New York: Rizzoli International, 1986).

Anderson, Margaret Lavinia, "Who Still Talked About the Extermination of the Armenians: German Talk and German Silences," in Suny, Ronald Grigor, Göçek, Fatma Müge, and Naimark, Norman M., *A Question of Genocide: Armenians and Turks at the End of the Ottoman Empire* (Oxford/New York: Oxford University Press, 2010), 199–220.

Andonian, Aram, *Exile, Trauma and Death: On the Road to Chankiri and with Komitas Vartabed* (London: Gomidas Institute and Tekeyan Cultural Association, 2010).

Aquinas, Thomas, *Summa Theologica*. Translated by Fathers of the English Dominican Province. 5 vols. (Westminster, Md.: Christian Classics, 1948).

Arendt, Hannah, *Eichmann in Jerusalem: A Report on the Banality of Evil* (New York/London: Penguin Books, 2006).

Aristotle, *Nicomachean Ethics*, tr. Terence Irwin (Indianapolis: Hackett Publishing Company, 2nd edition, 1999).

Arslanian, Artin, "British Wartime Pledges, 1917–18: The Armenian Case," *Journal of Contemporary History*, 13.3 (1978), 517–530.

Artinian, Vartan, *The Armenian Constitutional System in the Ottoman Empire 1839–1863* (Istanbul, 1989).

Aust, Helmut Philipp, "From Diplomat to Academic Activist: André Mandelstam and the History of Human Rights," *European Journal of International Law*, 25 (2014), 1105–1121.

Berkley, George E., *Hitler's Gift: The Story of Theresienstadt* (Boston: Branden Books, 2001).

Bilsel, Can S. M., "Our Anatolia," *Muqarnas*, 24, History and Ideology: Architectural Heritage of the "Lands of Rum" (2007), 223–241.

Bloxham, David, "The First World War and the Development of the Armenian Genocide," in Suny, Ronald Grigor, Göçek, Fatma Müge, and Naimark, Norman M., *A Question of Genocide: Armenians and Turks at the End of the Ottoman Empire* (Oxford/New York: Oxford University Press, 2010), 260–75

Bonifas, Amié, "A 'Paradisiacal' Ghetto of Theresienstadt: The Impossible Mission of the International Committee of the Red Cross," *Journal of Church and State* (1992), 805–18.

Bozarslan, Hamit, *Violence in the Middle East: From Political Struggle to Self-Sacrifice* (Princeton, NJ: Marcus Wiener Publishers, 2004).

Brenner, Hannelore, *The Girls of Room 28: Friendship, Hope and Survival in Theresienstadt* (New York: Schocken Books, 2009).

Browning, Christopher R., "The Nazi Decision to Commit Mass Murder: Three Interpretations. The Euphoria of Victory and the Final Solution: Summer–Fall 1941," *German Studies Review* (1994), 473–81.

Bryce, Viscount, *The Treatment of Armenians in the Ottoman Empire 1915–16* (New York/London: G. P. Putnam's Sons, 1916).

Carr, E. H., Radek, Karl and Price, M. Philips, "Radek's 'Political Salon' in Berlin 1919," *Soviet Studies*, 3.4 (1952), 411–30.

Clay, Catrine and Leapman, Michael, *Master Race: The Lebensborn Experiment in Nazi Germany* (London/New York/Sydney/Toronto: BCA, 1995).

Cruickshank, A.A., "The Young Turk Challenge in Postwar Turkey," *Middle East Journal*, 22.1 (1968), 17–28.

Dadrian, Vahakn, *The History of the Armenian Genocide: Ethnic Conflict from the Balkans to Anatolia to the Caucasus* (Providence/Oxford: Berghahn Books, 1995).

Dadrian, Vahakn, and Akçam, Taner, *Judgment at Istanbul: The Armenian Genocide Trials* (New York/Oxford: Berghahn, 2011)

Dalrymple, William, *From the Holy Mountain: A Journey Among the Christians of the Middle East* (New York: Henry Holt & Co., 1997).

Davison, Roderic H, "The Armenian Crisis 1912–14," *The Armenian Historical Review* (1948), 481–505.

Deringil, Selim, "'The Armenian Question Is Finally Closed': Mass Conversions of Armenians in Anatolia During the Hamidian Massacres of 1895–1897," *Comparative Studies in Society and History* 51.2 (2009), 344–71.

Der Matossian, Bedross, *Shattered Dreams of Revolution: From Liberty to Violence in the Late Ottoman Empire* (Stamford: Stamford University Press, 2014).

Dündar, Fuat, *Crime of Numbers. The Role of Statistics in the Armenian Question (1871–1918)* (New Bruswick/London: Transaction Publishers, 2010).

———. "Pouring a People into the Desert. The 'Definitive Solution' of the Unionists to the Armenian Question," in Suny, Ronald Grigor, Göçek, Fatma Müge, and Naimark, Norman M., *A Question of Genocide: Armenians and Turks at the End of the Ottoman Empire* (Oxford/New York: Oxford University Press, 2010), 276–86.

Edib, Halide, *Memoirs of Halidé Edib* (New York/London: The Century Company, 1926).

Erimtan, Can, "Hittites, Ottomans and Turks: Ağaoğlu Ahmed Bey and the Kemalist Construction of Turkish Nationhood in Anatolia," *Anatolian Studies*, 58 (2008), 141–71.

Erol, Emre, "'Macedonian Question' in Western Anatolia: The Ousting of the Ottoman Greeks Before World War I," in Kieser, Hans-Lukas, Öktem, Kerem, Reinkowski, Maurus, *World War I and the End of the Ottomans: From the Balkan Wars to the Armenian Genocide* (London/New York: I. B. Taurus, 1915), 103–30.

Ersoy, Ahmet, Górny, Maciej and Kechriotis, Vangelis (eds.), *Discourses of Collective Identity in Central Southeast Europe (1770–1945): Texts and Commentaries, Vol. III/1, Modernism: The Creation of Nation-States* (Budapest/New York: Central University Press, 2010).

Farré, Sébastien, Schubert, Yan, "L'illusion de l'objectif. Le délégué du CICR Maurice Rossel et les Photographies de Theresienstadt," *Le Mouvement social* (2009), 65–83.

Frankfurt, Harry, *On Truth* (New York: Alfred Knopf, 2009).

Frisk, Robert, "Living Proof of the Armenian Genocide," *The Independent* (2010).

Gaunt, David, *Massacres, Resistance, Protectors: Muslim-Christian Relations in Eastern Anatolia During World War I* (Piscataway, NJ: Gorgias Press, 2006).

Gerlach, Christian, "The Wannsee Conference, the Fate of German Jews, and Hitler's Decision in Principle to Exterminate All European Jews," *The Journal of Modern History* (1998), 759–812.

Ginio, Eyal, *The Ottoman Culture of Defeat: The Balkan Wars and Their Aftermath* (London: Hurst and Company, 2016).

Göçek, Fatma Müge, *Denial of Violence: Ottoman Past, Turkish Present and the Collective Violence against Armenians* (New York: Oxford University Press, 2014).

Gökay, Bülent, "The Battle for Baku (May–September 1918): A Peculiar Episode in the History of the Caucasus," *Middle Eastern Studies*, 34.1 (1998), 30–50.

Gottfried, Ted, *Deniers of the Holocaust: Who They are; What They do; why They do it* (Brookfield: Twenty-First Century Books, 2001).

Grobman, Alex, and Shermer, Michael, *Denying History: Who says the Holocaust Never Happened and why do they say it?* (Berkley/Los Angeles/London: University of California Press, 2009).

Gruner, Wolf, "'Peregrinations into the Void?' German Views and Their Knowledge about the Armenian Genocide during the Third Reich," *Central European History* (2012), 1–26.

Hanioğlu, M. Şükrü, *Atatürk: An Intellectual Biography* (Princeton/Oxford: Princeton University Press, 2011).

———. *A Brief History of the Late Ottoman Empire* (Princeton/Oxford: Princeton University Press, 2008).

———. *The Young Turks in Opposition* (Oxford: Oxford University Press, 1995).

Henry, Clarissa, and Hillel, Mark, *Of Pure Blood,* tr. Eric Mossbacher, (New York: Pocket Books, 1978).

Hovannisian, Richard G, *The Republic of Armenia,* 4 volumes (Los Angeles/Berkley: University of California Press, 1971–1996).

———. "Armenia and the Caucasus in the Genesis of the Soviet-Turkish Entente," *International Journal of Middle East Studies,* 4.2 (1973), 129–47.

———. "The Allies and Armenia, 1915–18," *Journal of Contemporary History,* 3.1 (1968) 145–68.

———. *Armenia on the Road to Independence, 1918* (Berkley/Los Angeles: University of California Press, 1967).

Ihrig, Stefan, *Justifying Genocide: Germany and the Armenians from Bismarck to Hitler* (Cambridge, MA/London: Harvard University Press, 2016).

Joannides, Paul, "Colin, Delacroix, Byron and the Greek War of Independence," *The Burlington Magazine* (1983), 495–500.

Kant, Immanuel, "On the Supposed Right to Lie Because of Philanthropic Concerns," *Grounding for the Metaphysics of Morals* (2nd ed.), ed. and tr. James W. Ellington (Indianapolis: Hackett, 1981).

Kévorkian, Raymond, *The Armenian Genocide* (New York: I.B. Tauris & Co Ltd., 2011).

Kieser, Hans-Lukas, Öktem, Kerem, and Reinkowski, Maurus, *World War I and the End of the Ottomans: From the Balkan Wars to the Armenian Genocide* (London/New York: I. B. Taurus, 1915).

Kieser, Hans-Lukas. "The Ottoman Road to Total War (1913–15)," in Hans-Lukas Kieser, Kerem Öktem, and Maurus Reinkowski (eds.), *World War I and the End of the Ottomans: From the Balkan Wars to the Armenian Genocide* (London/New York: I.B. Taurus, 1915), 29–53.

Köroğlu, Erol, *Ottoman Propaganda and Turkish Identity: Literature in Turkey During World War I* (London/New York: I.B. Tauris & Co. Ltd., 2007).

Kuyumjian, Soulahian, *Archaeology of Madness. Komitas Portrait of an Armenian Icon* (London: Gomidas Institute Books, 2010).

Leapman, Michael, *Master Race: The Lebensborn Experiment in Germany* (London/New York/Sydney/Toronto, 1995).

Lenin, V.I., *Collected Works, September 1917–February 1918*, Vol. 26, ed. George Hanna, trans. Yuris Dobnikov and George Hanna (Moscow: Progress Publishers, 1964).

Lewis, Bernard, *The Emergence of Modern Turkey*, 3rd ed. (Oxford/New York: Oxford University Press, 2002).

———. "Watan," *Journal of Contemporary History, 26. The Impact of Western Nationalism: Essays Dedicated to Walter Z. Laqueur on the Occasion of His 70th Birthday* (Oxford University Press, 1991) 523–533.

Lieven, Dominic, "Dilemmas of Empire 1850–1918. Power, Territory, Identity," *Journal of Contemporary History*, 34.2 (1999), 163–200.

———, "Dilemmas of Empire 1850–1918. Power, Territory, Identity," *Journal of Contemporary History* (1999) 495–500.

Lifton, Robert J., *Nazi Doctors: Medical Killing and the Psychology of Genocide* (New York: Basic Books, 1986).

Lipstadt, Deborah, *Denying the Holocaust: The Growing Assault on Truth and Memory* (New York/London/Victoria/Toronto/Auckland: Plume, 1994).

Maksudyan, Nazan, "Walls of Silence: Translating the Armenian Genocide into Turkish and Self-Censorship," *Critique* (2009), 635–49.

———. "The *Turkish Review of Anthropology* and the Racist Face of Turkish Nationalism," *Cultural Dynamics*, 17.3 (2005), 291–322.

Melson, Robert, "A Theoretical Inquiry into the Armenian Massacres of 1894–1896," *Comparative Studies in Society and History*, 24.3 (1982), 481–509.

Markusen, Eric, and Smith, Roger W, "Professional Ethics and the Denial of the Armenian Genocide," *Holocaust and Genocide Studies* (1995).

Morgenthau, Henry, *Ambassador Morgenthau's Story* (Detroit: Wayne State University Press, 2003).

Nash-Marshall, Siobhan, "Genocide," *The New Catholic Encyclopedia of Philosophy Supplement* (Detroit: Gale, 2009), 387–91.

Nash-Marshall, Siobhan, and Rita Mahdessian, "Lies, Damned Lies, and Genocide," *Metaphilosophy*, 44.1–2 (2013), 116–44.

Niepage, Martin, *The Horrors of Aleppo* (London: T. Fischer Unwin Ltd., 1917) and reprinted on the 60th anniversary of the Armenian Genocide by Plandome, N.Y.: New Age Publishers, 1975).

Öktem, Kerem, "The Nation's Imprint: Demographic: Engineering and the Change of Toponymes in Republic Turkey," *European Journal of Turkish Studies* (2008), 1–27.

Orwell, George, *1984* (Fairfield, Iowa: www.1stworldlibrary.org, 2004).

Palmer, R. R., "Reflections on the French Revolution," *Political Science Quarterly* (1952), 64–80.

Panian, Karnig, *Goodbye Antoura: A Memoir of the Armenian Genocide* (Stanford: Stanford University Press, 2015).

Panossian, Razmik, *The Armenians: From Kings and Priests to Merchants and Commissars* (New York: Columbia University Press, 2006).

Prager, Brad, "Interpreting the Visible Traces of Theresienstadt," *Journal of Modern Jewish Studies*, 7.2 (2008), 175–94.

Pringle, Heather, *The Master Plan: Himmler's Scholars and the Holocaust* (New York: Hyperion, 2006).

Reynolds, Michael A., *Shattering Empires: The Clash and the Collapse of the Ottoman and Russian Empires 1908–1918* (Cambridge/New York: Cambridge University Press, 2011).

———. "Buffers, Not Brethren: Young Turk Military Policy in the First World War and the Myth of Panturanism," *Past and Present*, 203 (2009), 137–79.

Safarian, Alexander, "On the History of Turkish Feminism," *Iran & the Caucasus* (2007), 141–51.

Salt, Jeremey, "The Narrative Gap in Ottoman Armenian History," *Middle Eastern Studies* (2003), 19–36.

Sarafian, Ara, *Talaat Pasha's Report on the Armenian Genocide* (London: Gomidas Institute, 2011).

Sarkiss, Harry Jewell, "The Armenian Renaissance 1500–1863," *The Journal of Modern History* (1937), 433–48.

Shankland, David, "Integrating the Rural: Gellner and the Study of Anatolia," *Middle Eastern Studies*, 2 (1999), 132–49.

Shermer, Michael and Grobman, Alex, *Denying History: Who Says the Holocaust Never Happened and Why Do They Say It?* (Berkeley/Los Angeles/London: University of California Press. 2009).

Smith, Robert W., Markusen, Eric, and Lifton, Robert Jay, "Professional Ethics and the Denial of the Armenian Genocide," *Holocaust and Genocide Studies*, 9 (1995) 1–22.

Sönmez, Emel, "The Novelist Halide Edib Adivar and Turkish Feminism," *Die Welt des Islams* (1973), 81–115.

Strauss, Johann, "The Millets and the Ottoman Language: The Contribution of Ottoman Greeks to Ottoman Letters (19th–20th Centuries)," *Die Welt des Islams* (1995), 189–249.

Suciyan, Talin, *The Armenians in Modern Turkey: Post-Genocide Society, Politics and History* (London/New York: I.B. Taurus, 2016).

Suny, Ronald Grigor, *"They Can Live in the Desert but Nowhere Else." A History of the Armenian Genocide* (Princeton/Oxford: Princeton University Press, 2015).

Suny, Ronald Grigor, and Göçek, Fatma Müge, and Naimark, Norman M., *A Question of Genocide: Armenians and Turks at the End of the Ottoman Empire* (Oxford/New York: Oxford University Press, 2010).

Travis, Hannibal, "Turkey Past and Future: Did the Armenian Genocide Inspire Hitler," *Middle East Quarterly* (2013), 27–35

Troller, Norbert, *Theresienstadt: Hitler's Gift to the Jews* (Chapel Hill/London: The University of North Carolina Press, 1991).

Trumpener, Ulrich, *Germany and the Ottoman Empire, 1914–1918* (Princeton, New Jersey: Princeton University Press, 1968).

Uğur Ümit Üngör, *The Making of Modern Turkey: Nation and State in Eastern Anatolia, 1913–1950*, (Oxford/New York: Oxford University Press, 2012).

———. "'Turkey for the Turks': Demographic Engineering in Eastern Anatolia, 1914–1945," in Suny, Ronald Grigor, Göçek, Fatma Müge, and Naimark, Norman M., *A Question of Genocide: Armenians and Turks at the End of the Ottoman Empire* (Oxford/New York: Oxford University Press, 2010), 287–305.

Uğur Ümit Üngör, and Polatel, Mehmet, *Confiscation and Destruction: The Young Turk Seizure of Armenian Property* (London/New York: Continuum International Publishing Group, 2011).

Walker, Christopher J., "Between Turkey and Russia. Armenia's Predicament," *The World Today*, 44.8/9 (1988), 140–44.

Ye'or, Bat, Kochan, Miriam (tr.) and Littman, David G. (tr.), *The Decline of Eastern Christianity under Islam: From Jihad to Dhimmitude* (Madison/Teaneck: Farleigh Dickinson University Press, 1996).

Yeşil, Faith, "Looking at the French Revolution through Ottoman Eyes: Ebukir Ratib Efendi's Observations," *Bulletin of the School of Oriental and African Studies, University of London*, 70.2 (2007), 283–304.

Zahra, Tara, *The Lost Children: Reconstructing Europe's Families after World War II* (Cambridge/London: Harvard University Press, 2011).

Zenkovsky, S. A., *Pan-Turkism and Islam in Russia* (Cambridge: Harvard University Press, 1960).

Zürcher, Erik J., "Renewal and Silence," in Suny, Ronald Grigor, Göçek, Fatma Müge, and Naimark, Norman M., *A Question of Genocide: Armenians and Turks at the End of the Ottoman Empire* (Oxford/New York: Oxford University Press, 2010), 306–16.

———. *The Young Turk Legacy and Nation Building: From the Ottoman Empire to Atatürk's Turkey* (London/New York: I.B. Tauris & Co., 2010).

———. *Turkey: A Modern History* (London/New York: I.B. Tauris, 2004).

———. "The Ottoman Legacy of the Turkish Republic: An Attempt at a New Periodization," *Die Welt des Islams* (1992), 237–53.

INDEX

OTHER TITLES OF INTEREST:

Prophetic Witness: Catholic Women's Strategies for Reform
By Colleen M. Griffith

Presenting practical strategies for reform and renewal of the Church, this strikingly direct volume brings together the voices of leading Catholic theologians who offer ideas for change while still showing that feminist reflection can work in support of the Church.

978-0-8245-2526-2 paperback / 128 pages

Handing on the Faith: The Church's Mission and Challenge
By Robert P. Imbelli, Ed.

Renowned theologian and teacher Robert P. Imbelli introduces the work of leading Catholic theologians, writers, and scholars to discuss the challenges of handing on the faith and to rethink the essential core of Catholic identity.

978-0-8245-2409-8 paperback / 264 pages

Finding Beauty in the Other:
Theological Reflections across Religious Traditions
Edited by Peter Casarella and Mun'im Sirry

This valuable collection of essays features a host of highly respected scholars, presenting a unique treatment of the concept of beauty as seen in a variety of religions and cultures. These include Catholicism, Hinduism, Buddhism, and Islam. In addition, beauty as seen in various African cultures is discussed.

978-0-8245-2336-7 paperback /
978-0-8245-2335-0 hard cover / 398 pages

Anatomy of Misremembering:
Von Balthasar's Response to Philosophical Modernity

The most comprehensive account of the relationship between Hans Urs von Balthasar and Hegel. For the author, it is essential to engage and correct Hegel, whose thought is a comprehensive misremembering of the Christian thought, practices, and forms of life.

978-0-8245-2562-0 paperback / 688 pages